The New Foundations of Labour Law

Kerstin Ahlberg / Niklas Bruun (eds.)

The New Foundations of Labour Law

PL ACADEMIC RESEARCH

Bibliographic Information published by the Deutsche Nationalbibliothek
The Deutsche Nationalbibliothek lists this publication in the Deutsche Nationalbibliografie; detailed bibliographic data is available in the internet at http://dnb.d-nb.de.

Coverabbildung: © Sondem / Fotolia.com

Library of Congress Cataloging-in-Publication Data
Names: Ahlberg, Kerstin, editor. | Bruun, Niklas, editor.
Title: The new foundations of labour law / Kerstin Ahlberg, Niklas Bruun (eds.)
Other titles: New foundations of labor law
Description: Frankfurt am Main ; New York : Peter Lang, 2017.
Identifiers: LCCN 2017019267 | ISBN 9783631718506
Subjects: LCSH: Labor laws and legislation. | Labor laws and legislation, International.
Classification: LCC K1705 .N49 2017 | DDC 344.01--dc23 LC record available at https://lccn.loc.gov/2017019267

ISBN 978-3-631-71850-6 (Print)
E-ISBN 978-3-631-72677-8 (E-PDF)
E-ISBN 978-3-631-72678-5 (EPUB)
E-ISBN 978-3-631-72679-2 (MOBI)
DOI 10.3726/b11540

PL Academic Research is an Imprint of Peter Lang GmbH.

Peter Lang – Frankfurt am Main · Bern · Bruxelles · New York · Oxford · Warszawa · Wien

This publication has been peer reviewed.

www.peterlang.com

Table of contents

Foreword

In 2009, the Swedish Research Council for Health, Working Life and Welfare (FORTE) decided to fund a six-year research program called 'Regulating Markets and Labour – Nordic, European and Global Perspectives' (ReMarkLab). Through the program, a closely collaborating group of researchers was formed at the Institute for Social Private Law, Department of Law, Stockholm University. The research group consisted of Niklas Bruun (director, Stockholm and Helsinki), Kerstin Ahlberg (Stockholm), Filip Dorssemont (Leuven), Thomas Erhag (Gothenburg), Jonas Malmberg (Uppsala), Mia Rönnmar (Lund), Cesar Rosado Marzán (Chicago), and Silvana Sciarra (Florence). Silvana Sciarra withdrew from the group when she was appointed Judge of the Italian Constitutional Court and Jonas Malmberg resigned when he became President of the Swedish Labour Court. Petra Herzfeld Olsson (Uppsala) replaced him.

The starting point for ReMarkLab was that globalisation is the major driving force for change of labour law, industrial relations, and labour markets. This globalisation consists of two closely interlinked processes.

The first is the rapid globalisation of the economy. The globalisation of the world economy is likely to contribute to economic growth, but it also causes challenges for labour. The second is the network economy and the digitalisation, which also change the foundations of labour law. Globalisation has shifted the balance of power between the nation state, workers, and employers, to the benefit of the latter.

The application of labour law and social security in cross-border situations was in focus for the ReMarkLab. Furthermore, we studied the process of the internationalisation of law itself. Today, the actual content of labour law at the national level is decided through a complex interplay between different actors (legislators, courts, social partners, multinational companies etc.) at different levels (national, regional and global). Further, the internationalisation of both economic law and labour law entails a territorial struggle between the aspirations of both fields of law in re- or deregulated markets and labour respectively, within the context of a complex structure of multi-level governance.

The funding allowed the group to have common meetings and activities while the individual researchers continued their normal work at their home universities. The group has especially followed the ongoing changes on the labour market, transnational developments and developments within the regulatory paradigms regarding work and the future of work, and its members have published different contributions relating to this development individually as well as jointly.

To mark the conclusion of the research program, ReMarkLab organized an international conference under the title 'New Foundations of Labour Law in the Globalized Economy?' in Stockholm in May 2016. The conference was divided into four blocks: 1) Precarious Work – the New Normative Model for Labour Law?; 2) Labour Law and New Forms of Labour Mobility; 3) Human Rights and International Labour Standards; and 4) Emerging Forms of Labour Law: Soft, Hybrid or Reactive?

As organizers, we were extremely happy with the outcome of the conference and its highly qualified presentations, which are significant contributions to the present debate on the future of labour law. We therefore wanted to collect the contributions into a common volume, and we are grateful that most of the speakers at the conference were willing to rework and develop their presentations for this publication. The book includes the main contributions from this conference.

We have structured the book in three sections. The first section, 'The changing foundations of labour law', focuses on the law itself. Here, four authors discuss how a changing political setting influences the very foundations of contemporary labour law. The contributions in the second section, 'Precarious work – the new normative model?', deal with the challenges that various new business models put to regulating working life and social welfare. The contributions in the final section, 'New forms of labour mobility', treat the specific difficulties related to the protection of workers who move over borders between countries and continents.

Now that the six years ReMarkLab journey is over, we want to thank the group, all participants in the conference, and the numerous colleagues and friends who have contributed in one way or another to our work during this period.

Niklas Bruun and Kerstin Ahlberg

I. The Changing Foundations of Labour Law

Niklas Bruun

The Old and New Foundations of Labour Law

1. Introduction

The starting point for the ReMarkLab research program was the deep changes that the preconditions for regulating labour markets and work have undergone worldwide during the last three decades of globalization.

This starting point is not very original. In fact, there is an abundant literature and widespread debate on the relevance of the classic labour law ideas in the world of today, sometimes declaring the death or disappearance of labour law, but more often trying to redefine the basic idea or ideas of labour law.[1]

Within the ReMarkLab program, we have had the privilege and opportunity to discuss this issue from different angles and this paper is an effort to sum up some main features of the analysis and to explain the tensions and different views that underpin the present debates. This analysis of the state of labour law of today has the high ambition of forming a synthesis of our discussions and efforts. The present paper, however, in no way represents any collective outcome of our efforts; it is the views of the undersigned, but I hugely benefit from what I learned from my colleagues and partners in the program. Furthermore, I have had the privilege of being entrusted with some international tasks, which have enabled me to get direct insights into some developments of the functioning of international labour law.[2]

2. The Development of Labour Law – The Starting Points

The starting point for this effort has been – following in the footsteps of Hugo Sinzheimer, Otto Kahn-Freund, Folke Schmidt and many others – that it is an important task for labour lawyers to identify the principles which could be read

1 See especially G Davidov and B Langille (eds), *The Idea of Labour Law* (Oxford University Press 2011), K Stone and H Arthurs (eds), *Rethinking workplace regulation* (Russel Sage Foundation 2013) and G Davidov, *A purposive approach to labour law* (Oxford University Press 2016).

2 I have had several tasks within the International Labour Organization (ILO) system (e.g. member of the Committee of Freedom of Association), as well as in the United Nations (UN) system (member of the Committee on the Elimination of Discrimination against Women, CEDAW).

or abstracted from the legal instruments adopted and to make them explicit and coherent, but also to point at inconsistencies and fragmentation. The latter has become increasingly predominant in the present phase of globalization.

Although labour lawyers disagree on many things, it is generally accepted that classic labour law, as it evolved in the aftermath of industrialization after World War II, was in essence a two-dimensional phenomenon. On the one hand, there was individual labour law regulating the individual contractual relationship between the employer and the worker from the starting point that the worker is the weaker party and needs protection. As many authors have pointed out, the relation between an employer and an isolated employee or worker is typically a relation between a bearer of power and one who is not a bearer of power.[3] Traditionally it has been understood as a relationship of subordination. Davidov underlines that it is misleading to argue that the employment contract is an agreement like any other, since the employer agrees to pay the employees' wages, a sum that is known and which the employee has no power to change later as he or she sees fit. On the other hand, the employee agrees to an open-ended clause, giving the employer the right to issue commands which will change from time to time as the employer sees fit.[4] There is a structural inequality between the parties of this contract. Therefore, the protective aim has been regarded as the rationale for the entire individual labour law as a mandatory field of law applying to the employment relationship.

In contrast, there was collective labour law, where contractual balance was achieved by freedom of association for both employees and employers and the formation of trade unions that could conclude collective agreements with their employer counterparts. A well-functioning collective bargaining system required autonomy for the social partners in which they could operate, as well as a legitimate position for them as subjects within the legal system. This was what Sinzheimer called the labour constitution[5] or economic constitution of labour law. These

---

3 See P Davies and M Freedland, *Kahn-Freund's Labour and the Law* (3rd ed Stevens 1983) 18.

4 Davidov, *A purposive approach to labour law* (1) 54.

5 In Sinzheimer's 1927 edition of *Grundzüge des Arbeitsrechts*, he used the term 'labour constitution' to refer to the collective labour law parts of German law: the law regulating works councils, trade unions, collective agreements, industrial action and arbitration. See further R Dukes, *The Labour Constitution. The Enduring Idea of Labour Law* (Oxford University Press 2014) 20–22.

starting points have also formed the basis for the Constitution of the ILO, as well as its basic Conventions on the issue of freedom of association.[6]

The classic labour law has many limitations as many scholars have pointed out and it covers only a limited part of the governance of the world of work. It does not cover the informal sector, which traditionally has been huge in many, especially developing, countries. It has not been concerned about the labour market as a whole, but has mainly focused on those who are employed. Its main traditional context was the industrial society. For a long period, it was very much part of a nation state building project, building a national labour constitution.

Generally speaking, classic labour law has had a private law core with some public law elements. However, in many countries, the whole welfare society was built around the employment contract. Taxation, welfare benefits, and pensions were in a regulatory manner linked to the employment relationship. The governance of these benefits and their detailed regulation have been seen as falling outside of labour law (work governance) and forming a separate social security field. I do not think it is necessary to change this approach.

In this context, I am not going to discuss the classic labour law postulates, but I want to emphasize that we still have a very strong inheritance from the classic labour law that actually was developed on the national level and was anchored in international law up until the early 1980s. Some academics argue that the basic ideas of labour law are out of date.[7] I strongly disagree, but the changed reality in which work is performed has brought up complementary and partly competing regulatory mechanisms, which have an impact on how the classic labour law principles and rules are implemented and function. While some argue that these new elements are external factors undermining or broadening the labour law regulatory regime, others see it as a fundamental crisis of labour law as we know it.[8]

Here I only want to present a very general picture of these well-known postulates. My point of view is that labour law of today can no longer adequately be described as two-dimensional, but that, actually, we have to picture it as a

6 Dukes, *The Labour Constitution* (n 5) 12 ff, see also H Sinzheimer, *Grundzüge des Arbeitsrechts* (Jena G Fischer 1927).

7 See B Langille, 'Labour Law's Theory of Justice' in Davidov and Langille (eds) *The Idea of Labour Law* (n 1) 105–106.

8 See Davidov; *A purposive approach* (n 1) 6, whose justification for a narrow labour law is not very convincing: 'This book uses the term "labour law" in the meaning common in most of the world – including employment law and workplace discrimination law. This makes sense because of the shared characteristics of these laws, and particularly that they address the same set of problems.'

four-dimensional field of law. I argue that we need to acknowledge the four-dimensional structure of labour law in order to somehow rationalize the discussion and also recognize existing new developments. At the same time, we need to develop tools to understand and tackle these new developments in a consistent and coherent way, in order to put them into a context and to be able to create a functioning regulatory governance of future work.

So where do we stand now? According to many critics, we are facing the crisis of labour law, the decline of trade unions, and the complete change of work in the new evolving network society. They argue that traditional tools of labour law are not enabling us to adequately address the upcoming new problems. However, while it is true that there are many indications of the crisis, there are still enough employees and workers out there in the labour market, which makes it justified to argue that labour law still has a role to play. Especially in an era of rising populism, nationalism and extremism, there is every reason to revisit the spirit of the Philadelphia Declaration and its central postulate: 'labour is not a commodity' and 'poverty anywhere constitutes a danger to prosperity everywhere'.[9] We do not have a unified regulation of the world of work. Besides the two still relevant basic ideas of labour law, there are two new basic ideas which clearly are forming a base for regulation of work on a global scale.

The first one is the human rights approach to labour and work. The other one is about access to work or access to the labour market. Although its theoretical framework is often formulated in economic and not legal terms, the latter forms such a forceful goal of work governance worldwide that it cannot be ignored when we try to adequately describe current labour law. In a normative sense, we can of course argue that this access justice should not be given such a prominent role, but if we want to understand and describe the present situation, we cannot ignore it.

3. Labour Rights as Human Rights

The recognition of the significance of human rights on the labour market has grown considerably, first in the aftermath of World War II, and then also after the collapse of the Soviet Union and the Soviet Bloc of states in Eastern Europe.

The protection of labour rights as fundamental rights regulates the world of work partly directly and partly indirectly, through some spill-over effects. I think

---

9 See A Supiot, *The Spirit of Philadelphia. Social Justice vs. the Total Market* (Verso 2012). The Philadelphia Declaration was adopted by the General Conference of the ILO in May 1944 in Philadelphia, and it laid the foundations for the post-war ILO agenda which included the adoption of Conventions 87 and 98.

there is a large international consensus that the eight core labour Conventions of the ILO, as well as the relevant provisions in several UN fundamental rights instruments – starting with the UN Declaration of Fundamental Rights from 1948 – reflect a global consensus regarding core labour rights. A related development towards this emphasis on fundamental human rights is the introduction into working life of extensive non-discrimination legislative rules. Today many authors describe individual labour law as consisting of individual labour law and non-discrimination law, but in fact, the evolution of non-discrimination law has taken place mainly since the 1970s.

There are many critical views regarding the content and design of fundamental labour standards. For instance, one could ask why health and safety, the right to life, is not better protected as a fundamental right. However, this kind of architectural defect does not change the fact that there has been a paradigmatic shift in the national labour law constitution in many countries because of the enactment of different human rights instruments. And although we must have in mind that the employment relationship is basically a two-party relation between private parties, the state has undertaken several obligations to make sure that these rights are respected and promoted and that there are sanctions in place against those who do not fulfil their obligations in this regard.

In 1998, the ILO Labour Conference decided to proclaim eight of the existing labour Conventions as Core Labour Standard Conventions. These Conventions were divided into four categories. The categories are: freedom of association and the effective recognition of the right to collective bargaining, the elimination of forced or compulsory labour, the abolition of child labour, and the elimination of discrimination in respect of employment and occupation.

The decision on the Core Labour Standards has the form of an ILO Declaration on Fundamental Principles and Rights at Work. The Declaration commits ILO member states to respect and promote principles and rights whether or not they have ratified the relevant Conventions. This declaration makes it clear that these rights are universal, and that they apply to all people in all states regardless of the level of economic development. It particularly mentions groups with special needs, including the unemployed and migrant workers. It recognizes that economic growth alone is not enough to ensure equity, social progress and the eradication of poverty.

The commitment by all member states to abide by the core Conventions is supported by a follow-up procedure. Member states that have not ratified one or more of the core Conventions are asked each year to report on the status of the relevant rights and principles within their borders, noting impediments to ratification, and areas where assistance may be required. These reports are reviewed by the Committee of Experts. In turn, their observations are considered by the ILO's Governing Body.

3.1 Dynamic Interpretation

When discussing the interpretation of the ILO core Conventions, it is important to note some basic facts. Most of these core conventions are rather old. The only exception is the new legally binding Protocol on Forced Labour, supported by a Recommendation (No. 203), aiming to advance prevention, protection and compensation measures, as well as to intensify efforts to eliminate contemporary forms of slavery. The Convention regulating the worst forms of child labour is as recent as 1998. The older instruments are rather short and many of the interpretations concerning their content have gradually been developed in practice.

For many good reasons, the drafting policy when regulating fundamental rights which should be applied globally and universally is often driven by intentions and a will to produce instruments that are formulated in a concise and declaratory manner.

If human rights instruments contain very detailed rules, they might not function in diverse contexts, which again might create problems regarding numbers of ratifications or for implementation. Within the ILO with its tripartite structure, slightly different views have traditionally been held regarding the preferable drafting approach. Employers have tended to prefer short and general instruments, while trade unions often argue for detailed regulation in order to avoid what they see as watering down or downgrading of certain rights in the context of national implementation.

Both approaches can be defended. Short, very general texts create problems with predictability and may lead to legal uncertainty. It is a legitimate requirement that state parties should know what obligations they undertake when they ratify a convention. If the text is short and general, we might find out the real content only after the implementation phase, when the supervisory bodies have assessed what the implementation requires.

On the other hand, detailed rules may create problems not only for member states with different labour market institutions. They may also block the possibility for a dynamic legal evolution of interpretation in accordance with the development of values in society.

Such a dynamic interpretation has clearly been prevailing regarding the ILO Conventions adopted in the aftermath of World War II. This is very clear if we look at Conventions 100 and 111 on equal treatment and non-discrimination.

The views and even the conceptual framework regarding discrimination have developed considerably since the adoption of these Conventions in the 1950s. For instance, the concept of sexual harassment at the workplace is not explicitly mentioned in the text of Convention 111, but there is widespread recognition that it is one important form of discrimination that the Convention covers. Also regarding the Freedom of Association Conventions No. 87 and No. 98, there are examples of generally accepted interpretations that actually cannot be found in their wording. One example is that the right to strike is not mentioned in the language of Convention 87. Another example is that the obligation for state parties to promote collective bargaining has been given a rather far-reaching interpretation in the practice of the ILO supervisory bodies.

3.2 Expansion of the Scope of Labour Law

The international labour standards are important in many senses. They have found their way into a number of public and private regulations and are significant elements in the globalized labour law. Here we can shortly mention five examples of how international labour standards are used in the globalized world:

- in international trade agreements
- in public procurement, for example in the European Union (EU)
- in fair trade labelling
- in Corporate Social Responsibility (CSR)
- in transnational company agreements.

In this context, I cannot enter into a deep analysis of these developments, but can only try to shortly illustrate what I mean.

It has become a standard content of international trade agreements to include a chapter on trade and labour. Such a clause is standard in agreements in which the United States (US), as well as the EU, take part. The common denominator here is that ILO labour standards are referred to, and that parties to these agreements commit themselves to following ILO fundamental standards and to uphold existing levels of protection. In addition, the parties shall make 'continued and sustained efforts to ratify fundamental ILO Conventions if they have not yet done so'.[10] For example, Article 23.3 in the new trade agreement between Canada and the EU reads as follows:

---

10 Here quoted from the recent free trade agreement between Canada and the EU, the Comprehensive Economic and Trade Agreement (CETA), Article 23.3 p. 4.

Multilateral labour standards and agreements

1. Each Party shall ensure that its labour law and practices embody and provide protection for the fundamental principles and rights at work which are listed below.

   The Parties affirm their commitment to respect, promote and realise those principles and rights in accordance with the obligations of the members of the International Labour Organization (the "ILO") and the commitments under the ILO Declaration on Fundamental Principles and Rights at Work and its Follow-up of 1998 adopted by the International Labour Conference at its 86th Session:

(a) freedom of association and the effective recognition of the right to collective bargaining;
(b) the elimination of all forms of forced or compulsory labour;
(c) the effective abolition of child labour; and
(d) the elimination of discrimination in respect of employment and occupation.

2. Each Party shall ensure that its labour law and practices promote the following objectives included in the ILO Decent Work Agenda, and in accordance with the ILO Declaration on Social Justice for a Fair Globalization of 2008 adopted by the International Labour Conference at its 97th Session, and other international commitments:

(a) health and safety at work, including the prevention of occupational injury or illness and compensation in cases of such injury or illness;
(b) establishment of acceptable minimum employment standards for wage earners, including those not covered by a collective agreement; and,
(c) non-discrimination in respect of working conditions, including for migrant workers.

The common criticism towards labour clauses in trade agreements is that the enforcement mechanism often is 'toothless'. A panel can be established, but there are usually no fines, no penalties and no possibility of trade retaliation.[11] These features, however, do not change the fact that clauses in trade agreements on fundamental labour standards can be an important element in bringing in formal or informal economic sanctions towards a trade party which does not fulfil its ILO obligations.

Public procurement is another context in which fundamental ILO standards are of importance. The EU Directive on public procurement of 2014 explicitly requires that, among others, subcontractors must respect ILO standards and that EU member states shall stipulate this in national law: 'Member States shall take appropriate measures to ensure that in the performance of public contracts economic operators comply with applicable obligations in the fields of environmental, social and labour law established by Union law, national law, collective agreements

11 This is the case in the CETA.

or by the international environmental, social and labour law provisions listed in Annex X'.[12] In Annex X, all the eight core ILO Conventions are listed.

Free trade agreements and public procurement are driven by states or public authorities. Fundamental ILO standards are however extensively used by private actors as well, which is an interesting new development.

The trend towards labelling of products and services has led to new forms of control and requirements of the fundamental ILO standards. For instance, the 'Fairtrade' label or mark cannot be used for products or services unless they have been produced with full respect and compliance of ILO standards. The Fairtrade foundation also exercises control in this regard.[13]

The frequent references to ILO standards, both in CSR codes of conduct and in transnational company agreements, are interesting in the sense that here private parties are using the ILO standards in order to declare commitment to certain basic values and to make such commitment visible.

The commitments in instruments such as the CSR-codes or the transnational company agreements are often described as soft law instruments, since their enforceability is often limited. They are often declarations of good intentions and ambitions, but they usually do not entitle employees or trade unions to rights or benefits that could be enforced.

This new feature of international human rights based 'labour law' has led to the introduction of the concept of 'hybrid labour law' in order to describe the difference between 'hard' traditional labour law stipulating rights and obligations for employees and employers, and this new 'soft law'.[14]

These developments have undoubtedly increased the significance of the core ILO Conventions since they are not only used by states, but also by private

12 Article 18.2 of Directive 2014/24/EU of the European Parliament and of the Council of 26 February 2014 on public procurement and repealing Directive 2004/18/EC. See further *Upphandling och villkor enligt kollektivavtal.* (SOU 2015:78), which formed the basis of the Swedish legislation that came into force on 1 June 2017.

13 See J Bowes (ed), *The Fair Trade Revolution* (Plutopress 2011).

14 The concept "hybrid labour law" has been developed by Ulrich Mückenberger. See U Mückenberger, 'Civilizing Globalism: Transnational Norm-Building Networks as a Lever of The Emerging Global Legal Order?' (2010) 1 (4) Transnational Legal Theory, and U Mückenberger, 'Hybrid global labour law' in R Blanpain and F Hendrickx (eds), *Labour Law between Change and Tradition: Liber Amicorum Antoine Jacobs* (Bulletin of Comparative Labour Relations Series 78 Kluwer Law International 2011). See also N Bruun, 'New Developments in Labour Law – towards a Hybrid Type of Labour Law?' in P Wahlgren (ed) *Soft Law* (Scandinavian Studies in Law Volume 58 Stockholm 2013) 63–74.

organisations and corporations. On the other hand, there are no mechanisms for the ILO to control that the interpretations adopted and agreed upon among private actors are following the ILO standards as defined within the organization. There is a clear risk that the interpretation will become fragmented and inconsistent, especially in light of the fact that the texts of the fundamental Conventions are short and general.

The entering of human rights into labour law has had a significant effect on expanding the scope of labour law as it generally has been understood. The strict limitation of labour law to a traditional employment relationship is difficult to uphold if we can identify 'vulnerable workers' outside the labour law protection.

One such group is domestic workers, who in many jurisdictions have been regarded as being outside the labour market, working in the private sphere, outside the control of labour inspectorates and similar institutions.[15] From a human rights perspective, it is clear that domestic workers cannot be ignored, as they are a huge group of employees internationally, which includes a significant share of migrant workers indicating the feminization of migration. In some countries, domestic work is not only an issue of workers' rights, but issues regarding forced labour as well as discrimination on grounds of gender and ethnicity might be involved. With the ILO Convention on domestic workers, the issue has become part of the labour law discourse in many countries.

4. Access to the Labour Market – Access Justice

The contemporary approach to labour law cannot be understood without taking into account the existence of a significant population that does not have access to the labour market. It is not controversial to see the reduction of social exclusion as one important goal for labour law. Work is important for people not only for being dignified members of society, but also for being part of a community. Unemployment is a huge problem in the developed market economies, and together with competition for jobs between workers, it can create significant tensions.

For many years, economists have debated the difference between insiders and outsiders on the labour market, where the insiders are often described as employees who are active in trade unions and have good benefits and protection against dismissals, while the outsiders are those who circulate between short-term contracts and unemployment.

15 See ILO Convention No 189, see further J Fudge, 'Domestic Work, Mobility and Labour Law: Challenging Borders' in this volume.

Many labour law innovations have their background in the idea of granting access for disadvantaged groups to the labour market. The right to priority for full-time jobs granted to those working part-time is one example. Another example is the Finnish system for alternate leave, where a senior employee can take leave for studies or similar activities, if an unemployed person can be granted the job as replacement for him or her.

Some of the labour law reforms that have been controversial for reducing the protection of employees have been justified by the legislator as attempts to actually improve access to the labour market for certain groups. Weaker protection against dismissals and less strict seniority rules might make it easier for employers to dismiss older employees and recruit younger ones.

The reason why I think that we can speak of a fourth dimension of contemporary labour law is because it does not only include some regulatory elements that clearly aim towards inclusion and access for individuals to the labour market. In addition, my argument is that within the framework of contemporary law, the worker has been given a completely new role and new responsibilities. Earlier the worker had rights and obligations towards the employer and towards the trade union within the collective bargaining system. These legal positions more or less exhaustively defined the role of the worker. Today the worker has many obligations towards the state, and if these obligations are not fulfilled, sanctions, mainly in the form of reduced unemployment benefits or social security, will be applied.

Today, the worker or jobseeker has to be an active subject, looking for work in a systematic and controlled manner. There can be a legislated demand for an individual job-seeking plan combined with a study plan, and the worker should be prepared to take the job offered even on less favourable terms. The worker should also continuously make sure that he/she remains employable by upgrading different skills. Thus, in this new context, the responsibility for working skills and flexible adjustments is on the worker, not the employer.

The more radical form of this thinking argues that 'obstacles for access to work' must be removed by the worker him/herself, and work providers (employers) must be supported and encouraged. Such support can be subsidies paid to employers who hire young workers etc.

The EU labour law and labour market regulation has significantly strengthened this new dimension of labour law. The EU labour market regulation is essentially about access to the internal EU labour market. The term 'access justice' was launched by Hans Micklitz who argued that European regulatory private law is united by a social orientation and by a particular conception of justice, which sets it apart from typical national welfare legislation.[16] The employability-pillar of the EU employment policy emphasizes the role of the individual, and the same is true for the other pillars as well; that is to say, entrepreneurship, adaptability and equal opportunities.

Kaarlo Tuori, who has developed some theories about European constitutionalism, makes a distinction between the economic and the juridical constitution of Europe. He also discusses whether we can adequately introduce the concept of social constitution for describing the social dimension of the EU.[17] He argues that, in any case, the economic constitution has primacy over the social constitution and that access justice is yet another example of this. Furthermore, he argues that there is a tension between the European access justice and the solidarity-based social justice underpinning national welfare regimes.[18]

One example of the evolution of labour market access justice is the casualization of work, which has taken place in several member states of the EU. Valerio De Stefano has done an extensive study that shows mechanisms for excluding casual workers totally or partially from labour protection in many instances. The main justification for these new mechanisms are that they create labour market access and work opportunities for vulnerable groups and that, therefore, severe decent work deficits can be accepted.[19]

Access justice forms a hybrid between social welfare law (labour law) and its traditional values, and market law and its economic rationale. In that sense, it can form part of the hybrid labour law, where soft regulation and the rationality of markets prevail.

Access justice is very state-oriented (or designed by global institutions). Social partners do not play any significant role. Within the European employment policy, some kind of role for social dialogue has been reserved, but it has clearly been an exercise where the EU institutions have interacted primarily with the member states.

Access justice can be understood in different ways. The radical neo-liberal approach could most probably be that most traditional labour law is actually creating

---

16 H Micklitz, 'Social justice and access justice in private law' in H Micklitz (ed), *The Many Faces of Social Justice in Private Law* (Elgar 2011) 3–60 (also published as EUI Working Paper 2011/2).

17 See K Tuori, *European Constitutionalism* (Cambridge University Press 2015) 227–232.

18 ibid 232.

19 V De Stefano, 'Casual work beyond casual work in the EU. The underground causalisation of the European workforce – and what to do about it' (2016) 7(3) European Labour Law Journal 421–441.

obstacles for access to the labour market. Therefore, we should adopt a radical deregulatory agenda. I am arguing that this kind of discourse actually cannot be described as a labour law discourse. Instead, it is to be classified as an economic agenda, abandoning the basic postulates and goals for labour law. When some states argue that they must demolish all labour law regulation in order to attract foreign investments and create jobs, they are no longer focusing on the problems within labour law.

In this chapter, I want to stay within the limits of labour law. My argument is that access justice forms an element and causes a tension within the labour law discourse in most developed western countries. If we want to understand the ongoing debates, we have to include all four dimensions of labour law in our discussion. Therefore, we cannot ignore access justice as the fourth labour law dimension. Furthermore, access justice seems to gain ground in the new 'gig' economy. Uber and other actors strongly emphasize that they provide access to the labour market for excluded groups, and the same is true for employers hiring employees on so-called zero hours contracts.

5. The Four Dimensions of Contemporary Hybrid Labour Law

I have described contemporary labour law as consisting of four dimensions. I think all four dimensions are present in most jurisdictions, but it is clear that the differences between national labour law systems are significant, and that the single different dimensions might have a very different weight within different national systems.

We know from before that many countries have rather weak trade unions and that collective labour law does not play a significant role. This might result in stronger emphasis on individual labour law and the human rights dimension, and vice versa.

The role of the state in the new areas of labour law is crucial, although it is not beyond the realms of the imagination to include some collective elements in access justice. In practice, however, the role for social partners seems to be limited in this field.

In order to illustrate the interaction between the four dimensions of labour law, I will finally exemplify the discussion with some snapshots from Sweden and Lithuania. There are very different labour law paradigms in place in these countries, but in both jurisdictions there is an active discourse on how to develop labour law from within labour law.

In Figure 1 below, I have tried to illustrate the four dimensions of contemporary labour law, the elements of the new hybrid labour law. Different labour law systems can position themselves in different ways within this four-dimensional field and generally speaking, developed labour law has historically moved from left to right in the figure, from a mix of individual and collective labour law towards a situation where emphasis is given to both a human rights approach and an access justice approach to labour law.

Figure 1. The four dimensions of contemporary labour law.

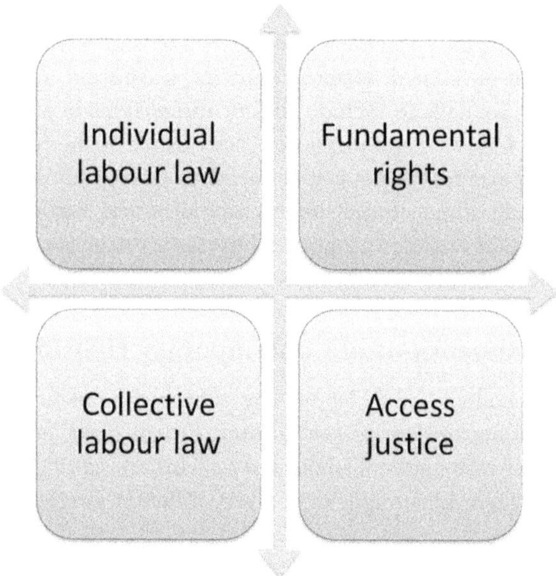

In Figure 2, I make an attempt to describe Swedish labour law within this four-dimensional field. Swedish labour law is still strongly driven by social partners, and the organisations on the employers' as well as the workers' side. Collective labour law is clearly primary to the individual labour law, but there is a significant traditional element of individual labour law present in the form of dismissals protection and individual rights.

Within the Swedish system, 'the Swedish model', there has clearly been a tension between the traditional left side of the picture (individual and collective labour law) and the right side with fundamental rights and access justice.

The tension in relation to human rights has clearly been felt in relation to the European Convention of Human Rights (ECHR) where the European Court of Human Rights (ECtHR) has interpreted human rights in a way which has to a varying extent intervened in the traditional functioning of the Swedish model.

In the well-known Gustafson case, the question was whether the employer was entitled to not enter into a collective agreement, and whether industrial action against him was actually in breach of his rights under Article 11 of the Convention.[20] The Court argued that the compulsion aimed at making an employer enter into a collective agreement was not, as such, protected by Article 11.[21] Further tensions have occurred regarding the control of the content of collective agreements where the ECtHR has held that the State Party to the Convention has a positive obligation to protect individuals' interests in cases where a collective agreement imposes a disproportionate burden, for instance costs, on an applicant.[22]

From this very short Swedish excursion, we can note that the fundamental human rights approach, which in many cases protects workers and trade unions in accordance with ILO practice, also in some cases can undermine collective labour law as a result of the fact that it has a strong emphasis on individual rights.

Swedish labour law has also moved toward labour market access justice. There are labour market measures focusing on getting young job seekers into the labour market, and there have also been many debates concerning wage setting (that is lower wages) for vulnerable groups such as migrant workers.

Posted workers have been a special case since the legal status of posted workers is regulated in detail by EU law. The well-known Laval judgment[23] that was handed down by the Court of Justice of the European Union (CJEU) has been described by Tuori as an example of a case where the transnational access justice collided with, and prevailed, over the Nordic welfare model and its social justice.[24]

In the following, we can position the 'Swedish Model' in the four dimensional picture of contemporary labour law. Although this regulatory model continues to have its base in collective labour law and also in individual labour law, it also contains some elements of fundamental rights and access justice.

---

20 Gustafson v. Sweden, no 15573/89, EHCR 1996-II.

21 See further I van Hiel, 'The Right to Form and Join Trade Unions Protected by Article 11 ECHR' in F Dorssemont, K Lörcher and I Schömann, *The European Convention on Human Rights and the Employment Relation* (Hart Publishing 2013) 287–308.

22 See further P Herzfeld Olsson 'Every Natural or Legal Person is Entitled to the Peaceful Enjoyment of His or Her Possessions: Article 1, Protocol 1 to the European Convention on Human Rights'. In Dorssemont, Lörcher and Schömann, *The European Convention on Human Rights* (n 21) 381–414.

23 Judgment 18 December 2007, *Laval un Partneri*, C-341/05, EU:C:2007:809 [2008] ECR I-2891.

24 See Tuori, *European Constitutionalism* (n 17) 267.

Figure 2: The Swedish Model

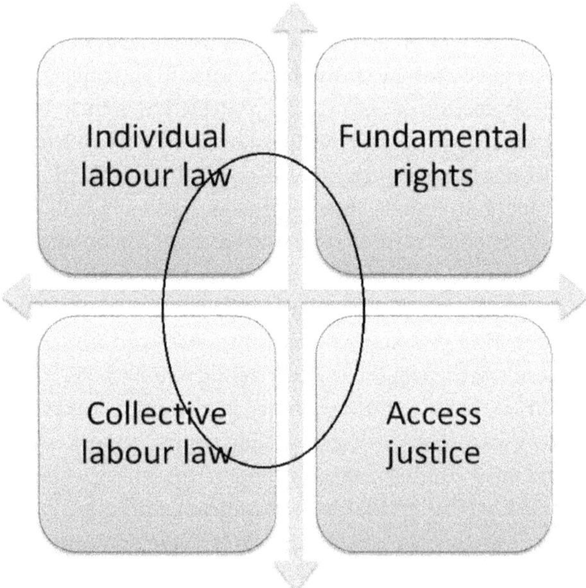

The figure looks rather different if we compare it with the labour law developing in the EU member states in Eastern Europe. The new legislation in Lithuania, which was approved by the Parliament in 2016 and is subject to some discussions still in the spring of 2017, can serve as an example.[25]

The problems with a lack of representativeness of trade unions seems to be solved by generally undermining collective bargaining. This takes place by promoting a general works council system and by a main rule restricting the application of collective agreements to the members of the trade union.

In this volume, it is not possible to enter into an in-depth analysis of the new Lithuanian labour law, but one may point to some of its features which seem to indicate that there is an evolving element of access justice present in this legal system.

The emphasis is very much on individual labour law, but not so much on individual rights for the workers as on encouraging the employees' efforts to stay employable and to acquire new skills and increase adaptability. Lifelong learning

25 The Law on the Approval, Entry into Force and Implementation of the Labour Code of the Republic of Lithuania. 14 September 2016, No XII-2603.

and the ability to absorb new skills and new opportunities will become vital elements for individual success, quality of employment and the sustainability of the labour market. According to the Lithuanian legislator, this cannot be left to self-regulation or private initiatives of the parties to the contract of employment. A more active involvement of the state has been manifestly introduced.

The new Labour Code 2016 provides detailed regulation on compensation of employer's investment in the employee's qualifications, and at the same time, it gives the employees opportunities to request time off, including paid time off, for the purpose of vocational training.[26] For example, the parties to the employment contract may make a special agreement that the employee, who resigns from the enterprise, will compensate the employer for its costs for the employee's training. The incentives to invest in an employee's qualifications is promoted with the new provision that if an employer pays for the employee's studies for a bachelor's or master's degree and (or) a professional qualification, the parties may agree that the employee may terminate the employment relationship only after having compensated the employer for its expenses. After completion of the studies, this obligation is valid for as many years as the employer has financed his or her studies.

If the employee looks for education opportunities on his or her own initiative, Lithuanian labour law already earlier allowed the employee to ask for leave for educational purposes. However, the leave was unpaid unless there was a special agreement with the employer. Article 135 of the new Labour Code 2016 entitles an employee to five working days leave per year in order to participate in non-formal adult education programmes. Such leave shall be granted upon notification of the employer at least 20 working days in advance and may be accumulated for no longer than three years. Employees whose employment relation with the employer has continued for more than five years have the right to at least half of the average wage for educational leave up to 10 working days per year, if they participate in non-formal adult education programmes aimed at improving their qualifications.

Here the main goal is to improve the employee's qualifications. This is seen as a common interest for the employee and the employer. At the same time, dismissals protection has been reduced. The Labour Code 2016 brings certain 'innovations' as far as grounds for the expiry of an employment contract, protection of individual groups of employees, formalization of the dismissal procedure and severance payments are concerned. The major changes though relate to the costs of dismissal. The notice period has been shortened to one month (two weeks if the employment relationship has continued for less than one year). Before, it

26 T Davulis, 'Main features of Lithuanian Labour Law Reform 2016'. Forthcoming.

varied from two to four months. The dismissed employee shall be paid two average monthly wages in severance pay, but in cases where the employment has continued for less than one year, the severance pay is lower, equal to only half of his or her monthly average wage.

Additional flexibility for the employers has been offered by the new ground of dismissal without any fault on the part of employee – if the law does not provide a formal ground for dismissal but dismissal is necessary, the employer may dismiss the employee by paying a severance payment of six monthly wages.[27]

The changes in dismissal protection were originally justified by the intention to introduce compensatory measures in the area of active labour market policies and financial support for the unemployed. These changes were, however, rather symbolic.[28]

The rough picture of Lithuanian labour will mainly integrate access justice with some elements of individual labour law and fundamental rights. The element of collective labour law is very slight.

Figure 3: The position of the 2016 Labour Law of Lithuania

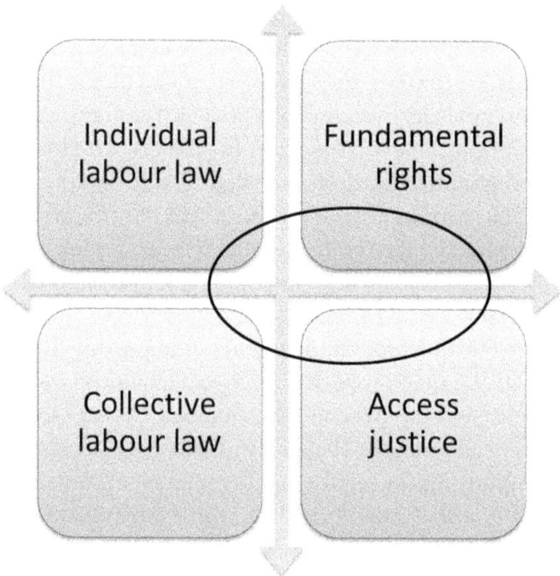

27 Article 59 of the Labour Code 2016.

28 Davulis, 'Main features of Lithuanian Labour Law Reform 2016' (n 26).

These short comparative highlights between some elements in Swedish and Lithuanian labour law do not only show how national models can consist of a specific mix of the four dimensions of contemporary hybrid labour law. They also show the significant variations in the regulatory framework within the European Union, which might cause us to ask whether a European social model actually exists and what the content of it might be.

Another relevant conclusion is that in the contemporary context of the four dimensions of labour law, there must be some minimum elements of the two traditional labour law dimensions (individual and collective labour law) present in order for us to label a regulatory regime or governance model as a labour law system. The question of how to define the borders here certainly deserves a separate discussion, but it falls outside the scope of this presentation.

Alan Bogg[1]

Brexit, Labour Law and the Twilight of Liberalism

1. Introduction

On 23 June 2016, the British people voted to leave the European Union (EU). With 51.9 per cent in favour of Brexit, the margin of victory was small but decisive. In political terms, Brexit is a seismic event for the United Kingdom (UK) and the other member states of the EU. Brexit is also a seismic event for labour law. In this chapter, I will argue that the political earthquake of Brexit has tipped the sphere of labour law on its head. It heralds the twilight of liberalism in British labour law and, perhaps, the wider European project.

In section two, the chapter sets out the historical development of UK labour law as largely contained within a liberal paradigm. The pivotal disagreements of labour law were between 'left-liberals' and 'right-liberals'. In section three, I explore the philosophical challenge posed to liberalism by 'communitarian' political philosophers. In section four, I examine the shift towards a more authoritarian style of communitarian politics in British labour law, the effect of which is to take British labour law beyond liberalism. It identifies three faces of communitarian labour law that are based upon an authoritarian conception of national community. In section five, I examine the potential of recent work on the 'labour constitution' to counter the shift towards authoritarianism in UK labour law. Drawing upon the work of Carl Schmitt, I suggest the need for caution given the central role of the 'political' in the 'labour constitution' concept. Until the contours of the political are developed, the enlivening of the political risks unleashing dark forces that are destructive of human freedom. The conclusion calls for a liberal counter-movement to repel the darkness that now threatens us.

2. Liberal Labour Law

Labour law is a field whose terrain is pock-marked with the scars of disagreement. Within the UK context, those disagreements have been fiercely contested.

1 The author is grateful to the Philip Leverhulme Trust for the support of his research work through the Philip Leverhulme Prize. The author is grateful to Mark Freedland for the discussion of some of the ideas in an earlier draft.

Nevertheless, those disagreements have generally occurred within a stable set of political parameters. We might describe those parameters as liberal. During the twentieth century, it is possible to identify two 'ideal types' that represent the main characteristics of the competing liberal conceptions of labour law across that period. We could describe these as the 'left-liberal' and the 'right-liberal' conceptions of labour law.[2] These ideal types should not be misunderstood. There are many nuances and disagreements between thinkers within each of these ideal types. And political practice has been a good deal messier than this simple picture of 'left-liberal' and 'right-liberal' models might imply. Yet there is some value in using this 'ideal type' analysis to identify, in broad terms at least, what the main bases of disagreement have been. Perhaps more importantly, we may also identify if there is an underlying consensus on certain matters that 'left-liberals' and 'right-liberals' might share as participants in a liberal tradition, even whilst disagreeing on other matters.

First we might identify some common normative commitments shared by 'left-liberals' and 'right-liberals'. Whatever else liberalism is, it is a political philosophy that is concerned with individual freedom or autonomy, and providing the rights and resources necessary for an individual citizen to formulate and pursue his or her own conception of the good. Liberalism is also a political philosophy that is committed to the anti-perfectionist or 'neutral' state, such that the state 'does not justify its actions by reference to some public ranking of the intrinsic worth of different (justice-respecting) ways of life, for there is no public ranking to refer to.'[3] The enforcement of liberal rights enables citizens to make those determinations for themselves. In the aftermath of World War II, liberalism provided a plateau upon which a basic consensus could be constructed that was anathema to political totalitarianism.

In political philosophy, the fault line between 'left-liberals' and 'right-liberals' centred on the role of the state in redistribution and the legitimacy of welfare state provision. For 'left-liberals', economic liberties such as freedom of contract play an important but subordinate role in the realisation of autonomy. While 'left-liberals' may applaud the role of markets in respecting citizens' free choice between occupations, and ensuring that citizens are responsible for the costs of their preferences between work and leisure, 'left-liberals' also acknowledge the egalitarian limitations of markets. In particular, success in the marketplace is

---

2 For discussion, see W Kymlicka, 'Liberal Egalitarianism and Civic Republicanism: Friends or Enemies?' in A L Allen and M C Regan (eds), *Debating Democracy's Discontent* (Oxford UP 1998) 131.

3 ibid 133.

often determined by 'morally arbitrary' characteristics such as intelligence and social class. 'Left-liberals' would allow for interventions to rectify those 'morally arbitrary inequalities'.[4] As such, 'left-liberals' might support the enactment of 'health and safety laws regulating working conditions, product safety provisions, minimum wage laws, and laws requiring overtime for more than a 40-hour week'.[5] For 'right-liberals', by contrast, economic liberties and market institutions play a critical role in the realisation of individual freedom. For liberals such as Nozick, the centrality of the free market to individual freedom flowed from inherent natural rights to property, life and liberty in the state of nature.[6] Other 'right-liberals', for example Hayek, did not base their arguments on inherent natural rights. Hayek's liberalism was based upon a theory of the Rule of Law, and the superior epistemic advantages of market institutions in assimilating and transmitting widely dispersed and fragmented knowledge in society.[7]

The tectonic friction between these two broad movements within the liberal tradition generated the great labour law controversies of the twentieth century. How much latitude should be given to collective bargaining? Should individual employment rights be 'deregulated' to enhance the contractual freedom of the parties to the employment contract? Does a minimum wage ensure a fair economic distribution? Should the closed shop be permitted in some circumstances or never at all? For all that, it should nevertheless be remembered that the great labour law scholar Otto Kahn-Freund and the political economist Friedrich von Hayek, for all their profound differences on matters of labour law, were liberals. The spectre of totalitarianism haunted their work, albeit with very different effects. The political significance of Brexit is that it may have precipitated a profound realignment of the fault lines of political disagreement. The disagreement is no longer about the meaning of individual freedom and how best to realise it. Nor whether liberal rights should extend beyond contract and property rights to encompass social rights, and so forth. Instead, the very idea of individual freedom as a value is now the subject of political contestation. This has been reflected in a shift to a more communitarian style of politics and statecraft in the sphere of UK labour law, especially in the aftermath of Brexit.

4 ibid 134.

5 S Freeman, *Rawls* (Routledge 2007) 57.

6 R Nozick, *Anarchy, State, and Utopia* (Blackwell 1974).

7 F A Hayek, *The Constitution of Liberty* (Routledge 1960). For an excellent critical overview and discussion, see A Gamble, *Hayek: The Iron Cage of Liberty* (Polity 1996).

3. The Communitarian Critique of Liberalism and the Resurgence of Communitarian Labour Law

The political philosopher Michael Walzer, while sympathetic to the basic tenets of liberalism, is also astute to the challenges faced by liberalism in the modern world.[8] Indeed, Walzer describes liberalism as a 'self-subverting doctrine',[9] for the freedoms that are protected through familiar liberal rights mean that communities are more fragile and precarious than they would otherwise be in illiberal societies. Thus, Walzer identifies what he describes as the 'Four Mobilities' which lie at the heart of liberal societies and generate disruptive pressures on communal attachments and local forms of life. Walzer lists these as 'geographic mobility', 'social mobility', 'marital mobility' and 'political mobility'.[10] 'Geographic mobility' is focused on the greater propensity of citizens to move their places of residence. 'Social mobility' identifies the ways in which children may lead different occupational, social and economic lives compared to their parents. 'Marital mobility' is concerned with the increasing rates of divorce and remarriage in modern societies. Finally, 'political mobility' is concerned with the ways in which individual political allegiances are now more fleeting, unstable, and less constrained by communal attachments and allegiances. These different forms of liberal mobility can lead to a situation where 'we liberals probably know one another less well, and with less assurance, than people once did…We are more often alone than people once were, being without neighbors we can count on, relatives who live nearby or with whom we are close, or comrades at work or in the movement.'[11]

The Brexit vote in the UK provides some vindication for Walzer's thesis about the precariousness of communities in liberal societies. In fact, the specific context of Brexit identifies ways in which Walzer's 'Four Mobilities' fail to fully capture the extent of the mobilities and their corrosive effects on the survival of communal attachments. In the light of Brexit, four features should be added to or given special emphasis within Walzer's account. First, Walzer's account of 'geographic mobility' was couched within the context of a single nation state, the United States, and it was concerned with the mobility of citizens within that country. The EU commitment to free movement of workers means that 'geographic mobility' within the European context displays a further dimension, which is the phenomenon of labour migration between European countries.

8 M Walzer, 'The Communitarian Critique of Liberalism' (1990) 18 Political Theory 6.
9 ibid 15.
10 ibid 11–12.
11 ibid 13.

Second, labour migration as a dimension of 'geographic mobility' has the potential to generate knock-on consequences for 'social mobility'. As Walzer observes, 'social mobility' 'carries people down as well as up and requires adjustments that are never easy to manage.'[12] When our children must weave different narratives to us because of reduced economic opportunities and different life experiences, this creates inter-generational cleavages which undermines or fragments communities. Where the causes of downward 'social mobility' are (rightly or wrongly) attributed to 'geographical mobility' and labour migration leading to the oversupply of cheap labour and the depression of living standards in the host state, this can create other forms of tension and resentment between different groups on national or ethnic lines.

Third, it is important to specify 'capital mobility' as a distinct form of liberal mobility that may have significant corrosive effects on communities. For example, the free movement of capital and the free movement of services may have significant dislocating impacts on local communities where firms decide to relocate in order to take advantage of cheaper labour costs or favourable tax or employment regimes in other countries. Finally, we might add another dimension to 'political mobility' which is the restructuring and realignment of legal and political sovereignty as between the EU and member states. In the political debates around Brexit, this was often reflected in discourse around the loss of national sovereignty over domestic laws and policies, and a failure of the EU and Council of Europe institutions to respect the authority of indigenous laws and practices. It was also reflected in political rhetoric emphasising a growing sense of political disempowerment, especially in those regional communities within the UK that experienced relative economic deprivation, such as in the post-industrial North of England.

According to Walzer, the social consequences of liberalism, particularly as manifested in atomism and the erosion of established forms of life, accounts for the recurrent appeal of communitarianism in political philosophy.[13] Its role is to operate as a corrective to liberalism's neglect of communal forms of life, both in its theory and political practice. In political philosophy, the 'communitarian critique' of liberalism was ascendant in the 1980s, where Amy Gutmann noted a 'revival' of communitarian theories in a famous review essay published in 1985.[14] Though 'communitarianism' encompasses a wide range of theories and concerns, meaning

---

12 ibid.

13 ibid 6.

14 A Gutmann, 'Communitarian Critics of Liberalism', in S Avineri and A de-Shalit (eds), *Communitarianism and Individualism* (Oxford UP 1992) 120.

that we need to be cautious in ascribing too much theoretical unity to the label, several themes in communitarian writings can be identified.

The first theme is the attachment of liberal theories to an impoverished conception of personhood that fails to recognise the constitute role of communal attachments in personal identity. According to some communitarian critics, liberals postulate the notion of a self that is essentially separate from its ends, whereas communitarians would point to the importance of constitutive obligations that are unchosen, such as obligations of loyalty to one's family or the nation.[15] As Michael Sandel has argued: 'To imagine a person incapable of constitutive attachments...is not to conceive an ideally free and rational agent, but to imagine a person wholly without character, without moral depth.'[16] The second theme is what Charles Taylor has described as the 'primacy of rights'.[17] In a similar vein, Sandel has criticised the tendency in liberal thought to elevate the position of rights based upon the protection of the fundamental autonomy of the citizen to choose her attachments and commitments.[18] Against this 'primacy of rights' position, communitarians tend to emphasise the importance of shared goods, and the civic responsibility to engage in collaborative practices of political participation. In this way, citizens join together in the public sphere to exercise democratic control over the common culture that gives individual freedom its particular value and meaning. The third theme is the tendency of liberal philosophies to support governmental practices that 'devalues, neglects, and/or undermines community'.[19] This is undesirable because communal attachments are 'a fundamental and irreplaceable ingredient in the good life for human beings.'[20] This has led communitarians to reject certain liberal commitments, such as the 'neutrality' of the state towards conceptions of the good, to provide perfectionist support for valuable forms of life that might otherwise disappear. The fourth theme is scepticism towards the 'universalism' of moral principles associated with liberal theories (particularly in respect of human rights). Instead, some communitarian thinkers have argued that morality is only intelligible within the specific contexts of particular communities. Sometimes this

15 M Sandel, 'The Procedural Republic and the Unencumbered Self', in Avineri and de-Shalit (eds) *Communitarianism and Individualism* (n 14) 12.

16 ibid 23.

17 C Taylor, 'Atomism', in C Taylor, *Philosophy and the Human Sciences 2* (Cambridge UP 1985) 187.

18 Sandel, 'The Procedural Republic and the Unencumbered Self' (n 15).

19 A E Buchanan, 'Assessing the Communitarian Critique of Liberalism' (1989) 99 Ethics 852.

20 ibid.

is manifested in a repudiation of rights discourse, such as in the work of Alasdair MacIntyre, for whom a belief in rights is akin to a belief in witches.[21] Other political philosophers have emphasised the important role of particular cultural and social meanings as a basis for understanding and critiquing the role of distributive principles in distributing social goods.[22] There is also scope for communitarians to maintain a discourse of human rights, whilst drawing attention to the ways in which the specific ranking and content of such rights is shaped by different political and social cultures.[23]

It must be acknowledged that communitarian criticisms of liberal theory and practice have been productive in prompting liberals to be more attentive to the good of community. For example, Sandel proposed that states guided by communitarian values might 'enact laws regulating plant closings, to protect their communities from the disruptive effects of capital mobility and sudden industrial change.'[24] This proposal was welcomed by Amy Gutmann as a progressive policy that could equally be endorsed by liberals.[25] In a similar vein, Walzer points to 'plant-closing laws designed to afford some protection to local communities of work and residence. Inhabitants are insulated, although only for a time, against market pressure to move out of their old neighbourhoods and search for work elsewhere.'[26] These examples demonstrate how labour law can be a site where the 'tyranny of dualisms' is transcended,[27] and the best features of liberal and communitarian thought are integrated to achieve progressive political outcomes.

It must nevertheless also be acknowledged that communitarian politics has the potential to manifest a darker side too. The idea that the ethical obligations attached to social roles are inescapable for the occupants of those roles has an oppressive and illiberal quality. Gutmann's cautionary observations on the authoritarian risks of communitarian politics remain arresting: 'The common good of the Puritans of seventeenth-century commanded them to hunt witches; the common good of the Moral Majority of the twentieth century commands them not to tolerate homosexuals. The enforcement of liberal rights, not the absence of settled community, stands between the Moral Majority and the contemporary

21 A MacIntyre, *After Virtue* (Notre Dame 1981) 67.

22 M Walzer, *Spheres of Justice* (Basic Books 1983).

23 D Bell, 'Communitarianism' <http://plato.stanford.edu/entries/communitarianism/> (accessed 14 October 2016).

24 Sandel, 'Morality and the Liberal Ideal' The New Republic, 7 May 1984, 17.

25 Gutmann, 'Communitarian Critics of Liberalism' (n 14) 134.

26 Walzer, 'The Communitarian Critique of Liberalism' (n 8) 18.

27 This phrase is used by Gutmann, 'Communitarian Critics of Liberalism' (n 14) 130.

equivalent of witch-hunting. The communitarian critics want us to live in Salem, but not to believe in witches. Or human rights.'[28]

It is certainly true that mainstream communitarian thinkers would repudiate oppressive and authoritarian government. Yet Guttmann's concerns are addressed to the practical political programmes that might be justified in the name of communitarian social philosophy. I want to suggest that Brexit has shed light on a disturbing shift towards communitarian politics in UK labour law. It represents a form of communitarianism that is highly authoritarian and illiberal. There are three main dimensions to this new 'communitarian' labour law: (i) a repressive approach to trade union regulation, reflected in an increasing reliance on direct criminal sanctions to promote 'social order' in industrial disputes and the coercive curtailment of the political voice of trade unions in the democratic process; (ii) the ratcheting criminalisation of 'irregular' migrant workers and employers, and the use of criminal law to police the employment of migrants; and (iii) a reassertion of indigenous ethical practices and 'British' human rights, rejecting the legitimacy of European human rights law and the European Court of Human Rights. Taken together, these movements take us on the road to the destruction of voluntary intermediate associations in civil society, such as trade unions and social charities, and the strong assertion of community in the form of the sovereign nation.

4. The Three Faces of Communitarian Labour Law

4.1 The Trade Union Act 2016 and the Authoritarian State

The main provisions of the Trade Union Act 2016 cover a wide range of trade union matters, although some of the provisions will require further specification through secondary legislation. The following three matters exemplify its authoritarian character as a piece of legislation, and each will be discussed briefly: (i) restrictions on the right to strike, especially in relation to new ballot thresholds and notice requirements; (ii) tightening the law on picketing and protest; and (iii) restricting the political voice of trade unions by switching to an 'opt-in' scheme for trade union political funds, applying to new members following a transitional period. The legislation thus constitutes a bold, ambitious and comprehensive attack on trade union freedoms.

Beginning first with the restrictions on the right to strike, the provisions in the Trade Union Act that have perhaps attracted the most sustained attention are the revised thresholds for pre-strike ballots. Section 2 stipulates a requirement that

28 ibid 132–133.

50 per cent of those entitled to vote do so, in order for the ballot to constitute a valid authorisation of the industrial action. Section 3 stipulates a further requirement where 'the majority of those who were entitled to vote in the ballot are at the relevant time normally engaged in the provision of important public services', and that 'at least 40 per cent of those who were entitled to vote in the ballot' supported industrial action. The meaning of 'important public services' will be confined to services falling within the categories of health services, education of those aged under 17, fire services, transport services, decommissioning of nuclear installations, management of radioactive waste and spent fuel, and border security.

In a valuable piece of work on strike law reforms during the 1980s in the UK, Simon Auerbach drew attention to the balance between 'internal' and 'external' justifications for the imposition of balloting requirements on trade unions.[29] 'External' justifications were especially concerned with the minimisation of the effects of strike action on external constituencies, such as employers, service users and customers, or the wider 'public'. Strict balloting requirements would tend to disinhibit precipitate strike action, so that the weapon was only deployed by trade unions as a last resort. 'Internal' justifications were especially concerned with the relations between the trade union leadership and its members. This often rested on a perception that a militant leadership might be subjected to internal democratic constraint by a more moderate 'rank and file' membership. In relation to the measures in the recent Trade Union Act on elevated ballot thresholds for strikes in 'important public services', it is the 'external' justification that has been most dominant. This represents a view of strike law that places a premium on maintaining social order, avoiding the disruptive impact of strike action on public services, and suppressing pluralist conflicts of interest between 'public sector' workers and users of public services. Taken together with the other measures in the legislation, it marks a repudiation of pluralism in civil society.

This is reinforced by considering the proposals to restrict public protest through criminal law. In July 2015, the Department for Business, Innovation and Skills (BIS) commenced a consultation on the reform of picketing and protest law in parallel with the introduction of the Trade Union Bill.[30] Ostensibly, this consultation was directed at considering new legal measures to prevent the 'intimidation of non-striking workers' during industrial disputes. The specific proposals for

29 S Auerbach, *Legislating for Conflict* (Clarendon Press 1990) 118.

30 Department for Business, Innovation and Skills, 'Trade Union Bill: Consultation on Tackling Intimidation of Non-Striking Workers' (BIS/15/415, July 2015). <www.gov.uk/government/uploads/system/uploads/attachment_data/file/445439/BIS-15-415-tackling-intimidation-of-non-striking-workers.pdf> accessed 9 June 2016.

consideration in the BIS Consultation disclose an important shift in governmental strategy. Thus, the Consultation states '[e]mployers report that enforcing civil offences through the courts can be time-consuming and potentially expensive and slow'.[31] The Consultation contemplated the increased use of criminal sanctions in the restriction of 'leverage' protest. It identified as a 'key challenge' the need to 'promote effective policing and prosecution of intimidation and other offences arising in the context of industrial disputes',[32] and suggested that the government would work with the police and the Crown Prosecution Service to ensure that the existing catalogue of criminal offences (including anti-social behaviour provisions) was used more extensively and effectively against protesters using 'leverage' tactics.[33] Alongside the push for greater utilisation of existing criminal offences by the police and prosecuting authorities, the Consultation also raised the prospect of *further* criminalisation in the form of a new offence of 'intimidation on the picket line'. In the end, these measures proposing extended criminalisation were not enacted. The responses to the Consultation were overwhelmingly hostile. Moreover, the government had been weakened politically by the impending vote on Brexit. Nevertheless, these proposals for criminalisation may be resurrected at a later date, and they give an important insight into the government's view of public protest and its role in a pluralist democracy.

Finally, the Trade Union Act 2016 contains important new provisions restricting the political role of trade unions. Section 11 states that it is unlawful for a union member to be required to make a contribution to the political fund if the member has not given the trade union an 'opt-in notice' (or if the member has given notice of withdrawal from an 'opt-in' notice). The trade union is also subject to an obligation to notify its members of their right to withdraw from the political fund. The 'opt-in' regime is subject to a transitional arrangement, and it applies only to members who join at the end of a period not less than 12 months following the entry into force of the relevant provisions. This is coupled with cumbersome reporting obligations. While the final provisions in the Act are intrusive enough, these measures are significantly diluted from the original proposals in the Bill, which had envisaged a universal 'opt-in' scheme for all members, requiring renewal on a five-year cycle.

The House of Lords Select Committee on Trade Union Political Funds and Political Party Funding considered that this switch to an opt-out system 'could have

---

31 BIS/15/415 (n 30) para 8.

32 ibid para 37.

33 ibid paras 37–38.

a sizeable negative effect on the number of union members participating in political funds',[34] translating into a significant drop in the funding for the centre-left opposition party, the Labour Party.[35] In the view of the Select Committee, 'If any government were to use its majority unilaterally to inflict significant damage on the finances of opposition parties, it would risk starting a tit-for-tat conflict which could harm parliamentary democracy'.[36] The suspicion that this is part of a longer game to undermine political opposition was given further support by the announcement in the Spending Review and Autumn Statement 2015, published on 25 November 2015, which proposed the reduction of Short Money allocations to opposition parties by 19 per cent and then freezing them for the remainder of the Parliament.[37] It is difficult to resist the conclusion that this represents an incremental strategy to undermine the ability of other political parties and civil society groups to mount a credible and effective opposition to the Conservative Government. In sum, the measures in the Trade Union Act contain some of the most repressive measures witnessed in living memory in the UK, and it represents a turn towards a much more authoritarian style of statecraft in the regulation of trade unions.

4.2 The Immigration Act 2016 and Nationalistic Community

One of the central political controversies in the Brexit referendum was control over immigration. Specifically, many Brexiteers objected to the loss of sovereign national control over borders that was a corollary of free movement of workers. In the field of labour law, it manifested itself in the populist slogan, 'British Jobs for British Workers'. It was here that concerns with the oversupply of cheap labour, particularly from Eastern European member states, were most acute. Sometimes this centred upon diffuse concerns with the impact of migration flows upon the cohesiveness and character of local communities. It mainly crystallized around specific concerns with the effects of an oversupply of cheap labour on the living and working conditions and employment opportunities of indigenous workers.

It is against this political backdrop that the interactions between migration law and labour law have occurred. These intersections have increasingly been

34 Trade Union Political Funds and Political Party Funding Committee, *Report of Session 2015–16* (HL 2015–16, 106) para 74.
35 ibid para 100.
36 ibid para 115.
37 R Kelly, 'Short Money' (Briefing Paper 01663, House of Commons Library 22 March 2016). <http://researchbriefings.parliament.uk/ResearchBriefing/Summary/SN01663#fullreport> accessed 6 June 2016

mediated by the role of criminal law. Criminal law has performed two main functions in this context. We might identify these as the 'worker-repressive' and 'worker-protective' functions of criminal law. First, from a 'worker-repressive' perspective, there has been a growing use of criminal law to regulate the employment of 'irregular' migrants. This has led to the creation of new criminal offences that target employers employing 'irregular' migrants *and* migrant workers who are working illegally. Second, from a 'worker-protective' perspective, criminal law is increasingly being used to target highly exploitative and abusive employment practices that tend to be associated with migrant labour. Most obviously, this has been reflected in the criminalisation of trafficking and 'modern slavery' practices.[38] New forms of criminalisation are also addressing more specific labour abuses, such as the failure to pay the minimum wage. These functions were brought together in the Immigration Act 2016, which constitutes an important piece of labour legislation, albeit one in which the Home Office had a decisive hand.

Let us begin with the 'worker-repressive' functions of criminal law, where the Immigration Act 2016 creates new offences for workers working illegally and for the employers employing them. Thus, section 34 creates a new offence of 'illegally working'. This offence is committed where the worker (P) works where he or she is disqualified from doing so on the basis of his or her immigration status, and 'at that time P knows or has reasonable cause to believe that P is disqualified from working by reason of P's immigration status.' It covers an extremely broad range of contractual arrangements for the provision of work, even extending to self-employment. Conviction for the offence may be punished by a maximum of 51 weeks' imprisonment and/or a fine. In addition, the legislation makes provision for a confiscation order under section 70 of the Proceeds of Crime Act 2002 which would cover the remuneration earned as a result of working illegally. Section 35 expands the existing criminal liability for employers engaged in the employment of 'irregular' migrants. Specifically, it states that an employer is liable for an offence where it employs a migrant who is disqualified from working where the employer 'has reasonable cause to believe that the employee is disqualified from employment by reason of the employee's immigration status'. This is accompanied by draconian new powers for immigration officers, to be able to order the closure of workplaces where the employer has previously been convicted or held civilly liable for employing migrant workers illegally.[39] These criminal law measures build

38 See, e.g., Modern Slavery Act 2015.

39 Section 38 and Schedule 6.

upon the extensive set of civil penalties regulating the behaviour of employers that already existed in the UK.[40]

The 'worker-protective' criminalisation in the Immigration Act 2016 is concerned with tackling the worst forms of exploitation through the techniques of criminal law. This involves using criminal sanctions as an auxiliary enforcement mechanism for certain established employment rights, such as the right to a minimum wage. Its effect is to create new mechanisms of public enforcement through criminal law, alongside civil litigation. In support of this public enforcement through criminal prosecution, the legislation creates a new position of 'Director of Labour Market Enforcement' to coordinate the enforcement activities of public agencies concerned with licensing of certain employing entities and the enforcement of labour rights. In some respects, this might be regarded as a positive development. It signals an acknowledgement of the practical reality that the most vulnerable migrant workers will often lack the wherewithal to enforce their employment rights through the civil process. However, as ACL Davies' powerful analysis of the Immigration Act framework demonstrates, the reality is rather more ambivalent.[41] Specifically, the legislative framework is designed 'to build, rather than break down, connections between labour law enforcement and immigration enforcement' by facilitating cooperation between the 'Director of Labour Market Enforcement' and the public authorities concerned with immigration enforcement.[42]

Overall, the new regime of the Immigration Act 2016 constitutes an intensification of the authoritarian character of state intervention in labour law. This is reflected in a greater willingness to use the stigmatic and punitive techniques of criminal law to enforce immigration control in the sphere of work. The ratcheting up of criminalisation is of great symbolic and practical importance, since the processes of criminal investigation, prosecution and punishment are a public matter, and so within the jurisdiction of public rather than private law. The web of civil and criminal liabilities effectively co-opts private employers into the public task of immigration law enforcement.[43] This blurring of the public and the private

---

40 For discussion, see B Ryan, 'Employer Checks of Immigration Status and Employment Law', in C Costello and M Freedland (eds), *Migrants at Work* (Oxford UP 2014) 239.

41 ACL Davies, 'The Immigration Act 2016' (2016) 45 ILJ 431.

42 ibid 441.

43 The food chain 'Byron Burger' cooperated with the immigration authorities, which led to the arrest and deportation of 25 workers. It has been subject to protests by campaigning groups in the light of its cooperation in the arrests of its workers. See 'Protesters target Byron burger branch over immigration raid', 1 August 2016

both intensifies the private coercive power of employers while simultaneously extending the public coercive power of the state, yoked to the common goal of migration control. It also reinforces a public discourse of national community that potentially legitimates xenophobic agendas. The rallying call of 'British Jobs for British Workers' provides cover for a range of political programmes, not all of them benign.

4.3 Human Rights: The Universal Versus the Particular

The final dimension of communitarian labour law is the strong assertion of particularised ethical values, embedded in the concrete practices of a national community and vindicated through national sovereignty. This is to be preferred to the universalist tendencies of international human rights law, where abstract rights are treated as predicated on the common humanity of right-holders. We might describe this in terms of 'British Rights for British Workers'.

Paul Craig has described this concern with the concrete and particular in the framing of rights as 'autochthony'.[44] It refers to 'the descriptive and normative ideal of attachment to indigenous or native values'.[45] The source of its appeal is closely linked to the underlying social and political anxieties that surfaced during the referendum debates, for 'autochthony' 'stands in counterpoise to themes of globalisation, expressive of the desire to maintain some degree of national control.'[46] Craig identifies three distinct levels of meaning in 'autochthony'. Firstly, it is concerned with the relative supremacy of judgments of the European Court of Human Rights and the judgments of national courts, and the extent to which national courts can develop their own jurisprudence that is at variance from the norms of European human rights law.[47] Secondly, it is concerned with the extent to which European rights are independently embedded in national laws, especially the English common law. Finally, and this is the strongest communitarian sense of 'autochthony', the substantive content of abstract rights can only be formulated within specific national contexts, informed by the culture and ethical practices of a distinct people. In this vein, Lord Hoffmann has described human rights as

---

<www.theguardian.com/uk-news/2016/aug/01/byron-burger-chain-asks-protesters-to-respect-customers-safety> accessed 12 October 2016.

44 P Craig, *UK, EU and Global Administrative Law: Foundations and Challenges* (Cambridge UP 2015) 272.

45 ibid.

46 ibid.

47 On the 'supremacy of Strasbourg', see C Gearty, *On Fantasy Island: Britain, Europe and Human Rights* (Oxford UP 2016) chapter 7.

'universal in abstraction but national in application', and this underpins an argument that has radically deflationary consequences for the European Court of Human Rights' role as an adjudicative institution.[48]

It is important to be balanced in the normative assessment of 'autochthony'. On the one hand, it 'embodies the positive desire for indigenous values, and encapsulates the natural yearning for culture locally framed'.[49] On the other hand, and in common with other dimensions of communitarian thought, it also displays a darker side. According to Craig, this is 'manifest in distrust of the "other", whomsoever that might be, whether the foreign court, the foreign person or the minority living in one's own land. It is thus not surprising that conceptions of autochthony have proved attractive to far-right groups, eager to exclude those who are felt not to "belong"'.[50] This has obvious affinities with the kind of exclusionary communitarianism that underlies the Immigration Act 2016. It has generated a hostile legal and political climate towards European human rights law in the UK, reflected most strongly in Prime Minister Theresa May's stated wish to withdraw from the Council of Europe during her tenure as Home Secretary.[51] At the current time, the government is proceeding with its plan to repeal the Human Rights Act 1998 and replace it with a 'British Bill of Rights'. This sustained attack on the legitimacy of European human rights law has had seismic political consequences for the future role of the European Convention as an external constraint on authoritarian state policies.

The first consequence is the general decline in prestige of European human rights standards at the domestic level. If we first take the role of Convention arguments in the legislative process, recent experience with the Trade Union Act 2016 gives some cause for despondency in that regard. For example, Ewing and Hendy have analysed the government's attention to pressing Article 11 issues in the enactment of that legislation.[52] The government's memorandum on the European Convention of Human Rights (ECHR) was regarded as unsatisfactory by those authors: 'If produced by a first year student, this would have been returned unmarked, with a request that it be resubmitted with proper analysis of the issues

48 Lord Hoffmann, 'The Universality of Human Rights' *Judicial Studies Board Annual Lecture* 19 March 2009.
49 Craig (n 44) 284.
50 ibid.
51 Mrs May retreated from this stated position on announcing her candidacy for leadership of the Conservative Party.
52 K Ewing and J Hendy, 'The Trade Union Act 2016 and the Failure of Human Rights' (2016) 45 ILJ 391.

involved…supported by proper citation of relevant authorities'.[53] The Joint Committee on Human Rights also produced a report that the authors assess as 'being incomplete and superficial'.[54] Given the government's increasingly open contempt for international human rights law,[55] it is probably a judicious conclusion that European human rights law does not impose significant constraints on the legislative activities of the government at the current time. It is unlikely that the indigenous 'British' version of freedom of association, at least in the vision of the current Conservative Government, extends to the protection of fundamental labour rights as protected by the core conventions of the International Labour Organization (ILO). There is an increasingly strong display of 'autochthony' amongst the senior English judiciary, and this has been manifested in strong criticism of the European Court of Human Rights' (ECtHR) 'living instrument' approach to Convention interpretation.[56] Whether the common law protects freedom of association, and whether that indigenous common law concept of freedom of association extends its protection to the right to strike, must be regarded as extremely doubtful at the current time. As the UK Government and the English judiciary cut loose from the constraints of European and international human rights law, it is doubtful that this will lead to a progressive evolution of 'British rights for British workers'.

The second consequence is the faltering political confidence of the ECtHR itself, in the face of strident political attacks by the UK Government and some senior English judges on the legitimacy of that court. The forward march of Article 11 to develop trade union rights was halted in *National Union of Rail, Maritime and Transport Workers v UK (RMT)*.[57] The Court determined that the elaborate and burdensome procedural requirements for notice in UK strike law did not constitute an 'interference' with Article 11; and the ban on secondary industrial action, interfering with an 'accessory' rather than a 'core' trade union freedom under Article 11, was within the State's wide margin of appreciation under Article 11(2). The decision is doctrinally odd, and may be explicable as a 'political' rather than a 'legal' decision, given the stated preference of some Government

53 ibid 395.

54 ibid 402.

55 A Bogg, 'Beyond Neo-liberalism: The Trade Union Act 2016 and the Authoritarian State' (2016) 45 ILJ 299, 330–331.

56 Lord Sumption, 'The Limits of Law', in NW Barber, R Ekins and P Yowell (eds), *Lord Sumption and the Limits of the Law* (Hart 2016) 15.

57 (2015) 60 EHRR 10. See also A Bogg and K D Ewing, 'The Implications of the RMT Case' (2014) 43 ILJ 221.

Ministers to withdraw from the ECHR.[58] The renewed concern for 'subsidiarity' in the lexicon of European human rights law no doubt reflects a political judgement by the Court as to how much external judicial intervention laggard states will tolerate before those states activate the nuclear option of withdrawal. The recent admissibility decision under Article 11, determining that the complaint concerning the abolition of the Agricultural Wages Board was inadmissible, is likely to fortify the suspicions of trade unionists that the ECtHR is no longer a constraint against oppressive governments.[59] It is also likely to fortify the boldness of those same states in fostering a culture of international impunity. While the concept of 'subsidiarity' is valuable in creating regulatory space for states to implement human rights norms in ways that are sensitive to local conditions, what we now seem to be witnessing is a political retreat by a Court that is cowed by the bullish intransigence of states such as the UK. There seems to be some truth in Ewing and Hendy's recent suggestion that there is now an 'Article 11 (3) opt out' for the UK in respect of trade union rights.[60] Since *RMT*, there has not been a single successful application by a British trade union bringing an Article 11 claim against the UK Government.

Taken together, these three communitarian movements reinforce a strong re-assertion of the nation state as the locus of community. The authoritarian curtailment of intermediate associations such as trade unions stifles pluralism and dissent in civil society, in the interests of social unity and public order. The use of criminal law to police the employment sphere reinforces the framing of a public discourse based on the preference for 'British workers'. Finally, even rights are particularized entitlements, with the ethical content of rights shaped by the culture, traditions and political history of a nation.

5. The 'Labour Constitution' and the Concept of the Political

One of the most important interventions in labour law scholarship in recent years has been the retrieval and reworking of older paradigms of labour law scholarship. In particular, the work of the German jurist Hugo Sinzheimer on the 'labour

---

58 C Cooper 'Theresa May Faces Huge Backlash over Call to Leave European Human Rights Convention' *Independent* (London, 25 April 2016) <www.independent.co.uk/news/uk/home-news/theresa-may-calls-to-withdraw-from-eu-human-rights-convention-a7000231.html> accessed 7 June 2016.

59 *Unite the Union v UK* App no 65397/13 (ECtHR, first section, 26 May 2016).

60 Ewing and Hendy, 'The Trade Union Act 2016 and the Failure of Human Rights' (n 52) 416.

constitution' has been given a fresh relevance to contemporary debates through the work of Ruth Dukes. Sinzheimer's theory of the 'economic constitution was based upon a view of labour law as a 'tool to be employed in the process of democratizing the economy.'[61] True democratization required an 'economic constitution' alongside a 'political constitution', so that citizens were emancipated in both the material and political dimensions of their lives. It was a theory of labour law that was at its base rooted in democratic values, and this was manifested in its developed account of *institutions of governance* in the economic sphere. According to Dukes, the 'constitutional function' of labour law envisaged that the law 'should be used to institute, or recognize, a system of workers' councils and bi-partite industrial councils, and to confirm the continued existence of the trade unions and employers' associations.'[62]

In Dukes' brilliant monograph, *The Labour Constitution*, she develops a rich account and application of these old ideas within the context of advanced globalisation and the complex interaction between different legal orders concerned with the regulation of work.[63] As with Sinzheimer's work, Dukes' theory is a democratic theory of labour law. This is counterpoised to modern theories of labour law based upon the 'law of the labour market'.[64] Specifically, Dukes challenges the idea that labour rights should be explained and justified as 'market-constituting' norms.[65] The effect of this theoretical move is to privilege markets as a form of ordering, and to insulate the market order from political challenge. Instead, there is nothing natural or inevitable about market ordering. It represents a political choice to do things in a certain way, and this political choice has profound allocative impacts on the various actors engaged in that ordering. We can also choose through politics to do things differently. In this way, Dukes reasserts the deeply political character of labour law and the transactional mechanisms of employment in society.[66] This exposes the inherently conflictual nature of productive activities and their regulation, whereas the 'law of the labour market' tends to conceal those conflicts by treating the evaluation of norms as a technical exercise in economic theory. Ultimately the 'labour constitution' affirms the normative case for the

---

61 R Dukes, 'Hugo Sinzheimer and the Constitutional Function of Labour Law', in G Davidov and B Langille (eds), *The Idea of Labour Law* (Oxford UP 2011) 59.

62 ibid 62.

63 R Dukes, *The Labour Constitution: The Enduring Idea of Labour Law* (Oxford UP 2014).

64 See, for example, S Deakin and F Wilkinson, *The Law of the Labour Market* (Oxford UP 2004).

65 Dukes, 'Hugo Sinzheimer and the Constitutional Function of Labour Law' (n 61) 206.

66 ibid 205.

ascendancy of politics *over* markets: 'If the definition of well-functioning markets and even the prior question of the inherent desirability of markets as a means of organizing social interactions are essentially matters of perspective, then workers ought to be in a position to argue for those laws and institutions which will better protect their interests.'[67]

Dukes' call for the primacy of politics is a stirring one. Indeed, the 'Brexiteers' who succeeded in the EU Referendum were keen to present this outcome as a challenge by the disenfranchised many against a narrow coterie of political and economic elites. In sum, this popular revolt at the ballot box represented the recrudescence of the political. My own view is that this is a plausible rendering of recent events. I also concur with Dukes that the normative ideal of the 'labour constitution' has a powerful normative appeal and has emancipatory potential in the face of global capitalism. Where I depart from Dukes is in my reticence about the 'political' and what that might mean in contemporary democratic practice. Politics is a central concept in Dukes' defence of the 'labour constitution'. She does not elaborate on the characteristics of the political in her work, and an account of the political is a vital prerequisite to any normative evaluation of the emancipatory potential of the 'labour constitution'. Indeed, the 'labour constitution' project may be compatible with a range of political programmes, not all of them benign.

As Sinzheimer was publishing the second edition of *Grundzüge des Arbeitrechts* in 1927, another German jurist, Carl Schmitt, was just publishing the first edition of *The Concept of the Political.*[68] Schmitt remains a controversial figure given his associations with Nazism. Nevertheless, his reflections on the concept of politics are insightful and challenging in our contemporary situation. According to Schmitt, the basic axis of politics is the distinction between 'friend' and 'enemy'. The basis of that distinction can only be understood in concrete and particular terms:

> 'The specific political distinction to which political actions and motives can be reduced is that between friend and enemy…The distinction of friend and enemy denotes the utmost degree of intensity of a union or separation, of an association or disassociation…The political enemy need not be morally evil or aesthetically ugly; he need not appear as an economic competitor, and it may even be advantageous to engage with him in business transactions. But he is, nevertheless, the other, the stranger; and it is sufficient for his nature that he is, in a specially intense way, existentially something different and alien, so that in the extreme case conflicts with him are possible.'[69]

---

67 ibid 206.

68 C Schmitt, *The Concept of the Political* (University of Chicago Press 2007).

69 ibid 26–27.

For Schmitt, then, conflict is central to his concept of the political. In contrast to 'labour constitution' perspectives, this conflict is something distinct from the material conflicts over production. According to Schmitt, the political is tied to the existence of the state. Ultimately, this friend-enemy conflict may be existential in character, where the very existence of the political community's way of life is threatened by the 'enemy'. The 'enemy' may be defined in national or ethnic or economic terms, and this will depend upon the concrete context. While Schmitt recognises the existence of intermediate associations within a political community, such as trade unions and churches, he rejects pluralist theories of the state: 'In reality there exists no political society or association but only one political entity – one political community. The ever-present possibility of a friend-and-enemy grouping suffices to forge a decisive entity which transcends the mere societal-associational groupings.'[70] He also rejects liberalism, which Schmitt regards as a doctrine whose denial of the 'political' imperils the very existence of the state. This is because in existential situations, 'the political entity must demand the sacrifice of life. Such a demand is in no way justifiable by the individualism of liberal thought.'[71] Only the 'political' has the urgency that is capable of underlying such a demand. Only the 'political' is capable of animating the life of the citizen and liberating him from the torpor of private affairs and material consumption.[72]

Schmitt's account of the political is no doubt an extreme one. In the current political climate, however, it has some currency, even if only to signal a warning about the destructive potential of unshackled politics. Across Europe, we are witnessing the resurgence of far-right political groups, and the mainstream political right is being reconfigured in more authoritarian and nationalist terms. Any plea for the primacy of politics must explain what is entailed by the political. As the Schmittian account of the political demonstrates, there are things much darker and more sinister than well-functioning markets, and the triumph of politics may bring terrible things in its wake. The shift towards communitarian labour law is dangerous precisely because it is framed around the notion of national community, underpinned by national sovereignty, with the nation state setting the concrete ethical horizons of the community (including its conception of rights). The challenge now for proponents of the 'labour constitution' is to develop a notion of social democratic politics that is anchored in liberal values. This enterprise will be as concerned to specify the limits of political creativity, such as through

70 ibid 45.

71 ibid 71.

72 For discussion of the possible justifications of the political in Schmitt's work, see L Vinx, 'Carl Schmitt', <http://plato.stanford.edu/entries/schmitt/> accessed 14 October 2016.

the constraints of liberal rights, as it is concerned to open up opportunities for popular democratic control.

6. Conclusion

Liberal labour law is now in retreat. Whether liberal principles can be restored to the centre ground of the reform agenda is an open question at the present time. What seems clear is that we may have all failed to appreciate the fragility of liberal institutions, and their vulnerability to the dark undertow of populist discontent in times of economic crisis and uncertainty. It is now time for liberalism to reassert itself in more muscular terms, in the face of a dominant populist agenda and authoritarian state policies.

What would a liberal reform agenda look like? Leaving aside questions of detail, it should be guided by the following principles: (i) respect for the Rule of Law including: respect for international law and a universalist core of fundamental human rights, the fundamental right of citizens to access a court and the independence of the judiciary under a constitutional regime of separation of powers; (ii) constitutional protection of the liberal 'mobilities', while acknowledging that some of those mobilities (especially free movement of capital) will sometimes need to be limited in the interests of social justice; (iii) recognition that free trade unions, collective bargaining and the right to strike are indispensable components of a free and fair society; (iv) constitutional protection of periodic elections between competing political parties, regulated by fair and balanced campaign finance laws; (v) protection of fundamental social rights of workers, such as those listed in the 'Solidarity' chapter of the EU Charter of Fundamental Rights. The market economy and liberal mobilities depend upon social consent. In turn, social consent depends upon social and economic arrangements that are fair and equitable for all. Social stability cannot simply be taken as a given in a globalised world. In that respect, liberals of all persuasions would do well to recall the Preamble to the ILO Constitution, that states '*Whereas universal and lasting peace can be established only if it is based upon social justice*'.

Kevät Nousiainen

Anti-Discrimination Law Setting the Standard for Social Europe?

1. Introduction

Those interested in European Union (EU) labour law have noted mandatory anti-discrimination law gaining ground, while regulation of the conditions of work by binding legislation has abated. EU employment law is largely defined by the free movement of 'economically active' persons, in practice migrant workers. A social counterweight to the economic rights based on the four freedoms was sought in the years before the millennium, with the aim of enhancing the legitimacy of European integration. In labour relations, anti-discrimination law has served the aim of increasing legitimacy through the social purposes connected to it. The European social dialogue, institutionalised with the Treaty of Maastricht (Treaty on European Union) in 1992, introduced the Euro as a common currency and provisions on fiscal policies aimed at limiting sovereign debt and annual budget deficits. These mechanisms were to keep expenditure on social welfare in the member states within strict limits. To counterbalance these monetarist policies, new mechanisms for 'social Europe' were adopted by the Commission led by Jacques Delors. The Maastricht Treaty opened a route for turning agreements negotiated by the European level social partners into directives. Collective labour law at the European level was expected to back up the legitimacy of EU social politics. Social rights, in the sense of rights of workers in the European labour markets, were added to the EU treaties. Such rights were held as a natural concomitant of free trade and free movement of labour.

The approach has met several setbacks in subsequent years. For example, a series of decisions by the Court of Justice of the European Union (CJEU) on the Posting Directive undermined much of the potential of collective bargaining for levelling up the pay of posted workers.[1] The decisions were particularly felt in the Nordic member states, with their strong collective bargaining traditions.[2]

1 B Bercusson, 'The Trade Union Movement and the European Union: Judgment Day' (2007) 13 (3) European Law Journal 279–308.

2 K Ahlberg, N Bruun and J Malmberg, 'The Vaxholm case from a Swedish and European Perspective' (2006) 12 (2) Transfer 155–166.

The recent years' financial and economic crises have further eroded the credibility of EU labour law. At the same time, anti-discrimination law has been evoked as a means to counteract social exclusion. In a sense, anti-discrimination norms seem to become the new standard for social and labour law, and anti-discrimination law has been seen as a tool for a more social EU and a means of improving the legitimacy of the Union.

The aim of this chapter is to consider reasons behind the turn to anti-discrimination law in the EU, and to assess legitimate as well as more problematic motivations behind it. Also, the chapter pays attention to the socio-economic and political backdrop of the decline of labour law and the rise of non-discrimination rights in the Union's legal architecture.

Two developments are discussed. First, that social and economic inequality has increased in most Western societies, and it seems that traditional socio-economic mechanisms have lost their capacity to tame class conflicts and produce social peace and order. The second development, which is here discussed as a concomitant of increasing social and economic inequality, is the expansion of non-discrimination law. Both European and national legislators have seemed to rely more and more on non-discrimination when social and economic inequalities increase in the developed economies of the world. The change indicates an abandonment of the idea, proposed for example by Ralf Dahrendorf during the post-World War II period, that societies become socially and economically more integrated through the combined forces of labour union driven collective bargaining, and protective legislative development.[3]

The growing inequality has several causes. It seems to have a connection with neo-liberal politics and with globalisation and related movement of capital, goods, labour and services across national borders. Neo-liberal politics are in this chapter seen as inimical to social welfare policies, but more compatible with non-discrimination. The second factor that is paid special attention to is the political trend towards identity politics. Identity politics stress the right to personal and group identities based on ethnicity, religion and other similar factors, rather than access to social and economic rights. In this sense, identity politics seem to have an affinity with non-discrimination law, rather than with general social and labour rights.

It should be pointed out at the outset that identity politics do not merely concern 'new' ethnic and religious groups, or women who are usually assumed to be the claimants for better protection against discrimination. Identity politics

---

3 R Dahrendorf, *Class and class conflict in industrial society* (Stanford university Press 1959).

have also become prevalent where established groups and nations are in question – often when such groups or nations fear the loss of privilege, entitlement or grandeur. National politics seem to evolve around issues of national identities and aversion to 'others', as lately exemplified by the refugee crisis in Europe, the Brexit referendum in Britain in June 2016, and the United States (US) presidential and senate elections in November 2016. Mr. Trump dominated among white, working class male voters in the US elections. The gender gap, racial split and age differences among voters was significant.[4] Right-wing populist parties have established themselves in the political institutions of many, or most EU member states since the 1990s. While the scholarly analysis of these political changes is still underway, it is already clear that conservative parties in the Western world are becoming fragmented, as discontented constituencies turn to nationalist and often racial values and politics. Such values and a wish to prevent further migration appeals to a considerable part of the constituencies of former left-wing parties. The discontent that both 'new' and 'old' groups express has an impact on anti-discrimination law and politics. The idea of using anti-discrimination as a building block for 'social Europe' has encountered a severe backlash.

The boost of anti-discrimination law in Europe is seen in this chapter as a promise of a turn to more substantive equality and an attempt to decrease social exclusion by focusing on factors that cause harm to groups of people whose equal rights have been historically denied, and who are even today stigmatised by characteristics they either cannot change, or cannot be reasonably asked to change. As described below, anti-discrimination law has changed the content of what the legal principle of equality stands for.

The impact of anti-discrimination law is limited, however. The severest limitation of anti-discrimination law consists of its inherent incapacity to introduce substantive social and economic welfare for minorities, where rights for such welfare do not exist for the majority. In the era of discontent among middle class groups who have lost jobs and whose income has decreased, minorities may appear as enemies who may be held responsible for this downhill development. Nationalist, racist and anti-feminist movements evoke identity politics. Identity politics partly motivate anti-discrimination law as well. These movements make use of the complex concept of equality as non-discrimination. The promise of

4 At the moment of writing, only preliminary exit poll surveys are available. The information above is from a survey by Edison Research that was conducted for the Associated Press and television networks on 9 November 2016.

anti-discrimination is likely to suffer from the backlash that is taking place in the Western world.

2. Increasing Inequality, its Political Causes and Counterweights

It is excessive for the purposes of this chapter to attempt to convince every reader of the globally increasing economic inequality. For our purposes, it is sufficient to refer to some statistics and scholarly works on income and property differentials. Organisation for Economic Co-operation and Development (OECD) sources show that income inequality in the OECD countries is at present at its highest levels for the past half century, with the average income of the richest 10 per cent of the population being about nine times that of the poorest 10 per cent.[5] Thomas Piketty shows in his study based on taxation related information that property differentials decreased in the 20th century until the 1970s, and then started to increase.[6] Economic growth has since then been slower than the growth of income from capital. In the US, the income share of the top 0.5 per cent of all income earners fell sharply in early 20th century, but has increased rapidly since the 1970s. Wage differentials compressed in the mid-century, but the high differentials prevalent in the early decades of the century returned towards the end of it. 'Top wage shares were flat before World War II and dropped precipitously during the war. Top wage shares only started recovering from this shock since the 1970s but are now higher than before World War II'.[7] The economist Joseph Stiglitz claims that the gap between what the political and economic systems were supposed to do, and what they actually do, has become too large to be ignored. He refers to radical protests of the Arab spring, the Occupy Wall Street movement, and the Spanish '*los indignados*' as a sign of indignation at the failure of the markets, as evidenced by the erosion in the standard of living.[8]

In Finland, income differentials decreased until the 1990s, but started to increase rapidly after that. The proportion of the richest one percent shows a U-shaped pattern, as a major equalization of income took place from the 1960s

---

5 B Keeley, *Income Inequality: the Gap between Rich and Poor* (OECD Publishing 2015).

6 T Piketty, *Capital in the Twenty-First Century* (Belknap Press 2014).

7 T Piketty and E Saez, 'Income Inequality in the United States, 1913–1998' (2003) The Quarterly Journal of Economics CXVIII.

8 J E Stiglitz, *The Price of Inequality* (W.W. Norton & Company 2013).

to the 1990s. After that point, equality diminished.[9] The change took place with the taxation reform of 1993, which introduced a flat-rate capital income tax, while income tax on labour earnings remained progressive. Simultaneously, social transfers to lower income groups started to decrease.[10] Since the 1990s, income differentials have remained more static, but in the 2010s differentials have somewhat risen again due to the growing number of retired and unemployed persons.[11]

Changes in taxation coincide with the fall and rise of income differentials. Progressive taxation of the highest income groups was quite high while property differentials decreased, but was reduced especially in the US and in Britain under the Ronald Reagan and Margaret Thatcher regimes and has remained low since then. Taxation of capital has decreased, as states compete by offering benefits to multinationals and other enterprises that settle under their jurisdiction.

To put it crudely, the rich become richer and the poor become poorer, due to politics that reduce social transfers and progressive taxation. The group to gain most from the increasing economic inequality is a select group, a small part of the highest decile of income earners. The OECD recommends that government policies should aim towards better inclusion of all, especially women and young people, in the workforce, by means of policies aimed at education and equal opportunity. The OECD also stresses a need of taxation and social policies for a more equal distribution of wealth.[12] For Thomas Piketty, redistribution through taxation is the measure to be taken for a retour to more egalitarian economics.

Inequality within societies is discussed under different terminologies. The OECD recommendation for better social policies uses the terms social inclusion and exclusion. These terms originate in the French debate of the 1970s, where they became popular in discussions on social rights and obligations between the state and citizens. The terms appeared in EU documents during Jacques Delors' presidency in the 1980s. In the EU context, the use of the terms underwent a subtle change. Exclusion now referred to specific groups of persons, and the grounds for their exclusion, such as race, sex and age.[13] The choice of terminology in the EU

9 M Riihelä, R Sullström and M Tuomala, *Trends in top income shares in Finland 1966–2007* (Government Institute of Economic Research 2010 Research Reports 157).

10 M Tuomala, 'Tuloerot kasvavat Suomessa' (Income differentials increase in Finland) (2000) 18(7) Tieteessä tapahtuu.

11 Tuloerojen muutos Suomessa pitkällä aikavälillä, 1966–2013 (Tulonjakotilastot [Statistics Finland] 2013).

12 Keeley, *Income Inequality* (n 5) 80–81.

13 D Allman, 'The Sociology of Social Inclusion' (Sage Open 8 January 2013) accessed 29 October 2016.

context indicates a turn in European politics towards 'social Europe', but does so by stressing group-based access to labour and related rights, rather than levelling up social and economic rights generally.

The ratification of the Maastricht Treaty countered intense opposition in many member states, as the Treaty deepened integration in areas of traditional national sovereignty. European community law was criticised for its lack of a 'social dimension', but the aim of strengthening the social dimension to correspond to the economic impact of the Union was and is far from being shared by all EU member states. Despite contested views concerning the need of regulation, European labour law and labour market related social policies were institutionalised in legal instruments, such as the Community Charter of the Fundamental Social Rights, the Social Protocol annexed to the Maastricht Treaty, and later the chapter on employment policy in the Treaty of Amsterdam. The ambition to establish binding legislation and to develop fundamental rights at the European level finally led to the adoption of the Charter of Fundamental Rights in 2000, and its Treaty status under the Treaty of Lisbon. Among the most disputed provisions of the Charter were those under Chapter VII on workers' rights.

On the other hand, much of the social dimension policies adopted by the Maastricht Treaty were in practice solutions that channelled European decision-making away from binding legislation, which was blocked due to interlocking member state and EU legislative mandates. The use of the open method of coordination, adopted in the Maastricht Treaty, is based on policies that do not require mandatory EU legislation. The adoption of the European level collective agreement steered regulation towards new corporatist channels. The new 'soft law' type measures were expected to bring results through social learning among member states, and by naming and shaming the laggards among them. The turn to less binding regulatory tools was in line with neo-liberal politics, which stressed the necessity to 'reduce regulatory burdens'.

The lack of traditional sanctions, rules and even guidelines that was a hallmark of the new regulatory tools, was from the outset seen to involve risks that could undermine the effectivity of these new measures. The financial and economic crisis has brought the shortcomings of 'soft' policies to the fore.[14] Even primary EU law has not provided a real protection against interventions into the social rights and policies in the era of financial and economic crises. The European crisis management has allotted extensive powers to introduce policies, including

14 N Bruun, K Lörcher and I Schömann (eds), *The Economic and Financial Crisis and Collective Labour Law in Europe* (Hart Publishing 2014).

austerity measures, to the European Central Bank and the European Commission. In constitutional terms, the crisis has meant a return to economy-steered integration.[15] Austerity measures have introduced social policies that are not within the ambit of the legislative framework of the EU, yet have a deep impact on social rights and policies. Soft law measures follow a similar trajectory. Before the crisis, an open method of coordination was used for balancing social and economic considerations in employment policy, but the crisis management policies are limited merely to economic ones.[16]

3. The Boost of European Anti-Discrimination Law

Anti-discrimination law has its *raison d'être* in the historical exclusion of certain groups of people from rights. Slavery, subjugation of women, prohibition of same-sex sexual relations, or rights of persons who are non-believers of the state religion, all involve a systematic historical exclusion of groups of people from equal rights. Similarly, persons classified as mentally or physically disabled have been deprived of even the most fundamental rights. Discrimination is the legal term to cover such deprivation. Semantic roots of the term discrimination lie in making distinctions, or discriminating between, for example, good and bad, but the present main meaning of the word refers to making false distinctions among human beings. The meaning now attached to the term discrimination was adopted first after World War II.

The roots of anti-discrimination law in racial discrimination are connected to slavery and colonialism. The end of traditional forms of slavery did not end differential treatment and segregation on the grounds of race. Recognition of equal civil and political rights did not give equal access to employment, housing and services. Thus, the aim of anti-discrimination is to extend protection against discrimination to private law relations, rather than only to public law ones.

The US Civil Rights Movement and other political actors demanded federal legislation against discrimination in the 1950s, and the US anti-discrimination law (Equal Pay Act 1963, Civil Rights Acts 1964 and 1968) was adopted primarily to deal with racism. Other grounds of discrimination under US federal law (religion, sex, age and disability) were prohibited, inspired by the prohibition of

15 K Tuori and K Tuori, *The Eurozone Crisis: a Constitutional Analysis* (Cambridge University Press 2014).

16 N Bruun, 'Social Policy and Labour Law during Austerity in the European Union' (2015) European policy analysis (2015:2epa) Swedish Institute for European Policy Studies.

discrimination on the grounds of race and colour. Sex as a prohibited ground of discrimination was added to the proposal for the Equal Pay Act first in the House of Representatives. The Civil Rights Act 1964 concentrated largely on issues that were relevant in the context of racial discrimination, such as voter registration and access to private and public services. Title VII of the Act prohibits an employer to discriminate on the grounds of race, colour, religion, sex or national origin. In subsequent years (1978 and 1990), Title VII was supplemented by legislation against discrimination on the grounds of pregnancy, age and disability. Title VII is enforced by the federal Equal Opportunity Commission, which was given the right to litigate in its own name by the Equal Opportunity Employment Opportunity Act in 1972. Title VII on labour market discrimination thus has a relatively broad personal scope. The rights of employees under Title VII are also protected by allowing accessible remedies.

Many national legislatures in Europe, as well as the European Community law, first prohibited discrimination on the grounds of sex. All Nordic states, for example, adopted anti-discrimination law that only covered sex discrimination in the 1970s and 1980s. In the 1970s, the women's movement demanded women's access to the labour market, and even economic reasons spoke for women's participation in paid work. The emphasis on gender in the first European anti-discrimination law reflects the importance of including women in the labour force, as well as the relatively small number of immigrants in many member states at that time.

For example, in the Nordic area, immigration at that point often took place within the Nordic area, and was made easy by the common Nordic labour market (The Nordic Council had introduced the Nordic Passport Union in the 1950s, thus allowing not only the crossing of borders, but even a common Nordic labour market). Nordic labour law, as well as related work-based social insurance of the time, was motivated by a belief in social integration through collective bargaining and mandatory social welfare norms. Only in the last decades, immigration from non-Nordic states has become the main form of net migration in the Nordic area. In European states with colonial history, or with significant national minorities, the emphasis of early anti-discrimination law lay on ethnic or racial discrimination. For example, in Britain, the Race Relations Act 1965 prohibited racial discrimination and set up a body to investigate discrimination, and later, the Equal Pay Act 1970 and the Sex Discrimination Act 1975 prohibited discrimination on the grounds of sex.

European Community anti-discrimination law started to develop in the 1970s, with a clear emphasis on labour market discrimination against women. For more than two decades, European law only prohibited discrimination on the grounds of nationality and sex. The prohibition of nationality-based discrimination (which refers to member state nationality) is the logical consequence of the free market and related four freedoms, which require that nationality cannot be a ground of preference or exclusion in the common market.[17] Primary EU law now in force gives protection against discrimination on the grounds of nationality through provisions on international market activities (Articles 45, 49 and 56 Treaty on the Functioning of the European Union, TFEU).

The modest beginnings of European law on discrimination on the grounds of sex was the equal pay principle, adopted in the Treaty of Rome (Article 119) and in subsequent treaties (now Article 157 TFEU). The equal pay principle had made little progress by the 1970s. Through case law and legislation, discrimination on the grounds of sex was banned. Case law was important in establishing that the article on equal pay identified the criteria of discrimination sufficiently to create direct effect in member states.[18] The article could also be the legal base for secondary legislation banning sex discrimination. The first directives against discrimination on the grounds of sex were adopted in mid-1970. The most important of these were the Equal Pay Directive,[19] and the Equal Treatment Directive.[20] These directives and related case law were consolidated into what is known as the Recast Directive in 2006.[21] Mandatory legislation against discrimination of self-employed

17 Originally, nationality discrimination was placed under regulation of free movement, such as Council Regulation 1612/68/EEC on freedom of movement for workers within the Community. Provisions against discrimination on the grounds of nationality are usually not discussed as a part of European anti-discrimination law. Neither have the prohibitions against discrimination of persons doing part-time or fixed-term work usually been considered in the context of proper anti-discrimination law. The prohibitions of discrimination in non-typical work were introduced by European level collective agreements, later adopted as Council directives (see Council Directive 97/81/EC concerning the Framework Agreement on part-time work concluded by UNICE, CEEP and the ETUC, and the Council Directive 1999/70/EC concerning the framework agreement on fixed-term work concluded by ETUC, UNICE and CEEP).

18 In the second Defrenne case (Judgment of 8 April 1976, *Defrenne v SABENA*, C-43/75, EU:C:1976:56), the CJEU held that the equal pay provision had direct effect on member states, and that the provision also extended to employers.

19 Directive 75/117/EEC on the approximation of the laws of the Member States relating to the application of the principle of equal pay form men and women.

20 Directive 76/207/EEC on the implementation of the principle of equal treatment for men and women as regards access to employment, vocational training and promotion, and working conditions.

21 Directive 2006/54/EC of the European Parliament and of the Council on the implementation of the principle of equal opportunities and equal treatment of women and men in matters of employment and occupation.

persons on the grounds of sex (Directive 2010/41/EC), and on discrimination in access to goods and services (Directive 2004/113/EC), extend the material scope of EU anti-discrimination law outside the labour relation, but the scope is still restricted to market related discrimination.

Since the 1990s, increasing Euro-scepticism and criticism against excessive mandatory legislation made it difficult for the EU to respond to the call for a social Europe with mandatory social protection. Anti-discrimination law was more palatable for many. The boost of anti-discrimination law started with the Amsterdam Treaty (1997), which contained a mandate to legislate on new discrimination grounds (Article 13 of the Treaty of Rome, now Article 19 TFEU). The new grounds included racial or ethnic origin, religion or belief, disability, age and sexual orientation. The mandate allows the EU to legislate on discrimination based on sex, race or ethnic origin, religion or belief, disability, age and sexual orientation. Harmonised legislation on discrimination requires a unanimous Council decision, and consent by Parliament. Thus, a high level of consensus among member states is needed.

Within its mandate and legislative resources, the EU could now boost social inclusion by introducing more anti-discrimination law, while strengthening other types of social rights was politically precluded.[22] The pressure to enhance the 'social dimension' of the EU was one of the reasons for consent among member states to adopt legislation on new grounds of discrimination. The EU used its legislative powers by introducing new anti-discrimination law already in 2000, when the Racial Equality Directive (2000/43/EC) and the Employment Equality Directive (2000/78/EC) were given. Racial and ethnic discrimination now have the widest material scope of the grounds recognised under EU anti-discrimination law.

The expansion of EU anti-discrimination law also coincides with an increasing tendency to consider societies in terms of group advantage and disadvantage, and with the rise of 'politics of recognition' or 'identity politics'. Nancy Fraser coined the term, noting that in the post-socialist world of the 1990s, a struggle for recognition was replacing the conflict on socioeconomic redistribution.[23] Fraser claimed that cultural domination was supplanting economic exploitation as the core issue of felt injustice. Groups claiming recognition for their identities

---

22 G Falkner, 'The European Union's Social Dimension' in M Ciri and N Perez-Soórzano Boragán (eds), *European Union Politics* (Oxford University Press 2016).

23 N Fraser, *Justice Interruptus* (Routledge 1997); N Fraser, 'Social Justice in the Age of Identity Politics: Redistribution, Recognition, and Participation' in N Fraser and A Honneth (eds), *Redistribution or Recognition? A Political-Philosophical Exchange* (Verso 2003).

(national, ethnic, gender and others) seemed to displace social classes presenting claims of social justice. The development raised the question of how the two axes of injustice could be balanced.

The rise of the EU anti-discrimination law was influenced by the rise of identity politics. Race and religion became political issues with the increase in immigration outside of Europe, and with the rise of racist political parties in Europe. EU level activism aiming at making good the promise of anti-discrimination law on the grounds mentioned in the Treaty increased. On the other hand, the rise of the EU anti-discrimination law also reflects the discontent felt with the national social policy measures against poverty and marginalisation. Neo-liberal political regimes in the member states had undercut such policies. Using anti-discrimination as a social policy measure was more easily reconciled with neo-liberal economics than social protection measures, as they may be seen to promote the inclusion of new groups in the labour market, which could be expected to increase productivity.[24]

Human rights law and even constitutional law has always addressed more grounds of discrimination than national anti-discrimination law, especially due to the open-ended lists of prohibited grounds of discrimination. EU law is defined by the mandate of the Union to legislate, which only covers a limited number of grounds. The grounds recognised by EU law are counted as 'suspect' in international human rights law. While the main human rights instruments prohibit discrimination on a non-exhaustive list of grounds, the protection they give to different grounds varies. The European Convention of Human Rights, for example, prohibits on several explicitly mentioned grounds, but also on 'any such ground'.[25] Yet, the protection against discrimination required of the states parties varies by ground. The European Court of Human Rights requires 'very weighty reasons' to justify differential treatment on 'suspect' grounds, while a legitimate aim and proportionate means to realise such an aim is needed to justify differential treatment on non-suspect grounds.

4. Dimensions of the Principle of Equality

Equality is one of the core concepts and principles of law. The principle has a long history. It has several dimensions or aspects, however, each with its specific historical roots and social connotations. The formal principle of equality, equal protection of human and fundamental rights, non-discrimination (or anti-discrimination), and promoting equality by positive action, are such aspects.

---

24 A Somek, *Engineering Equality* (Oxford University Press 2011).

25 Article 14 of the European Convention of Human Rights.

The overall impact of the legal equality principle depends much on which of these dimensions is preferred, or is taken to express the core of the concept, from which the other dimensions are to be derived.

In practice, the dimensions of equality are often in opposition, or even contradict each other. The formal equality principle is of old seen to be at odds with requirements of substantive equality. The formal aspect of equality is related to rational decision-making and good administration, in the sense that it is rational to treat similar situations in a similar manner. The equality principle in this sense precedes the modern idea of human beings being equal – as its well-known formulation is found in Aristotle's Nicomachean ethics. Nor is the formal principle of equality as such concerned with social or substantive equality. From the point of view of formal equality, it is irrelevant whether a high or low level of rights is adopted. For example, the demand for equal pension rights for men and women in EU law could be met by 'levelling down' the rights of the privileged sex as well as by 'levelling up' the rights of the disadvantaged group. Neutrality as to social effects of the legal equality principle has been the target of criticism in the modern age, which has been politically premised on the ideal of social equality. As the famous dictum of Anatole France puts it, the law in its majestic equality forbids the rich and the poor alike to sleep under bridges, beg in the streets and steal loaves of bread. The justification of such neutrality is usually found in the importance of distinguishing law from politics. Distributive justice is usually seen as the prerogative of politics. Therefore, decisions on redistribution of resources are to be made by political, and not legal, decision-making.

5. The General (Formal) Principle of Equality; Anti-Discrimination as its 'Other'

The general principle of equality is recognised by EU law, as well as by the law of the member states, usually in the sense of formal equality. The case law of the CJEU has often defined the equality principle in terms of the Aristotelian idea of formal equal treatment, which requires that like cases are treated alike. The Aristotelian definition – to treat what is like alike and what is different differently to the extent it is different – is radically open as to what cases are similar and what are not. Legal provisions usually define what are to be considered like cases. Even so, many difficult discrimination cases turn on the question of comparability, that is, whether the persons or situations in the case are like and thus merit equal treatment, or not.[26]

Formal equality may be considered as an empty shell which allows either more or less social equality – or it may even be seen as a basis for an ideal of more substantive equality, yet to be completed. The dimensions of equality that supplement the formal one are related to issues of substantive justice in different ways. The modern constitutional and human rights principle that the rights of all are to be protected is understood to involve positive state duties to ensure these rights equally.

For Aristotle, human beings were not equal by nature. The modern theory of human rights, however, is based on an assumption of the natural equal dignity and rights for all human beings. The link between equal treatment and social justice has been strengthened by human rights and constitutional provisions directed at the legislator. In human rights law, the equality principle is usually defined in terms of non-discrimination, and requires that all human beings have the right to equal protection of their human and basic rights. The equality principle was adopted into the French Declaration of the Rights of the Man and Citizen in 1789, and has by now become a standard clause in modern constitutions. The constitutions of all EU member states (except those of Denmark and the United Kingdom) contain a provision on the right to equality.[27] In human rights, as well as constitutional terms, the equality principle requires that not merely the administrative decision makers but even the legislator respects non-discrimination. The protection of human rights requires that states fulfil not only their negative duties by not discriminating against persons or groups, to some extent states even have a positive duty to ensure their access to rights.[28] Three United Nations (UN) human rights conventions discussed below require that signatory states extend protection against discrimination to private actors and market actors.

States have traditionally been held responsible when they themselves, or their representatives, violate human rights. Today, both human rights instruments and international case law also hold states responsible for not taking measures against private persons who violate the rights of other private persons. The expansion of human rights has made it possible for new issues to be considered as human

26 M Banton, 'Discrimination Entails Comparison' in T Loenen and P R Rodrigues (eds), *Non-Discrimination Law: Comparative Perspectives* (Kluwer Law International 1999).

27 C McCrudden and S Prechal, *The concepts of equality and non-discrimination in Europe: a practical approach* (European Network of Legal Experts in the Field of Gender Equality, European Commission 2009).

28 S Fredman, *Human Rights Transformed* (Oxford University Press 2008).

rights violations. The development has far-reaching consequences for discrimination. For example, protection of the right to life; the right not to be subjected to torture or to cruel, inhuman or degrading treatment or punishment, and the right to liberty and security of persons under human rights law has traditionally involved the responsibility of the states parties to human rights treaties to respect these rights. Today, states may for example be held responsible for violence against women (more exactly, gender-based violence against women) which violates the rights mentioned above, if the state has not offered effective protection against such violence.[29] The concept of discrimination has from the beginning extended the responsibility for harm caused to persons because they have certain characteristics, to responsibility for private persons that cause such harm. The principle of equality in human rights law thus requires that states not only refrain from discriminating themselves, but even prevent discrimination by private persons against other private persons.

Prohibition of discrimination, and especially positive measures to promote equality, may appear as a limit and even violation of formal equality. They are a 'dangerous supplement' to formal equality, in the sense that anti-discrimination law and positive measures are felt necessary due to inherent failings of formal equality. These 'substantive' dimensions of the concept are needed to fill a void in the concept of formal equality.[30]

The principle of non-discrimination links legal equality to collective categories, or 'suspect grounds'.[31] Certain groups of persons are very likely to be discriminated against, and therefore any differential treatment of these groups must be assumed *prima facie* illegitimate. The term 'suspect ground' has its origin in US constitutional case law and legal doctrine, which requires that discrimination on certain

---

29 The legal response to the problem of violence against women in international law has been developed by the UN Committee on the Elimination of Discrimination against Women (CEDAW), by regional human rights bodies, and in Europe by the Council of Europe. In Europe, the European Court of Human Rights has by now an extensive case law on the issue, and the Istanbul Convention of 2011 (Council of Europe Convention on Preventing and Combating Violence against Women and Domestic Violence) defines violence against women as discrimination.

30 Jacques Derrida refers to the 'dangerous supplement' in his text on Jean-Jacques Rousseau's Essay on the Origin of Languages, describing how Rousseau gives precedence to speech above written word as a mark of presence, but goes on writing to make this point. The self is thus always constituted in relation of its supplement, the other, J Derrida, *Of grammatology* (The Johns Hopkins University Press 1997) 141–164.

31 P Westerman, 'The Uneasy Marriage between Law and Equality' (2015) 4(1) Laws 2015 82–90.

'hard core' discrimination grounds always merits a strict scrutiny by the legislator. The doctrine is now widely recognised by human rights law. International human rights instruments prohibit discrimination on a large number of explicitly listed grounds, and often also on other grounds that are not mentioned, as the lists of grounds are non-exhaustive. Human rights instruments require the signatory states to respect those rights, and restrict them only if necessary and then only to the extent that they are proportionate to the pursuance of legitimate aims of the restrictions in question. For example, the European Court of Human Rights has held that discrimination on the grounds of ethnic origin is practically never justified, and considers several other grounds suspect. The margin of appreciation of the signatory states is more limited where differential treatment is based on a 'suspect ground' than where it concerns other discrimination grounds.

Anti-discrimination law thus differs in some important respects from the concept of formal equality. Anti-discrimination legislation of the late 20th century was developed to face the fact of continuing differential treatment of people on 'suspect grounds'. Anti-discrimination law is aimed at employers, service or education providers and other similar actors, as well as public bodies.

The effectivity of the anti-discrimination law depends on many factors, such as the material and personal scope of the legislation, on how discrimination is defined, the number of derogations and exceptions allowed from the prohibition, and what justifications are allowed, as well as the remedies and sanctions that are available. EU member states have different solutions in these respects, despite the common requirements of mandatory EU anti-discrimination law, and there would be room for strengthening the institutional requirements.[32]

The definitions of direct and indirect discrimination in EU law are similar concerning all discrimination grounds. Under the Race Directive, direct discrimination occurs where 'one person is treated less favourably than another is, has been or would be treated in a comparable situation on grounds of racial or ethnic origin' (Article 2 (2) a). The main difference with the traditional formal equality principle lies in an emphasis that prohibited treatment of a person is 'less favourable', not merely different.

The notion of indirect discrimination broadens the prohibition of discrimination further. Indirect discrimination draws attention to the effects of a measure, rather than the differential treatment as such (in US law, indirect discrimination

32 The report published by the European Fundamental Rights Agency compares national solutions, and puts forward amendments that could enhance access to rights for victims of discrimination, *Access to justice in cases of discrimination in the EU: steps to further equality* (European Union Agency for Fundamental Rights 2013).

has even been called 'disparate effect').[33] The notion of indirect discrimination tries to get at rather subtle forms of discrimination, and outlaws institutional and structural factors that are harmful for certain groups of persons. EU law defines indirect discrimination by its detrimental effect on persons belonging to a protected group. Even direct discrimination needs not always to be intentional, but the concept of indirect discrimination is based even less on the intentionality of acts. Common law has tended to consider discrimination as a type of tort law, where civil law compensation is required for acts that cause harm. Indirect discrimination seems to fit badly with this idea. It has been explained, however, that under EU law, justification of discrimination is only admissible in cases of indirect (and not direct) discrimination, because the causality requirement is lacking in indirect discrimination – there is merely evidence of a correlation between the act and the harm. Therefore, the respondent must be allowed to defend him/herself by showing that the act had a justified end and that the measures taken were suited and not excessive for reaching it.[34] Thus direct and indirect discrimination are in fact two faces of a single coin, the difference between them being merely in how the causal relation is proved. Still, the notion of indirect discrimination tries to achieve substantive equality, or ensure equal outcomes, and involves group claims rather than individualistic ones. It thus differs from the traditional formal principle of equality.

6. Positive Measures for Promoting Equality: A Step beyond Law?

Positive measures for promoting equality (also known as affirmative action) are used in many jurisdictions in different forms and to a varying extent. Positive action consists of many types of measures, which allocate benefits to members of a disadvantaged group with the aim of eradicating discrimination and achieving more substantive equality. Equality law that requires mandatory positive action oscillates between two ideas of equality. On one hand, positive action often aims at promoting the equality of opportunities, or creating a 'level playing ground', which makes positive action compatible with the general principle of formal equality.

33 On differences between the US and EU anti-discrimination law, see L Roseberry, *The Limits of Employment Discrimination Law in the United States and European Community* (DJØF Publishing 1999).

34 E Ellis, *EU Anti-Discrimination Law* (Oxford University Press 2005) 88–90; E Ellis, 'The Fight against Discrimination: The Equal Treatment Directives of 2000' (Seminar at the Academy of European Law in Trier, Germany on definitions of key concepts in discrimination law 2007).

On the other hand, some forms of positive action aim at increasing *de facto* or substantive equality. Many lawyers find such measures unpalatable, as they involve distributive justice and seem to trespass into the area of politics, rather than to remain in the traditional legal ambit of formal equality.

Some international human rights treaties, notably the UN Conventions on the Elimination of All Forms of Racial Discrimination (Article 1 (4), on the Elimination of All Forms of Discrimination against Women (Article 4 (1)) and on the Rights of Persons with Disabilities (Article 5 (4)), define positive measures as non-discriminatory, provided they are necessary for achieving *de facto* equality. Positive action against racial and gender discrimination should be temporary and be discontinued when its purpose has been achieved. The parties to the Disabled Persons' Convention have the duty to ensure reasonable accommodation (Article 5 (3)) by adjusting conditions to provide enjoyment of rights of the disabled on equal basis with other persons, as well as access to services and other social goods, including an adequate standard of living and social protection. The positive duties to provide access and accommodation are comparable to positive action measures, and under the Disabled Persons' Convention, they are mandatory. On the other hand, only reasonable accommodation is required, and reasonableness is measured against the burden it causes. Accommodation is to be necessary and appropriate, and not cause disproportionate or undue burden (Article 2).

Positive measures were in use in several EU member states in the 1980s. Such measures included, among others, gender quotas and employer duties to promote equality. In a series of decisions, the CJEU limited the use of positive measures considerably.[35] At the time, there was no provision on positive action in EU law. The Court restricted preferential treatment in access to work to tie situations, where there were equally qualified male and female candidates for a job, provided that even in these cases there was room for considering the individual situations of the candidates, and reasons of greater legal weight than the gender balance at the workplace could be taken into account. Like the UN conventions referred to above, the CJEU required that positive measures be temporary. Radical positive action was outlawed by these decisions. Many politicians wished to give positive measures more room, and a new provision on positive measures was added to the article on equal pay in the Treaty of Amsterdam. However, the provision

35 Judgement of 25 October 1988, *Commission v France*, C-312/86, EU:C:1988:485; Judgement of 17 October 1995 *Kalanke v Freie Hansestadt Bremen*, C-450/93, EU:C:1995:322; Judgement of 11 November 1997, *Marschall v Land Nordrhein-Westfalen*, C-409/95, EU:C:1997:533; Judgement of 7 December 2000, *Schnorbus*, C-79/99, EU:C:2000:676; Judgement of 6 July 2000, *Abrahamsson and Andersson*, C-407/98, EU:C:2000:367.

(Article 144 (4) of the Treaty of Amsterdam, now Article 157(4) TFEU) brought no radical change. The provision does not require member states to take positive measures; it merely allows the use of such measures to a certain extent. The provision states that the principle of equality does not prevent any member state from adopting measures that provide 'specific advantages' that make it easier for the underrepresented sex to pursue vocational activity or prevent or compensate for disadvantages in professional careers. The impact of positive measures or affirmative action at the national level has often been disappointing, as preferential treatment of women or other disadvantaged groups tends to produce a backlash. The disadvantaged are assumed to be given a privilege, rather than being compensated for the disadvantage they suffer from.[36]

The social dimension that was to supplement the economic one as an aim of the EU is evident in the Amsterdam Treaty provision that lists those aims (Article 2 Treaty on European Union, TEU, now Article 3 TEU). The Union is to combat social exclusion and discrimination, to promote social justice and protection, equality between women and men, solidarity between generations and protection of the rights of the child. Another novelty in the Amsterdam Treaty was Article 3(2), now Article 8 TFEU, which requires the Union to aim to eliminate inequalities, and to promote equality between men and women in all its activities. The provision introduced a cross-cutting gender equality duty, in particular, a duty to use gender equality mainstreaming in all policies of the institutions of the EU, as well as in the policies of the member states when these implement EU policies.

The idea of gender or equality mainstreaming originates from the UN, and was first documented in the UN Beijing Platform of Action (which is not a legally binding instrument). It appeared in the EU in the Third Action Programme on Equal Opportunities. The idea is to ascertain that gender equality is taken into account in all policies and decision-making, instead of being observed only by specific equality bodies and in separate gender equality policies. Equality mainstreaming requires that the gender impact of all planned action, such as legislation and policies, is to be assessed. Since 1997, it has been a part of the European Employment Strategy. It has been claimed that gender mainstreaming took the place of positive action in European equality politics.[37]

---

36 C L Bacchi, *The Politics of Affirmative Action: Women, Equality and Category Politics* (Sage 1996).

37 M Stratigaki, 'Gender Mainstreaming vs Positive Action: An ongoing Conflict in EU Gender Equality Policy' (2005) 12(2) European Journal of Women's Studies 165–86.

The introduction of equality mainstreaming caused great expectations among feminists and scholars. Ten years later, these expectations were beginning to fade.[38] In the context of neo-liberal politics, national social welfare agendas withered, and new private-public institutional frameworks made gender mainstreaming difficult.[39] Mainstreaming policies have not made their way to the important economic and social decisions taken due to the financial and economic crises, for example in the decision making of the European Central Bank. The crises have gendered impacts, but these vary depending on national economic structures. The policy responses to the crises by both global actors (such as the World Bank and the International Monetary Fund [IMF]) and regional ones (the EU in particular) seldom paid attention to gendered impacts of the policies. Where austerity policies are relied on, women tend to bear the negative impacts.[40]

At the national level, gender mainstreaming duties are considered political, not legal. Thus, austerity politics have been carried out without being hampered by gender impact studies. In Britain, for example, the Equality Act placed an obligation on public authorities to promote equality of opportunity between women and men, as well as to produce gender equality impact assessments of policies and practices on gender equality. No such impact assessment was made on the gendered impacts of budget cuts. The Fawcett Society, a UK charity promoting gender equality, filed in 2010 for a judicial review of the government's budget for 2010, claiming that the budget had not been made in accordance with the Equality Act. The request for judicial review was not granted.[41]

Gender mainstreaming policies motivated other disadvantaged groups to demand similar measures to assess the impact of decision-making on the position of these groups. However, there is little legal foundation in EU law for equality mainstreaming where other 'suspect grounds' are concerned. Austerity policies have a negative impact on, for example, both old and young people and the disabled.

---

38 Y Benschop and M Verloo, 'Sisyphus' Sisters: Can Gender Mainstreaming Escape the Genderedness of Organizations?' (2006) 15 (1) Journal of Gender Studies 19–33; E Hafner-Burton and M A Pollack, 'Mainstreaming in the European Union: Getting the Incentives Right' (2009) 7(1), Comparative European Politics 114–138.

39 J Kantola and K Nousiainen, 'Institutionalising Intersectionality in Europe: Legal and Political Analyses' (2009) 11 (4), International Feminist Journal of Politics 382–400.

40 S Walby, 'Gender and the Financial Crisis' (Paper for UNESCO Project on Gender and the Financial Crisis, Lancaster University, 9 April 2009).

41 Fawcett's bid for a Judicial Review of the 2010 budget <www.fawcettsociety.org.uk/2013/02/fawcetts-bid-for-a-judicial-review-of-the-2010-budget-2/> accessed 2 November 2016.

Discrimination grounds intersect, which means that people at the intersection of several 'suspect grounds' have been especially vulnerable to cuts in employment and social welfare policies. Anti-discrimination may be the most influential aspect of the principle of equality to give substance to the social dimension in the EU.

7. Anti-Discrimination Law in Today's Economic and Political Crisis

The development of anti-discrimination law has changed the meaning of the legal principle of equality. The very reason of the notion's existence lies in acknowledging that the formal principle of equality has not been able to remove social exclusion. The boost of EU anti-discrimination law was premised on the need to enhance the social dimension of the Union. Certain features of anti-discrimination law imply that it may be used as a tool of substantive equality – something that the formal principle of equality as equal treatment is not. The prohibition of direct discrimination in EU law is clearly based on the idea of equal treatment, and follows the Aristotelian tradition. An extension of the notion of discrimination that would cover consequences of social structures that uphold social divisions by racial and gender and other 'suspect' grounds is difficult. The concept of indirect discrimination could in principle allow a consideration of many unfair practices and measures. However, it goes against the grain of traditional beliefs and understandings. Even noticing indirect discrimination often requires access to statistics or other systematic information, and finding the legal evidence is often demanding. Allegations of indirect discrimination are often met with annoyance, perhaps because the duty to compensate harm is traditionally connected with some degree of intentionality.

The impact of anti-discrimination law may be precarious, also due to the symmetricity of the prohibitions of discrimination. Such prohibitions do not prescribe detrimental treatment on the grounds of black skin, female sex or homosexual orientation. Discrimination is prohibited on the grounds of race, ethnicity, or sex, for example. The idea of anti-discrimination law is to tackle detrimental treatment of groups with a history of such treatment, with the tacit assumption that the categories of sex, race and other 'suspect grounds' in fact consist of binary oppositions, where white, male etc. are the favoured opposites. The symmetrical structure of the prohibitions allows the privileged, as well as the disadvantaged groups, to evoke their right to non-discrimination.

Migration from outside and inside Europe has become a ground for discontent and anger in many EU member states. The arrival of circa 10 million refugees to Europe from the Middle East (Syria, Afghanistan and Iraq) caused negative responses both within and among EU member states. The number of refugees and migrants that arrived in Europe in 2015 is not very great compared to the number of migrants in the whole world, which was estimated to be circa 232 million in 2013.[42] The burden faced by the member states varied considerably, depending on where within the EU the migrants originally arrived, and national policies in receiving them. The refugee crisis of 2015 has shown that there is a considerable lack of consensus and effective EU legislation concerning asylum seeking and migration.[43] The yearly migration flows among EU member states are, both from those with and without EU citizenship, also considerable. The number of migrants was estimated at 3.8 million migrants in the EU in 2014.[44]

The economic crisis has made a stronger 'social dimension' in the EU and its member states both more desirable and difficult. Austerity politics seem to be here to stay, and the economic doctrine on which they are based is not seriously challenged. A return to welfare state politics and more inclusive labour law protection does not seem probable. If it is so, anti-discrimination law will remain the main 'social dimension' in EU labour law. It will be difficult to face expectations of fair social policies based on anti-discrimination law alone. It is an inherent feature of anti-discrimination that it does not as such provide new rights and benefits. The very important idea of anti-discrimination lies in the attempt to remove unfair differences in access to rights already in place. Anti-discrimination law as such is indifferent as to what rights and benefits are fair, as long as they are enjoyed on an equal basis. Anti-discrimination law cannot effectively take the place of social and labour rights.

The middle classes that feel disinherited by politics that have led to their loss of employment, as well as their relative loss of welfare and status, seem discontent with both traditional right and left wing politics. The discontent often are members of groups in the favoured pole of binary oppositions such as white-black, and man-woman. Demands on retrieving the lost position easily turn on those groups who, having been historically excluded from the labour market, are attempting to find a place there under the protection of anti-discrimination law. Privileged categories of persons may claim discrimination under the symmetrical prohibitions of anti-discrimination law even more self-evidently than earlier.

---

42 ILO, *Global estimates on migrant workers: results and methodology* (International Labour Office 2015).

43 The EU has responded to the crisis, among others, by establishing the Asylum, Migration and Integration Fund for the period 2014–2020.

44 *Migration and migrant population statistics* (Eurostat 2016).

Non-discrimination has become an increasingly important meaning of the principle of equality. That means that the law pays more attention to groups and categories of people. Does this leave more room for what Martha Nussbaum calls 'politics of disgust'? Nussbaum refers to Lord Devlin's dictum that legislation that restricts the rights of gay persons may be given simply because homosexual acts 'disgust the average man'. According to Nussbaum, politics of disgust deny the principles of equality and non-discrimination.[45] The idea of equal rights is based on a belief that any subject of rights is also a subject worthy of esteem and respect.[46] Politics of disgust deny rights to persons who are found 'disgusting' on grounds such as their ethnicity, sex or sexual orientation. Social psychologists have referred to disgust as an emotion related to sexual, bodily or spiritual purity. Such emotions have been found to correlate with authoritarian and conservative attitudes,[47] which may be related to a manner of political persuasion through gut feelings rather than rational arguments.

Anti-discrimination law has faced strong opposition from the beginning. The present dilemmas of anti-discrimination in Europe relate to the feelings of loss for 'ordinary people' caused by long-term economic politics, combined with a need to accommodate the acute needs of newcomers to share in the rights and benefits. Many newcomers are seen as 'others', and it may be tempting to oppose their rights not with rational claims, but by politics of disgust. Then, anti-discrimination law may again be a tool needed against very crude forms of intentional abuse, rather than as a means capable of deconstructing subtle forms of structural discrimination. On one hand, there may be more need for anti-discrimination law, but on the other, the far-reaching promises of positive equality measures and a radical expansion of the notion of indirect discrimination may become foregone conclusions.

---

45 M Nussbaum, *From Disgust to Humanity: Sexual Orientation and Constitutional Law* (Oxford University Press 2010).

46 P Ricoeur, *Reflections on the Just* (University of Chicago Press 2007) 1–10.

47 Y Inbar, D Pizarro, R Iyer and J Haidt, 'Disgust Sensitivity, Political Conservatism, and Voting' (2012) Social Psychological and Personality Science 537–544.

Kari Tapiola

The Future Role of the International Labour Organization

1. Introduction

Although labour law from its origins onwards embodied a clear economic interest – avoiding competition at the cost of the health and safety of workers – there has been a constant struggle regarding the extent of how explicitly this economic interest is recognized. Labour legislation has been drafted primarily for the purpose of protecting collective and individual interests of the workers. The assumption, of course, has been that good working conditions contribute to productivity and healthy competition. The arguments presented to the International Labour Organization's (ILO's) 1941 Conference in New York are a case in point. The argument was made in detail, based on wartime needs of the economies of the allied countries, that even in bad times, basic conditions of work need to be respected.[1]

This link between the basic conditions of work – especially freedom of association and the potential of tripartite cooperation – was carried on to the 1944 Declaration adopted by the first International Labour Conference after World War II, in Philadelphia.[2] For decades to come, it inspired the policies for European

---

1 ILO: *The ILO and Reconstruction*, Report by the Acting Director of the International Labour Office, Conference of the International Labour Organisation, New York, October 1941 (Montreal 1941).

2 Article I of the Declaration of Philadelphia states:

The Conference reaffirms the fundamental principles on which the Organization is based and, in particular, that

(a) labour is not a commodity;
(b) freedom of expression and association are essential to social progress;
(c) poverty anywhere constitutes a danger to prosperity everywhere;
(d) the war against want requires to be carried on with unrelenting vigour within each nation and by continuous and concerted international effort in which the representatives of workers and employers, enjoying equal status with those of governments, join them in free discussion and democratic decision with a view to the promotion of the common welfare.

References to the Declaration of Philadelphia often restrict themselves to subparagraphs (a) and (c) of this key article. The Declaration is incorporated in the Constitution of the ILO.

reconstruction and the development of the Western welfare state model, and it was applicable to both decolonization and human rights during the Cold War period. Yet by the late 1970s, this approach started to be questioned. The argument was made that too much protection through regulation created rigidities in the labour market. From the early 1980s onwards, this spurred a growing trend favouring deregulation and labour market flexibility.

After the end of the Cold War, with various approaches to the opening of formerly closed markets, there has been an increased focus on improving the conditions for competition. This has led to increased tensions between the goals of economic and social legislation and regulation, to an extent that today labour law is shaped – or reshaped – increasingly openly with considerations of promoting economic circumstances and competitiveness.

Yet it is difficult to translate economic concepts into labour law. Many recognized and historical priorities of the ILO are seen from different perspectives, which are not always connected to one another. To give an example, eliminating child labour has been one of the recognized priorities since 1919. In that year, the first International Labour Conference also adopted the first Convention to deal with the issue: Convention No. 5 setting the minimum age for industrial employment.

In fact, child labour ranked together with long working hours among the concerns that fed early debate on labour law in the 19th Century. Convention No. 5, 1919, was the first one in a string of instruments that led to the 1973 Minimum Age Convention No. 138, which in itself is a consolidation of seven earlier Conventions. The normative approach concentrated on setting the minimum age, or the range of acceptable minimum ages, for employment, first for specific branches of activity and then for all forms of employment.

In the 1980s, the ILO analysed and treated the work of children more as an economic and development question without references to the ILO's minimum age standards.[3] At that time and well into the 1990s, Convention No. 138 was not highly ratified. In fact, the conventional wisdom was difficult to apply. Even Sweden had taken 17 years to ratify it. The Convention was often characterized as obsolete, and an example of inflexible and overly detailed regulation.[4]

---

3 See for instance G Rodgers and G Standing, 'Economic roles of children in low-income countries' International Labour Review (1981) 120 (1) 31–47.

4 Prior to the ratification campaign of fundamental ILO conventions, launched in 1995, the Minimum Age Convention No. 138 had 44 ratifications. The current number of ratifications for it is 169, the latest being by Canada where it will enter into force in June 2017.

2. Debate on Core Labour Standards

Yet the Minimum Age Convention was the only child labour instrument at hand when the discussion of core labour standards in the globalized economy started in the early 1990s. Child labour resurfaced as one of the key issues in the debate on the link between trade and labour standards. This was a sometimes highly emotional debate moving between the areas of competence of the ILO and the newly established World Trade Organization, with sharp differences on the proposal of introducing a 'social clause' in international trade agreements.

The notion of fundamental or core labour standards was largely accepted due to the inclusion of child labour in it. I recall that at an international conference of the sporting goods industry in London, in late 1996, some representatives of the leading brands told me that if the social clause would only be about child labour, they would not have problems with it. After listening to a detailed explanation of what Convention No. 138 actually contained – and what it did not – some of the participants said that if that was all there was to it, they did not see any problems in complying with its provisions.

Because there was no other ILO instrument directly addressing child labour, the Minimum Age Convention became by default the reference point in the debate on core labour standards. It was not at first recognized as a priority Convention for more frequent reporting in the same way as the fundamental Conventions Nos. 87 and 98 on freedom of association, Nos. 29 and 105 on forced labour, and Nos. 100 and 111 on discrimination. The increasing global focus on gender issues, as manifested by the Fourth UN World Conference on Women in Beijing, 4–15 September 1995, served to give a boost to the Equal Remuneration Convention, 1951 (No. 100). It became one of the two normative reference points for the principle of non-discrimination in employment and occupation, the other one being the Discrimination Convention 1955 (No. 111).

The core Conventions became an object of the ratification campaign, initiated in 1995 by the Director-General of the ILO, Michel Hansenne. This campaign was a consequence of the discussions at the World Summit for Social Development, convened by the United Nations in Copenhagen in March 1995. The Conference confirmed the importance of the four categories of core labour standards. It specified that they were set out in ILO Conventions and that all countries, independent of ratification, had the obligation to strive to realize their aims.[5]

5 Declaration on Fundamental Principles and Rights at Work and its Follow-up, adopted by the International Labour Conference on 18 June 1998. Annex revised on 15 June 2010.

Throughout the 1990s, there was a discussion on whether another ILO Convention on child labour would be needed for a more targeted prohibition of the use of child labour. Donor support, first from Germany since 1992 and subsequently from most of the industrialized countries, had made the International Programme for the Elimination of Child Labour into the largest single technical cooperation programme of the ILO. The International Labour Conference developed the notion of targeting the most intolerable forms of child labour with immediate action, while not giving up a more comprehensive approach to the issue in general. Among others, this was developed in a resolution adopted by the Conference in 1996, and it was also the subject of a special high-level discussion at the Conference.[6]

The idea of focussing on the 'intolerable forms' of child labour was strongly criticized by some groups. The question was asked, if you focus your action – and a standard – on the worst forms of something which as a whole should not exist anyway, are you then not tolerating or even legitimizing other work which is not classified as intolerable? In my earlier function as Deputy Director-General of the ILO, I had some thorough debates with the Nordic trade unions on this issue. My argument was that if the notion of applying time-bound programmes to eliminate child labour was acceptable (as it had largely become), then you must accept that imperfections will persist for a certain time.

Such an incremental approach is difficult to translate into the normative sphere. But this first-things-first view is a very practical ILO answer, and it comes with a lot of history. At the end of 1928, the first Director of the ILO, Albert Thomas, visited China. As told by his close collaborator, Edward Phelan (later Director-General), in Nanking revolutionary reformers, showed Albert Thomas a draft for a new Labour Code in China for his comments.

As Phelan tells the story, many of the provisions went beyond what was possible in highly developed countries. Thomas argued that the draft was far too complicated for what was needed. 'You must begin by prohibiting the work of young children and the exploitation of female labour. You must build up step by step a corps of factory inspectors who will enforce these provisions. Employ all your means and energy on that first and consider the rest later.'[7]

---

6 ILO, 'Resolution concerning the elimination of child labour' International Labour Conference 83rd Session 4–20 June 1996.

7 E Phelan, *Yes and Albert Thomas* (Columbia University Press 1949) 263. Phelan exclaimed that this was '(s)trange advice from the man who was accused of being a theorist and a doctrinaire'.

Indeed, in the 1920s, China was one of the very first recipients of technical assistance by the International Labour Office, on labour law in general and also on child labour.[8]

3. The Evolving Standards Policy

Let us return to the standards policy of the ILO as it is currently developing. There is an underlying trend which has its roots in the debate on labour market rigidities and flexibility in Europe in the 1980s, as well as the new constellation that emerged after the end of the Cold War. Criticism was expressed in and after 1991 above all by the Swedish employers, who played an important role in the Employers' Group of the ILO.

The Managing Director of the Swedish Employers' Confederation, Ulf Laurin, asked whether the ILO was still needed. Communism was gone, democracy had won. What was the 'business idea' of the ILO in the new circumstances? One of the key arguments was that the ILO had become a machine producing Conventions, which subsequently were less and less ratified. Mr. Laurin saw this as proof that there was no longer any market for the ILO's products.[9]

The debate on the value of standards was to an extent redirected by the recognition that in the new global context, there was a need at least to respect core labour standards. The new global economy had labour problems, which had to be dealt with on the basis of certain agreed norms. Old problems, such as child labour, forced labour and discrimination and exploitation of non-organized workers, were still very much there. In a new, more transparent world, they had become even more visible and called for action.

In the ILO, this led into the adoption of the 1998 Declaration of Fundamental Principles and Rights and its Follow-up. As already agreed at the Social World

---

8 C Yifeng, 'The International Labour Organization and Labour Governance in China 1919–1949', in R Blanpain, U Liukkunen and C Yifeng (eds), *China and ILO Fundamental Principles and Rights at Work* (Wolters Kluwer 2014) 29.

9 Mr. Laurin expressed his concerns to Director-General Michel Hansenne, saying that 'the ILO must adapt itself to a changing world, its main objective to fight communism does not exist anymore and the ILO should therefore instead support sustainable economic growth and promote productive employment. … The standard-setting activity – Conventions and Recommendations – must be reconsidered'. Describing the discussion with the Director-General, Mr. Laurin said that '(we) made it quite clear to Mr. Hansenne that if nothing happens and if the ILO does not become much more effective, we have no reason to continue with this work'. Note by Sten Selander, SAF, dated 23 June 1993 (ILO archives).

Summit in Copenhagen, fundamental rights were to be observed by all – not only those who had ratified the relevant ILO Conventions.[10] Both the Copenhagen Summit and the new World Trade Organization's (WTO's) 1996 Singapore Ministerial Conference[11] had agreed that the ILO and its standards were the global reference point.

The follow-up mechanism of the 1998 ILO Declaration had specific procedures for the countries that had not ratified the fundamental Conventions. It consisted of annual reporting, an examination of reports by a small group of non-legal experts, and reviews by the Governing Body, all this with the purpose of advising countries and channelling technical assistance for the realization of the principles underlying the Conventions, although the legal obligations entered into through ratification were not there.

This new procedure was expected to give a lot of work, much of it potentially delicate. Information on the realization of principles tended, particularly when transmitted by the social partners, to turn into allegations of shortcomings and violations. There was no other template for dealing with such allegations in the case of non-ratification than the special procedure of the Committee on Freedom of Association.

However, something else happened. Instead of subjecting themselves to an annual reporting and examination process, non-ratifiers by and large chose to escape to the more familiar and predictable supervisory system by increasingly ratifying the fundamental Conventions. The ratification rate of the Conventions is now well over 90 per cent, and it is led by the latest of them, Convention No. 182

10 World Summit for Social Development Programme of Action (Copenhagen March 1995) Ch 3.c, paras 54 (b) and (c).

11 World Trade Organization, Singapore Ministerial Declaration 14 December 1996. Paragraph 4 of the Declaration is on labour standards:

We renew our commitment to the observance of internationally recognized core labour standards. The International Labour Organization (ILO) is the competent body to set and deal with these standards, and we affirm our support for its work to promote them. We believe that economic growth and development fostered by increased trade and further trade liberalization contribute to the promotion of these standards. We reject the use of labour standards for protectionist purposes, and agree that the competitive advantage of countries, particularly low-wage developing countries, must in no way be put into question. In this regard, we note that the WTO and ILO Secretariats will continue their existing collaboration.

on the Worst Forms of Child Labour, which in 1999 was added to the list of the fundamental instruments.[12]

The argument of non-ratification, advanced in the early 1990s by the Employers' Group, was thus no longer there. At the same time, ratification prospects had become a more explicit criterion in the process of standard-setting by the ILO. The issue was raised throughout the second discussion of the Worst Forms of Child Labour Convention No. 182, in 1999. For example, the commitment to universal basic education was qualified as an aspiration in the text of the Convention once it was noted that over 20 countries did not have a legal obligation to basic education. Including it in the binding Convention would have endangered a corresponding number of ratifications.[13]

At the beginning of the substantive second discussion, and not least for purposes of ratification, the title of the Convention was readjusted. Instead of outright prohibiting certain forms of child labour, it became a Convention for 'immediate action' for the designated purpose.[14] The notion of 'worst forms' came up only in the process of drafting, as words such as 'unacceptable' or 'exploitative' were discarded. When the Committee drafting the Convention decided on the short title of the instrument, the suggestion of designating the objective as 'worst forms' was made by the Swedish Government delegate.

4. The Changing Standard-Setting Agenda

Were the employers right in 1991 – was the standard-setting system of the ILO out of control? Had it become some kind of an automatic process?

It is useful to look at the situation that had developed over a number of decades. In 1970–1979, the ILO adopted 23 Conventions. Between 1980 and 1989,

---

12 The Forced Labour Convention No. 29 has 178 ratifications; the Freedom of Association Convention No. 87 has 153; the Collective Bargaining Convention No. 98 has 164; the Equal Remuneration Convention No. 100 has 172; the Forced Labour Convention No. 105 has 175; the Discrimination Convention No. 111 has 173; the Minimum Age Convention No. 138 has 169; and the Worst Forms of Child Labour Convention No. 182 has 180. The ILO has 186 Member Countries.

13 ILO, *Report of the Committee on Child Labour*, International Labour Conference 87th Session June 1998.

14 In the draft version, the Convention was to be on 'the prohibition and immediate elimination' of the worst forms of child labour. After a thorough discussion, taking one day of the Conference Committee's work, it became a 'Convention concerning the prohibition and immediate action for the elimination of the worst forms of child labour'.

the number was 16. In 1990–1999, a total of 13 Conventions were adopted. In 2000–2009, the number of adopted Conventions fell to six. In the current decade, that is from 2010 until now, the International Labour Conference has adopted one Convention and two Protocols.[15]

Are we then now worse off? Standard-setting continues, as do ratifications of adopted Conventions. But we may be coming to a situation where we will indeed adopt less standards, especially binding Conventions, but where they are more thought through, with better preparation and, hopefully, an active follow-up. What the experience of campaigns and other action for ratification shows is that we cannot only produce standards and leave them, as it were, outside the factory door, expecting the world to make its way to these goods. Possibly we have been too much affected by what I would call a 'Stalinist' approach to marketing our products (or rather not marketing them at all). Once adopted, the instruments were considered strong enough on their own to be carried through to parliaments and subsequent implementation.

One of the factors was the way in which the agenda of the International Labour Conference was decided by the Governing Body. I have some experience in this, as in the early 1990s I was Workers' Spokesperson for the Office at the Governing Body sessions. From 1996 to 2010, I was responsible for this item in the sessions of the Governing Body, both coordinating the proposals and assisting the tripartite constituents in reaching an acceptable decision on the Conference agenda. Consequently, I know at least 14 ways in which the Conference agenda should not be set. I am afraid that the ideal formula has remained elusive.[16]

In my view, minus the usual rhetoric, the employers had a point in questioning a practice which – usually – meant that every year, the Conference had a second discussion on one topic, resulting in the adoption of a standard, and a first discussion on another standard. The established practice was that each Conference had two standard-setting items and one for a general discussion, in addition to the Committee on the Application of Standards.

When the Governing Body Members had different views on whether to address a topic or not, or how to address it, the result could become the lowest common denominator, a compromise which no one was really satisfied with. In some years, the Governing Body had no enthusiasm for any of the topics proposed by

15 ILO, Information System on International Labour Standards. Conventions, NORMLEX www.ilo.org.

16 This discussion continues. See Proposals for the Agenda of the International Labour Conference, discussed at the March 2016 session of the Governing Body (GB.326/INS/2).

the Office. In the early 1990s, the Governing Body selected from outside the list the item of health and safety in mines, largely because media reports of recent accidents in mines in China and Ukraine.[17]

I was involved in the backroom negotiations in 1995, which led to a deal between the employers and workers on the agenda two years later. The employers wanted to revise the Convention prohibiting fee-charging employment agencies. The workers, in turn, gained acceptance for a long-standing request to set a standard on 'contract labour'.

This was a terrible deal. What succeeded was the one-year Conference discussion in 1997 with the parallel process for the adoption of the Private Employment Agencies Convention No. 181. The first discussion that same year on contract labour was an unmitigated disaster. The Office had had misgivings all along about the decision imposed by the Governing Body, and its experts faced considerable conceptual and even linguistic problems in preparing the documentation for the Conference. For instance, there was no generally agreed translation for contract labour; the French version *travail en sous-traitance* did not convey the same meaning.

The members of the Workers' Group had different and even contradictory views on what was to be discussed. The employers were, in the words of their spokesperson, implacably opposed to a standard on the topic. And for the Committee's Indian Chair, contract labour seemed to be another form of bonded labour.

The whole thing became a train-wreck, and by the end of the second discussion in 1998, it was clear that what was needed was returning to the drawing board.[18] The topic was later on saved by a general discussion, and nearly ten years later, Recommendation No. 198 on Employment Relations summed up the somewhat inconclusive agreement on this topic in 2006.

5. The Washington Agreement

A new consensus, although shaky at times, has emerged since the late 1990s. Key employer and worker representatives agreed on the parameters of standards policy at a bilateral meeting in October 2000 in Washington DC.[19] This took place in the

---

17 This resulted in the Safety and Health in Mines Convention, 1995 (No. 176). Currently it has 31 ratifications.

18 ILO, *Report of the Committee on Contract Labour*, International Labour Conference 86th Session June 1998.

19 Based on a draft by employer participants, the Washington meeting produced a position paper which was later submitted to the Employers' and Workers' Groups on the Governing Body.

context of informal consultations, which the International Labour Office had been promoting since the negotiations for the 1998 Declaration. In this case, the Office supported the bilateral meeting financially, but did not participate in it. The joint view of the employers and workers was further elaborated in a joint statement (entitled 'Basis for common understanding'), which was adopted by both of the two groups on 10 November 2000.[20]

The principle of continued standard-setting has been maintained, but there is agreement that the choice has to be prepared with more substantive discussion before finally opting for a particular standard. Such a substantive discussion, if needed in the Labour Conference, makes sense before setting out on a two and a half year voyage to a new instrument.

The value of Recommendations as standards has also been revisited. The recent process could be seen to testify to an increased – or maybe refound – recognition that Recommendations are useable standards too, and not only the 'waste-paper basket of Conventions', as they had become to be seen as in the 1970s and 1980s, when the main focus was on Conventions. The Recommendation would sometimes be patched together at the end of a negotiating process, from bits and pieces that had not been found acceptable enough to make it into the Convention.

A recent case in point that demonstrates this evolution is the Social Protection Floors Recommendation 2012 (No. 202). The question of ensuring social security coverage and rights needed to be revisited in terms of standards, but for various reasons, a revision of the landmark Social Security (Minimum Standards)

---

20 The 'Basis for Common Understanding', dated 10 November 2000, contained the following points:

> All decisions in the process of standard setting should be taken by consensus between Workers and Employers. Both parties have to exhaust all possibilities to reach a consensus before having a vote. The value of both new Conventions, revised Conventions and Recommendations is recognized. General Discussions are valuable for identifying issues, form, purpose and contents of standards as well as to debate important issues. Where appropriate, the follow-up to autonomous Recommendations by the social partners at national level should be encouraged. The integrated approach and General Discussions will identify the standard-setting items to be placed on the Conference agenda. Both groups will support the setting of new standards, where appropriate. The linkage between the adoption of Conventions and their subsequent ratification and implementation will be promoted. Both Workers and Employers should promote social dialogue and tripartism at national level (the ratification of ILO Convention No. 144 and the establishment of tripartite consultative procedures).

Convention 1952 (No. 102) was not a feasible option. A general discussion at the 2001 International Labour Conference had left the question of either revision or new standards unanswered.

Likewise, the HIV and AIDS Recommendation 2010 (No. 200) was found to be preferable to an attempt at a Convention with uncertain ratification perspectives, especially as much of the topic had already been covered by a code of practice which had proved itself to be an efficient and acceptable tool for work on the ground with the constituents.[21] The prospect of turning a successful code of practice into a binding Convention was not readily available. It is to be noted that while codes of practice regularly address all constituents, the purpose of a Convention is to set out the legal obligations of a ratifying state. It would also be damaging if the contents of an acceptable and widely used code of practice would fail to gain acceptance through the ratification process.

A Recommendation, after all, is addressed to all, and it creates obligations which can be activated through follow-up measures. Recommendations are subject to the regular standards supervisory mechanism of the ILO. When accompanying a Convention, a Recommendation is a guide to its application. In the case of the Worst Forms of Child Labour Convention, options for determining the coverage of the Convention are specifically given by the Recommendation.

A stand-alone Recommendation can also serve as an entry point into terrain, where more work will be needed to identify what could lend itself to a more binding approach through legal obligations set out in a Convention. In this perspective, entering the question of standards to be applied in the informal economy through a Recommendation makes sense.[22]

In the light of the political debate on standards following the end of the Cold War, standard-setting has focused more directly than earlier on employment. An increase in employment policy instruments generally favours the approach of a Recommendation (or a promotional Convention as opposed to a strictly 'regulatory' one). One might also say that this has been a certain price to be paid for maintaining the standard-setting process with adequate support from the employers.

The issues arising out of globalization have also favoured a search for priority areas. The work for what became the Worst Forms of Child Labour Convention No. 182 (1999) was characterized as "targeting the intolerable". The same urgency

---

21 ILO, *An ILO code of practice on HIV/AIDS and the world of work* (ILO 2001).

22 Recommendation No. 204 on the Transition from the Informal to the Formal Economy (2015).

can be seen in the HIV and AIDS Recommendation No. 200 and the Domestic Workers' Convention 2010 (No. 189). The development of a standard against violence against women and men at work, scheduled to start at the 2018 International Labour Conference, is a step in the same direction.

A search for measures to prevent and eradicate universal scourges, irrespective of differences of levels of economic development, can also be seen as an indication that the attempt to set the minimum global level of social standards did not stop with the 1998 ILO Declaration on Fundamental Principles and Rights at Work. On the contrary, the process set into motion by that Declaration gave a new impetus to the traditional aim of respecting and improving the basic levels of decent work.

6. Issues for the Next Review

The existing body of standards will again be revisited. After a tripartite exercise between 1995 and 2002 led by the French Government Adviser, Jean-Louis Cartier[23], the number of up-to-date Conventions is 71 out of 189. Of Recommendations, 72 are up to date. The number of obsolete Conventions is 66, and those scheduled for revision is 22. About half of the ILO's normative system is not up to date, and much of it has been revised already. The main issue still facing the Cartier group was to cut down and do away with deadwood. But moving ahead with a dynamic standards system calls for more. Not only weeding out what is not viable and harmful, it calls for gardening.

A big question, for which there is no one magic solution, is how to revise standards. One model is consolidation, recently successfully applied in the case of the 2006 Maritime Labour Convention. Such a comprehensive overhaul as that of the numerous instruments of the Maritime Labour Code is hardly feasible in other areas. At a smaller scale, it inspired the negotiations for the Work in Fishing Convention No. 188, which failed to pass after the second discussion, but was then adopted in 2007. There had been five earlier conventions on work in the fishing sector.

The Minimum Age Convention No. 138 of 1973 also replaced seven conventions on the same topic adopted between 1919 and 1965. The traditional method of revision has been to rewrite the Convention from beginning to end, as was done with the Maternity Protection Conventions Nos. 103 and 183. The 'original'

---

23 Working Party on Policy regarding the Revision of Standards (Cartier Working Party), Information note on the progress of work and decisions taken concerning the revision of standards <www.ilo.org/wcmsp5/groups/public/---ed_norm/---normes/documents/genericdocument/wcms_125644.pdf> accessed 17 March 2017.

Maternity Protection Convention was No. 3 from 1919. Instead of focusing on specifically out-of-date provisions, this practice opens the whole Convention – and the principles underlying it – to review and rewriting.

Negotiating new instruments to fill the gaps between existing ones can be a perilous and frustrating process, too. The Promotional Framework for Occupational Safety and Health Convention, 2006 (No. 187) resulted from the application of an 'integrated approach' to standard-setting, which aimed at reaching a political consensus on what was needed to complete the normative approach in a specific field before starting the work on an instrument or instruments. The idea was that each aspect of Decent Work, as defined in the Report by Director-General Juan Somavia to the International Labour Conference in 1999, should have an adequate normative coverage.[24] As it turned out, there was not much room between the up-to-date Conventions on the same topic for an efficient new instrument.

There is some unexplored territory. One option for revision might be to amend only provisions which need updating, not entire Conventions. This approach is widely applied in national legislation. Yet, in the case of international treaties, it would create complications for countries which have ratified the original Convention and adjusted their legislation correspondingly. One of the arguments of the German delegate against the Constitutional Amendment of 1997, enabling the ILO to scrap obsolete Conventions, was the consequences for those who have ratified the Conventions in question. Now that the Constitutional Amendment has entered into force after nearly two decades, it will be possible to see how real those fears were.

In a dynamic, forward-looking standards system, international and national labour law would normally move hand in hand together. This could permit different and pragmatic ways of revision of the existing Conventions while identifying the new needs for standard-setting. But in a world where the general tendency of labour and social legislation is towards more flexibility, and dismantling existing regulation, revision will tend to turn into a rear-guard action, aimed at preserving a known level of protection instead of adapting to some new paradigm.

The current situation appears to reflect another and possibly profound shift in the way labour law is being seen. For some two centuries, the primary aim of labour law has been to protect workers against negative consequences of domestic and international economic activity. Over the last 25 years, there has been an increased emphasis on the promotion of growth and competitiveness, which are

24 ILO, *Decent Work* Report of the Director-General to the 87th Session of the International Labour Conference June 1999.

taken to be preconditions for job creation. But if labour law is crafted with the primary aim of economic development, and not the protection of workers, it runs the risk of losing its unique and essential value for dealing with the needs of social justice in developing, developed and transitioning societies.

II. Precarious Work – The New Normative Model?

Jeremias Prassl and Martin Risak*

Uber, TaskRabbit & Co: Platforms as Employers? Rethinking the Labour Law of Crowdwork

1. Introduction

Crowdsourced work is on the rise – presenting opportunities and challenges for workers, businesses, and regulators alike. From an employment law perspective, the phenomenon of work supplied through digital platforms opens a new chapter in the age-old problem of determining the scope of employee-protective norms: are crowdworkers employees or workers in a technical sense, and thus deserving of legal protection, ranging from minimum wage and working time regulation to unfair dismissal and collective rights, depending on their jurisdiction? Are they independent contractors, operating as small businesses on their own account, and thus rightly exposed to the rough and tumble of the market? Or do they represent a genuinely novel form of work, deserving of its own legal status and regulatory apparatus?[1]

The answer suggested by the platforms themselves is straightforward: *Uber, Mechanical Turk, TaskRabbit* and others merely see themselves as digital agents, connecting customers and independent contractors. Individual platforms' terms and conditions vary from country to country according to local conditions, whilst always pursuing identical aims: the denial of worker status.

At the same time, however, the level of control exercised by a platform can be significant, from setting wage levels to specifying – and supervising – how work is to be done. It is unsurprising, therefore, that courts and administrative bodies have begun to find themselves tasked with determining crowdworkers' legal status:

---

* This contribution is based on Jeremias Prassl's and Martin Risak's joint piece in a special edition, edited by Valerio de Stefano, of the *Comparative Labour Law and Policy Journal* (2016) on work in the on-demand economy. The authors are grateful to the organisers and participants at the Wharton workshop for discussion and feedback of earlier stages of this work, and to the organisers of the ReMarkLab conference in Stockholm for further discussion and analysis. The usual disclaimers apply.

1 See e.g. the recent call for the introduction of a new 'independent worker' status in the United States: S. Harris and A Krueger, *A Proposal for Modernizing Labor Laws for Twenty-First Century Work: The "Independent Worker"* (Hamilton Project, 2015).

early litigation in the United States (US)[2] was soon followed by similar lawsuits in Europe.[3] The questions raised are both novel, given the constantly evolving technology and business models of various platforms, and eerily familiar after decades of judicial and academic argument over how the contractual models used to structure 'atypical' work in 'fissured' workplaces[4] might fit into our received regulatory categories.[5] As an exasperated District Judge noted in the course of on-going US litigation, the task of determining worker status is akin to being 'handed a square peg and asked to choose between two round holes.'[6]

In the present paper, we hope to propose a different way of approaching the legal problems arising from crowdwork. Instead of dwelling on the well-rehearsed debates as to employee or independent contractor status, we analyse the multilateral contractual relationships in the operation of online platforms from a different angle, *viz* that of questioning which party, if any, could be identified as a responsible employer: by adopting a functional concept of the employer, we suggest, the courts might be able to sidestep the current impasse, and allocate rights and responsibilities in a flexible yet coherent manner.

Before turning to that discussion, three important caveats remain to be noted: first, as with all forms of 'atypical' work, it is important not to underestimate the sheer heterogeneity and complexity of underlying fact patterns: crowdwork should not be understood as a single, unified phenomenon, let alone a novel category of work relationships calling for *sui generis* regulatory responses.[7] Any proposed solution must be able to flexibly respond to changing economic and organisational models, offering conceptual coherence in the face of factual complexity. Second, whilst the functional concept of the employer was originally developed by one of the present authors in the context of English and European law,[8] the present piece

---

2 See further M Cherry, 'Beyond misclassification: The Digital Transformation of Work', (2016) 37 CLLPJ 577.

3 H J Parkinson, 'Uber faces legal action in UK over drivers' rights' (*The Guardian*, 29 July 2015).

4 D Weil, *The Fissured Workplace* (Harvard University Press 2014).

5 See further E Albin and J Prassl, 'Fragmenting Work, Fragmented Regulation: The Contract of Employment as a Driver of Social Exclusion' in M Freedland et al. (eds), *The Contract of Employment* (OUP 2016).

6 *Cotter et al. v. Lyft Inc.*, United States District Court, Northern District of California, Order of March 11, 2015 Denying Cross-Motion for Summary Judgment (Case No. 13-cv-04065-VC) 19.

7 As was once thought to be the case with agency work in the United Kingdom: *Construction Industry Training Board v Labour Force Ltd* [1970] 3 All ER 220.

8 J Prassl, *The Concept of the Employer* (OUP 2015).

is deliberately not focused on a single jurisdiction – we hope instead briefly to introduce that model, and then to illustrate its application in the context of two different online platforms. Finally, given present space limitations, we will not be able to address the difficult jurisdictional and conflict of laws issues which may arise, particularly in the context of primarily digital crowdwork, when platforms, customers, and workers operate in different countries.[9]

2. Working in the Digital Crowd

As Antonio Aloisi[10] and Valerio De Stefano[11] noted in their contributions to a special issue of the *Comparative Labour Law and Policy Journal* (CLLPJ), developments in information and communication technology ('ICT') have led not only to fundamental changes in traditional working relationships, but also to the emergence of new forms of employment located in the grey and often unchartered territory between employment contracts and freelance work;[12] a difficult fit for the existing binary legal categories of dependent labour and self-employment.

A particularly salient instantiation of this phenomenon is crowdwork, a relatively recent model also known as crowdsourcing of labour or crowd employment. These notions describe an ICT-based form of organising the outsourcing of tasks to a large pool of workers. The work (ranging from transportation services and cleaning to digital transcription or programming tasks) is referred to in a variety of ways, including 'gigs', 'rides', or 'tasks', and is offered to a large number of people (the 'crowd') by means of an internet-based 'crowdsourcing platform'.[13]

9 See e.g. L Merrett, *Employment Contracts in International Law* (OUP 2011). Even purely digital platforms, however, are increasingly limiting their workers to single jurisdictions, such as the US in the case of Amazon's *M Turk*: <http://turkrequesters.blogspot.com/2013/01/the-reasons-why-amazon-mechanical-turk.html> accessed 13 February 2017.

10 'Commoditized Workers – The Rise of On-Demand Work, a Case Study Research on a Set of Online Platforms and Apps' [2016] 37 CLLPJ 653.

11 'The rise of the 'just-in-time workforce': on-demand work, crowd work and labour protection in the "gig-economy"' [2016] 37 CLLPJ 471.

12 Cf. Eurofound, *New Forms of Employment* (2015) 107.

13 Such as notably Amazon's Mechanical Turk (www.mturk.com), see S Strube, 'Vom Outsourcing zum Crowdsourcing – Wie Amazons Mechanical Turk funktioniert' in Ch Benner (ed), *Crowdwork – zurück in die Zukunft* (Bund Verlag 2014) 75 et seq.

This organisational model forms part of a larger set of processes known as 'crowdsourcing',[14] with customers (or indeed employers) referred to as 'crowdsourcers'. As detailed in Figure 1, the resulting contractual relationships are manifold and complex: whilst the work is usually managed through an intermediary (the crowdsourcing platform), some will insist on direct contractual relationships between crowdsourcer clients and crowdworkers, whereas others will opt for tripartite contractual structures, akin to traditional models of agency work and labour outsourcing.[15]

Figure 1: Parties involved in the crowdsourcing of labour.

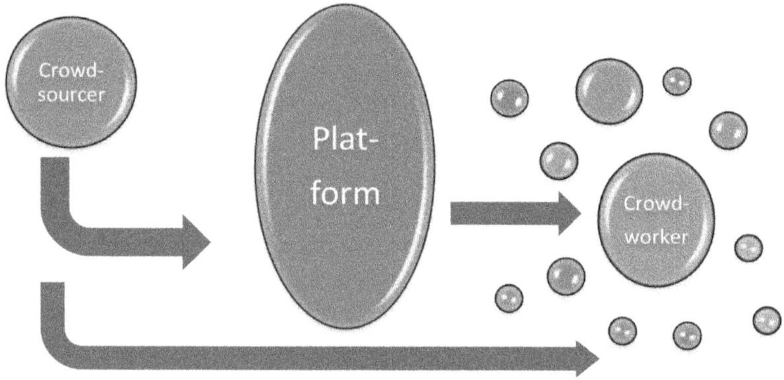

2.1 Characterising Crowdwork Platforms

We have already alluded to the nearly unlimited factual variety that characterizes the emergence of online platforms, both in terms of crowdsourcing in general (crowdfunding,[16] allocation of non-labour resources such as accommodation[17]), and crowdsourcing of labour, or crowdwork, in particular. It is therefore not useful, or indeed feasible, to construct an overall taxonomy of crowdsourcing

---

14 This term derives from a combination of the words "outsourcing" and "crowd", and was used by Jeff Howe for the first time, cf. J Howe, 'The Rise of Crowdsourcing' *Wired Mag* (14 June 2006) <www.wired.com/2006/06/crowds/> accessed 13 February 2017.

15 Cf. A Kittur et al., 'The Future of Crowd Work', paper presented at 16th ACM Conference on Computer Supported Coooperative Work, <www.lri.fr/~mbl/ENS/CSCW/2012/papers/Kittur-CSCW13.pdf> accessed 13 February 2017; J M Leimeister et al., 'Crowdwork – digitale Wertschöpfung in der Wolke' in W Brenner and T Hess (eds), *Wirtschaftsinformatik in Wissenschaft und Praxis* (Springer Verlag 2014) 51–64.

16 <www.KickStarter.com> accessed 13 February 2017.

17 <www.AirBnB.com> accessed 13 February 2017.

platforms. For present purposes, however, a few fundamental distinctions may be drawn.

Crowdsourcing, first, can take place internally or externally. In this contribution, we will look solely at external crowdsourcing, as internal crowdsourcing is generally arranged within the context of existing employment relationships, and therefore poses fewer fundamental legal problems,[18] regardless of whether the platform is operated by an independent enterprise or by the company itself.[19]

Work crowdsourced to an external crowd, on the other hand, can be seen as clustered along a spectrum of services and arrangements. On the one end, we find physical services to be undertaken in the 'real' (offline) world, where the crowdworker comes into direct contact with the customer. Examples include transportation delivered via apps such as Uber, domestic services (cleaning, repair work etc.) delivered via platforms such as *Helpling*,[20] and clerical work (e.g. customer service or accounting) provided by platforms like *UpWork*.[21] *Uber* customers, for example, use an app on their smartphones to request rides from a specific location, information that is instantly broadcast to drivers in the area.[22] Once the request has been accepted by a driver, she is directed to the passenger and onwards to the required destination, through her version of the Uber app. Payment is taken automatically from the customer by the platform, and after taking a commission between 20 and 30 per cent,[23] the platform passes payment on to the driver. Customers and drivers rate each other anonymously following each journey; the resulting scores are displayed to passengers and drivers respectively before the next trip commences.

On the other end of the spectrum, there is digital work delivered in the virtual world, usually via an interface provided by the platform. The tasks involved here are often very simple, repetitive activities involving low pay and highly standardised or automated processes. These 'microtasks' include digital labelling and the creation of image descriptions, categorising data and products, and the translation

---

18 Cf. Th Klebe and J Neugebauer, 'Crowdsourcing: Für eine handvoll Dollar oder Workers of the crowd unite?' [2014] AuR 4.

19 Cf. Eurofound (n 12) 110.

20 <www.helpling.com> – in the UK, this platform operates under a different brand, <www.hassle.com> accessed 13 February 2017.

21 <www.upwork.com> accessed 13 February 2017.

22 <www.uber.com/features> accessed 13 February 2017.

23 Though the platform continues to experiment with varying the amount of commission payable: <www.cnet.com/news/uber-tests-30-commission-for-new-drivers-in-san-francisco/> accessed 13 February 2017.

or proofreading of short texts; with larger tasks often broken down into smaller subtasks to be worked on independently. These microtasks are then posted on platforms, where crowdworkers can find and complete them. The leading platforms for this kind of 'cognitive piece work[24] or 'Neo-Taylorism'[25] include Amazon's Mechanical Turk[26] and *Clickworker*.[27] Survey research has shown that 25 per cent of the tasks offered on Amazon Mechanical Turk are valued at 0.01 United States Dollar (USD), 70 per cent offer 0.05 USD or less, and 90 per cent pay less than 0.10 USD per completed task; thus equalling an average wage of about 2 USD per hour.[28]

2.2 Working in the Crowd

Historically, the main advantage of hierarchical employment relationships over contracts with independent contractors was understood to be the entrepreneur's degree of control, and the resulting decrease in transaction costs, whether in the search, selection and training of workers, or the employer's tight control over the production process.[29] An increasing desire for labour flexibility, on the other hand, was the driver behind the more recent creation of different forms of atypical work, including agency work, part-time work and fixed-term employment.[30]

Crowdwork is a novel combination of these factors, in so far as platforms attempt to increase flexibility for the employer or customer and to reduce the cost of 'empty' or unproductive moments, whilst at the same time maintaining full control over the production process in order to keep transaction costs at a minimum. In order to meet these seemingly contradictory goals, two preconditions must be met: first, the crowd has to be large enough in order to always have individuals available when needed, and to maintain enough competition between crowdworkers to keep prices low. This is usually achieved through platforms' large and active crowds, with different platforms specialising in different segments of the crowdsourcing market.

---

24 F A Schmidt, 'The Good the Bad and the Ugly' in C Benner (ed), *Crowdwork – zurück in die Zukunft* (Bund Verlag 2014) 378.

25 J Leimeister et al., 'Crowdwork – Digitale Wertschöpfung in der Wolke' in C Benner (ed), *Crowdwork – zurück in die Zukunft* (Bund Verlag 2014) 32.

26 <www.mturk.com/mturk/welcome> accessed 13 February 2017.

27 <www.clickworker.com> accessed 13 February 2017.

28 Eurofound (n 12) 115.

29 R Coase, 'The Nature of the Firm' (1937) *Economica, vol* 4,386.

30 Eurofund, *Third European survey on working conditions* (2000); European Parliament, *Atypical Work in the EU* (1998).

Secondly, instead of the command-and-control systems inherent in 'traditional' employment relationships, crowdsourcers and platforms rely on 'digital reputation' mechanisms to guide the selection of crowdworkers and to ensure efficient performance control. Individual models vary, but the fundamental approach is consistent: crowdworkers are awarded points, stars or other symbols of status by the crowdsourcer or customer after completing a task.[31] Quality control itself can thus be crowdsourced by the platform to its customers or other crowdsourcers, tapping the 'wisdom of the crowd'[32] in order to determine the performance levels of each single crowdworker.

The potential upsides of this emerging model for firms and workers alike should not be underestimated.[33] Through the use of platforms, businesses ranging from restaurants to information technology service providers can draw on a large crowd of flexible workers to reduce or even eliminate the cost of unproductive time at work, and rely on reputation mechanisms to maintain full control over the production process or service delivery. The resulting competition between crowdworkers will ensure that quality remains high whilst wages remain low. As Lukas Biewald, the co-founder of the platform Crowdflower, put it bluntly in 2010, 'with technology, you can … get rid of [workers] when you don't need them anymore.'[34]

Crowdwork similarly offers significant potential upsides for (at least some of its) workers: first and foremost, in terms of flexibility, crowdworkers can decide when to work, where to work, and what kind of tasks to accept. Platform work might therefore be more compatible with other duties, such as childcare. The flexibility and potentially limited nature of individual engagements can also help the underemployed, providing additional income to their regular earnings,[35] and (at least through virtual work crowdwork) allow those excluded from regular labour

---

31 On some platforms, including *Uber*, customers are rated by crowdworkers in turn: cf. S Langlois, 'Don't tip your Uber driver? It could cost you a 5-star rating' (*Market Watch*, 12 August 2015) <www.marketwatch.com/story/dont-tip-your-uber-driver-it-could-cost-you-a-5-star-rating-2015-08-12> accessed 13 February 2017.

32 J Surowiecki, *The wisdom of the crowds* (Doubleday 2004).

33 <www.telegraph.co.uk/technology/uber/12086500/In-praise-of-the-gig-economy.html> accessed 13 February 2017.

34 As quoted in M Marvit, 'How Crowdworkers Became the Ghosts in the Digital Machine' *The Nation* (5 February 2014) <www.thenation.com/article/how-crowdworkers-became-ghosts-digital-machine/> accessed 13 February 2017.

35 <www.dailyworth.com/posts/3410-flexible-side-gigs-to-bring-in-extra-income/4> accessed 13 February 2017.

markets due to disabilities or other factors to find opportunities for gainful employment.[36] Finally, there is an increasing number of genuinely successful small entrepreneurs, focussed on particular niches or offering special skills, for whom crowdwork has become a very profitable source of new business.

At the same time, however, it is important to note that working conditions for the vast majority of crowdworkers appear to be poor, irrespective of the work being delivered.[37] The lack of unions or organising powers, the oligopoly of but a few platforms offering certain kinds of tasks, and constant economic and legal insecurity result in a massive imbalance of bargaining power, noticeable primarily in low wage-rates and heavily slanted terms and conditions in platform use agreements. In the case of virtual crowdwork, global competition and dislocated physical workplaces further aggravate these problems, as a lack of regulation leads to 'digital slaves'[38] working away in their 'virtual sweatshops'.[39]

Two problems in particular are repeatedly highlighted: low wages, and workers' dependence of their ratings with a particular platform. As regards the former problem, for example, some reports suggest that the average wage on Amazon's Mechanical Turk is less than $2 per hour[40], considerably below the US minimum wage.[41] A related aspect is insecurity with regards to payment: in accordance with the general terms and conditions of microtasking-platforms, crowdsourcers have

---

36 Cf. K Zyskowski et al.,'Accessible Crowdwork? Understanding the Value in and Challenge of Microtask Employment for People with Disabilities' <http://research.microsoft.com/pubs/228714/crowdwork_and_disability.pdf> accessed 13 February 2017.

37 M Marvit, 'How Crowdworkers Became the Ghosts in the Digital Machine' (n 34).

38 M Rosenblum, 'The Digital Slave – That would be You' *Huffington Post* (5 June 2013) <www.huffingtonpost.com/michael-rosenblum/the-digital-slave-that-wo_b_3222785.html> accessed 13 February 2017.

39 See for so "called gold farming" (professional online gaming to collect virtual money in games like World of Warcraft): J Dibbell, 'The unreal estate boom' *Wired Magazine* (January /2003) <www.wired.com/2003/01/gaming-2> accessed 13 February 2017; J Dibbel, 'The Life of the Chinese Gold Farmer' *NYT Magazine* (17 June 2016) <www.nytimes.com/2007/06/17/magazine/17lootfarmers-t.html?_r=2&oref=slogin> accessed 13 February 2017.

40 Cf. J Ross at al., 'Who are the crowdworkers? Shifting Demographics in Amazon Mechanical Turk', Paper prepared for Chi 2010 <http://dl.acm.org/citation.cfm?doid=1753846.1753873> accessed 13 February 2017; A Felstiner, 'Working the Crowd: Employment and Labour Law in the Crowdsourcing Industry', (2011) 32 Berkeley J. Emp. & Lab. L. 143.

41 In the US there are different minimum wages, depending on the Federal State. See <www.dol.gov/whd/minwage/america.htm> accessed 13 February 2017.

the right to reject the work without having to give a reason or providing payment, whilst still receiving the fruits of a worker's labour.[42]

Various systems of 'digital reputation', or rating mechanisms, which form one of the core elements of platform works, raise a second set of difficult questions:[43] a customer-input based system of stars or points not only puts crowdworkers in a state of permanent probation, but also infringes their mobility as it ties them to particular platforms.

3. The Regulatory Challenge

One of the very purposes of employment and labour law is to draw a distinction between the genuinely self-employed and those requiring protection against many of the problems just outlined, bringing the latter group within its protective scope. In this section, we briefly outline employment law's traditional approach to this crucial classificatory exercise and show that the multiplicity of contractual relationships and competing legal characterisations in the arrangements between platforms, workers, and customers, on the other hand, sits uneasily with the received binary divide.

3.1 The Received Analytical Approach

Most jurisdictions have developed a more or less elaborate legal framework regulating the employment relationship based on the idea of the existence of an imbalance of bargaining power when negotiating pay and conditions of work.[44] This usually includes the right to organise, to bargain collectively and to take collective action. Self-employed persons usually do not enjoy any of these rights, including minimum wages, sick pay or protection against unfair dismissal. Indeed, they may

---

42 For an illustration in the context of *Mechanical Turk*, see Strube, 'Vom Outsourcing zum Crowdsourcing' (n13) 78 (83); D Martin et al., 'Being a turker' in CSCW'14. Proceedings of the 17th ACM conference on Computer supported cooperative work & social computing [2014] <http://dl.acm.org/citation.cfm?id=2531602> accessed 13 February 2017.

43 There are also increasing reports of discrimination and bias hampering the operation of rating systems: see <www.bostonglobe.com/news/science/2013/08/08/the-pitfalls-crowdsourcing-online-ratings-vulnerable-bias/> accessed 13 February 2017.

44 M Freedland and P Davies, *Kahn-Freund's Labour and the Law* (Stevens 1983) 14, 69.

even be forbidden from coming to mutual arrangements over basic terms such as minimum payments, as this might contravene competition or anti-trust laws.[45]

Subsequent paragraphs look at the potential (bi-partite?) relationships underlying crowdsourcing arrangements, focussing on, in turn, crowdworkers and crowdsourcers, crowdworkers and platforms, and platforms and crowdsourcers, in order to briefly demonstrate the prevailing classification problems.[46] In addition to protracted questions as to the workers' legal status, a second problem emerges: even if the putative employee has been classified as such, he or she may struggle to point at the employer, which could be the platform or indeed the crowdsourcer.

3.2 Identifying Parties, Characterising Contracts

3.2.1 Contractual Relationship between the Crowdworker and the Crowdsourcer

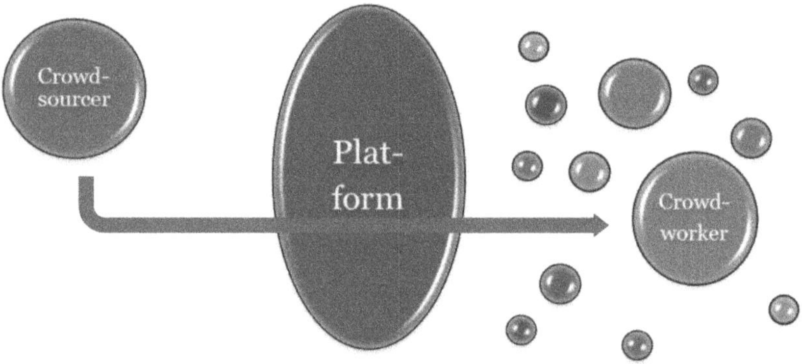

Figure 2: Contractual relationship between the crowdworker and the crowdsourcer.

The first question to be addressed concerns the existence of a direct contractual relationship between the crowdsourcer and the crowdworker. In some models, no such contract is in place. In other constellations, a direct contractual relationship exists between the crowdworker and the crowdsourcer – despite a lack of direct communication between the crowdworker and the crowdsourcer. In spite of its

45 Cf. ECJ Judgment of 4 December 2014, FVN Kunsten Informatie en Media, C-413/13, EU:C:2014:2411.

46 For present purposes, we focus primarily on the employee – independent contractor divide. Many jurisdictions have developed additional categories, such as the worker concept in the United Kingdom (see further ILO/ELLN, *Regulating the employment relationship in Europe: A guide to Recommendation No. 198* (ILO 2013) 23).

strong presence in this scenario, many platforms will claim only to act as a broker or agent when contracting with the crowdworker in these scenarios.[47]

As to legally classifying the relationship between the crowdworker and the crowdsourcer, we have to take into account that the relationship usually will only last for very limited time (e.g. for a ride or the fulfilment of a micro-task) and that contractual partners often change frequently. The contract will therefore – depending on the applicable tests in each jurisdiction – very likely not be an employment contract but a contract for services as the crowdworker is not integrated into the crowdsourcers business, the influence of the crowdsourcer on the work performed is limited, and there is no economic dependency on that contractual relationship alone.[48]

3.2.2 Contractual Relationship between the Crowdworker and the Crowdsourcing Platform

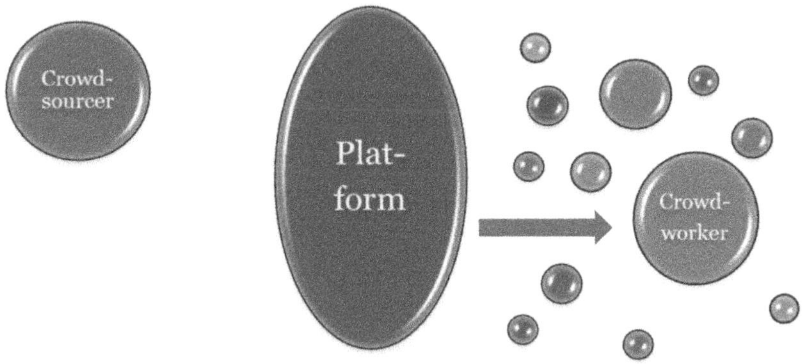

Figure 3: Contractual relationship between the crowdworker and the crowdsourcing platform.

In nearly all scenarios, there will be some form of contractual relationship between the crowdworker and the platform, in addition to any direct contractual relationship between the crowdsourcer and the crowdworker.[49] If they agree to work a task or job posted on the platform, the terms and conditions of the platform apply;

47 See e.g. the terms and conditions of *Uber*, as set out in the introductory section.

48 For an overview, see e.g. G Casale, *The Employment Relationship: A Comparative Overview* (ILO 2011).

49 E.g. Amazon Mechanical Turk Participation Agreement s 1.a https://www.mturk.com/mturk/conditionsofuse accessed 13 February 2017.

crowdworkers might also be asked to provide the platform with feedback on the crowdsourcer/customer.[50]

Any additional rights and obligations will strengthen the case for employee classification. Whilst there is no general obligation to accept any tasks, reputation systems built on the number of positive ratings will nonetheless put the crowdworker under pressure to work as much as possible to gain and maintain a positive rating. Platforms may introduce into their rating systems elements that take into account times of limited activity or inactivity and to make this part of the reputation of the crowdworker.[51] This puts crowdworkers' supposed freedom to accept tasks into a very different light.

Placement of the task on the platform might represent an offer to the crowd, which is subsequently accepted by accepting the task (e.g. accepting a ride) or simply through performance. Under the common terms and conditions of many platforms, the task may still be rejected by the crowdsourcer without either having to give a reason or to pay remuneration.[52] Alternatively, placement of the task may also be considered a mere invitation to treat (e.g. an offer to the crowd to make an offer).[53]

The underlying contract might be classified as a contract of employment or a contract for services, depending on the applicable tests in each jurisdiction. The relevant criteria may range from the intensity of the influence the contractual partner has on the work performed to economic dependency and permanence of the contractual arrangement. The flexible nature of the arrangement will often provide a serious hurdle to employee classification: the fact that both crowdsourcers and platforms are usually granted significant leeway in the terms and conditions, for example, suggests that the crowdworker might provide a service for which the recipient does not pay.[54]

If the crowdsourcing platform merely serves as the intermediary, providing but the infrastructure to allow a legal relationship in the above sense to be formed between the crowdworker and the crowdsourcer, it might be classified as no more than a placement service or temporary agency work; however, the lack

---

50 This is notably the case with *Uber* passengers: <https://help.uber.com/h/e9302f73-8625-427f-abf7-dbe7ab25af7d> accessed 13 February 2017.

51 *TaskRabbit*, for example, will deactivate accounts that have not completed tasks for more than 90 days: <https://support.taskrabbit.com/hc/en-us/articles/204409440-TaskRabbit-Community-Guidelines> accessed 13 February 2017.

52 E.g. Amazon Mechanical Turk Participation Agreement (n 49) 3.a.

53 Cf. e.g. *Partridge v Crittenden* [1968] 1 WLR 1204. Or even an offer for reward, see e.g. German Civil Code s 657, Austrian Civil Code s 860.

54 Cf. M Marvit 'How Crowdworkers Became the Ghosts in the Digital Machine' (n 34).

of integration into the crowdsourcer's business, as well as (supposed) the lack of managerial prerogative and control by the crowdsourcer, will often negate the latter. If, on the other hand, the work is provided for the crowdsourcing platform rather than for the crowdsourcer,[55] that legal relationship could in principle be deemed to be an employment relationship.[56]

The challenges quickly mount: in crowdwork arrangements, the tasks are often very short in duration – with the resulting relationships potentially characterised as a series of temporary employment relationships, which shift the risk of business downturns from crowdsourcers and platforms to individual workers, not unlike on-call work or zero-hours arrangements.[57]

3.2.3 Contractual Relationship between the Crowdsourcer and the Crowdsourcing Platform

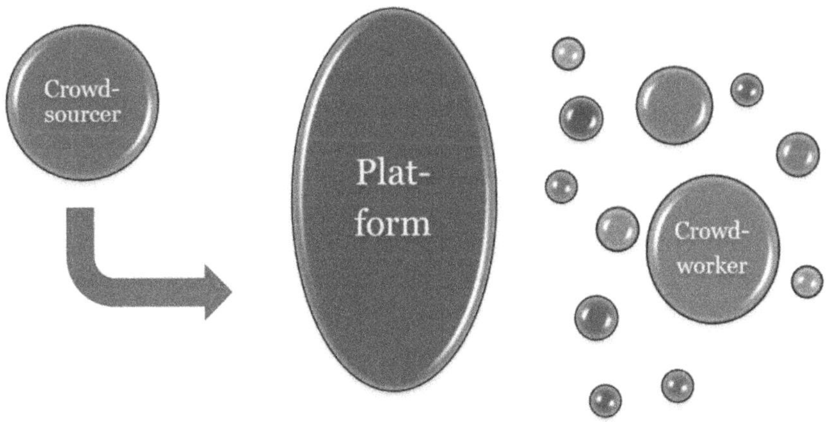

Figure 4: Contractual relationship between the crowdsourcer and the crowdsourcing Platform.

55 It is also possible to arrive at this estimation if it is concluded that, despite a bogus direct legal relationship between the crowdworker and crowdsourcer, the relationship actually exists between the crowdworker and the platform, due to the real economic content and the fact that the platform manages the relationship on its own behalf.

56 Cf. ILO/ELLN, *Regulating the employment relationship in Europe: A guide to Recommendation No. 198* (n 48) 28 et seq.

57 A Adams, M Freedland, and J Prassl, 'The "Zero-Hours Contract": Regulating Casual Work, or Legitimating Precarity?' (2015) 147 *Giornale di Diritto del Lavoro e di Relazioni Industriali* 529.

The final contractual relationship involved will be that between the crowdsourcer and the platform. This is likely always to be a contract for services, regardless of whether a direct relationship exists between the crowdworkers and the crowdsourcer.

3.3 Shortcomings of this Approach

The received analytical approach was developed in the context of two-party employment relationships. This is at the core of its shortcomings when faced with multiple parties: there is little analysis of contractual relationships as an interdependent net of contracts that only make sense as a whole.

This fragmented analysis makes employment law coverage fragile, given the wide variety of multi-entity employment scenarios: it becomes unclear, incoherent, and open to easy manipulation. Crowdwork thus serves as a clear illustration of the 'profound difficulties' posed by complex triangular or multilateral employment relationships:[58] it challenges the very existence of a contract of employment, thus leaving individual workers without recourse to the majority of domestic employment protective legislation. The complete breakdown of employment law coverage, e.g. in case of agency work in the UK, is a consequence of 'contractual arrangements that split, on the one hand, day-to-day control of work processes and, on the other hand, day-to-day securing and paying of people to work, [thus] prima facie prevent[ing] those working from being legally classified as anyone's "employees"':[59] neither the relationship with the crowdsourcer nor with the crowdwork platform is characterised as one of employment.

4. A Single Platform as the Employer

How, then, could we find ways to side-step this 'constant and increasing counterfactuality'[60] of the received approach? In suggesting that a focus on rethinking the concept of the employer could provide a starting point for a more fruitful analysis of crowdwork, this paper takes up the suggestion, first raised by Paul Davies and Mark Freedland (albeit in a different context), that the problems at stake might

58 M Freedland, *The Personal Employment Contract* (OUP 2003) 36 et seq.

59 L Barmes, 'Learning from Case Law Accounts of Marginalised Working' in J Fudge, S McCrystal and K Sankaran (eds), *Challenging the Legal Boundaries of Work Regulation* (Oñati International Series in Law and Society, Hart 2012) 308.

60 P Davies and M Freedland, 'The Complexities of the Employing Enterprise' in G Davidov and B Langile (eds), *Boundaries and Frontiers of Labour Law* (Hart Publishing 2006) 274.

> best be understood from an unfamiliar perspective, indeed initially a counterintuitive one, [where the] problem lies not in the binary analysis of the worker, but in the unitary analysis of the employer.[61]

In developing this line of thought, we suggest that the problems resulting from a unitary analysis of the employer, where the employing entity is defined as a single counterparty to the contract of employment or service,[62] can best be overcome through a more openly functional concept of the employer.

Subsequent discussion draws on recent work by one of us to set out the idea of the functional concept of the employer, in order to pave the way for an illustration of its operation in the crowdwork context. As *The Concept of the Employer* suggests, in order to restore congruence to the application of employment law norms, the very definition of the employer must carefully be reconceptualised as a more openly functional one.

4.1 The Functions of the Employer

For purposes of this analysis, a 'function' of being an employer is one of the various actions employers are entitled or obliged to take as part of the bundle of rights and duties falling within the scope of the open-ended contract of service.[63] In trawling the established tests of employment status such as control, economic dependence, or mutuality of obligation for these employer functions, there are endless possible mutations of different fact scenarios, rendering categorisation purely on the basis of past decisions of limited assistance.[64] The result of this analysis of concepts underlying different fact patterns, rather than the actual results on a case-by-case basis, is the following set of functions, with the presence or absence of individual factors becoming less relevant than the specific role they play in any given context.[65]

---

61 ibid 273.

62 J Prassl, 'The Notion of the Employer' (2013) Law Quarterly Review 380.

63 Prassl, *The Concept of the Employer* (n 8) 24–25.

64 Whilst subsequent examples are drawn primarily from Common Law jurisdictions, we suggest that the approach is capable of being similarly developed in Civilian jurisdictions.

65 The 'equipollency principle' (*Äquivalenzprinzip*): L Nogler, 'Die Typologisch-Funktionale Methode am Beispiel des Arbeitnehmerbegriffs' (2009) 10 ZESAR 459, 463.

The five main functions and their functional underpinning of the employer are:[66]

- Inception and termination of the employment relationship
- Receiving labour and its fruits
- Providing work and pay
- Managing the enterprise-internal market
- Managing the enterprise-external market

Key to this concept of the employer being a *multi-functional* one is the fact that no one function mentioned above is relevant in and of itself. Rather, it is the *ensemble* of the five functions that matters: each of them covers one of the facets necessary to create, maintain, and commercially exploit employment relationships, thus coming together to make up the received legal concept of employing workers or acting as an employer – and being subjected to the appropriate range of employee-protective norms.

A functional conceptualisation of the employer, then, is one where the contractual identification of the employer is replaced by an emphasis on the exercise of each function – whether by a single entity, as demonstrated immediately below, or in situations where different functions may be exercised from more than one *locus* of control,[67] a discussion to which we turn in section 5.

4.2 *Uber:* The Platform as a Sole Employer

The operation of transportation platforms causes significant problems when analysed through the traditional (contractual) lens of employment law – not least because the platforms will often go to great lengths to (mis-) characterise their relationships with workers and consumers alike. In the United Kingdom, for example, Uber stipulates that it 'accepts Bookings acting as disclosed agent for the Transportation Provider (as principal)'.[68] Its US version of the terms and conditions a customer must accept in order to download the required software ('app') is even more explicit, informing customers in capital letters that they 'ACKNOWLEDGE

66 For earlier attempts at such lists, see e.g. Freedland, *The Personal Employment Contract* (n 58) 40.

67 The term *locus* of control is designed to avoid additional complexities arising out of the fact, noted *inter al* by Freedland (n 58) 45–47, that even in traditional companies without external influence, management control is often exercised by more than one person amongst a group of relatively senior executives.

68 <www.uber.com/legal/gbr/terms> accessed 13 February 2017.

THAT UBER DOES NOT PROVIDE TRANSPORTATION OR LOGISTICS SERVICES OR FUNCTION AS A TRANSPORTATION CARRIER.'[69]

The moment we shift our analytical focus to Uber's exercise of employer functions, on the other hand, it becomes clear that the platform does in fact exercise all relevant employer functions usually involved in the provision of transportation or logistics services. The following paragraphs look at each function in turn, drawing on a range of qualitative accounts of drivers' experiences to demonstrate how Uber exercises full employer control, reaping the benefits of its drivers' work – and suggesting that it should therefore equally be responsible for related risks and costs.

At first glance, Uber's business model is very simple: customers download a small programme (the app) to their mobile phone, enabled with internet access and a Global Positioning System (GPS) locator. In order to create an account, a potential client must provide their credit card details; once these have been verified, the customer can begin to request rides. They are then connected to the closest driver (similarly equipped with a smartphone running an Uber app); billing, rating, and nearly all other interaction to be discussed take place exclusively through that online channel – indeed, the *Uber* app is designed specifically to hide passengers' and drivers' mobile numbers even when they speak to one another.[70]

4.2.1 Inception and Termination of the Employment Relationship

This employer function includes control over the very existence of an employment relationship, from the power of selection to the choice of dismissing a worker. At first glance, it might appear that the platform has little control over individual 'rides', their inception and termination: Uber customers use the app on their smartphones to request rides from a specific location, information that is instantly broadcast to drivers in the area.[71] Drivers may accept a ride request, and are then directed to the relevant customer. The relationship ends at the customer's destination, or – occasionally – if either party cancels the ride within a short timeframe after offer and acceptance.

---

69 ibid clause 2. cf the German version: 'Die Dienstleistung von Uber besteht lediglich in der Vermittlung der Beförderungsdienstleistung und in der Abrechnung der Beförderungsdienstleistung im Namen des Beförderungsdienstleisters. Uber selbst bietet keine Beförderungsdienstleistungen an und führt auch keine Beförderungen durch.' <www.uber.com/legal/deu/terms> accessed 13 February 2017.

70 <www.twilio.com/use-cases/masked-phone-numbers> accessed 13 February 2017.

71 <www.uber.com/features> accessed 13 February 2017.

In reality, on the other hand, the relationship between platform and workers is a much more long-term and durable one, irrespective of short individual engagements: the platform is fully in control of the existence of the relationship. Drivers have to sign up with Uber to use its app,[72] but the process is significantly more intensive than mere registration: the company will vet drivers' cars, check their licences, and demand proof of relevant insurance for the jurisdiction in question.[73] Uber is similarly in charge of terminating its driver's access to the platform. As a leading industry blog notes:

> It's every Uber driver's worst nightmare: To receive an email from Uber letting you know that you've been deactivated as an Uber partner, or a message in the app that says you can't drive. It's a huge disappointment to be fired from your ride sharing job, and to make things worse, you're given little to no warning or explanation about your deactivation. Instead, when you try to log on to drive, you're greeted with an error message.[74]

Reasons (where given) range from passenger complaints to average ratings dropping below 4.6 out of a possible 5. Reactivation is usually subject to an Uber-sanctioned re-training course, the low practical value of which has become a common cause for complaint.[75] The platform thus exercises full control over the existence of driver's work relationship.

Indeed, even at the short-term level of individual rides, it cannot be suggested that clients or drivers exercise the relevant functions: clients, for example, do not know who individual drivers are, or indeed which one of the cars shown on a schematic map will accept their transportation request. Drivers have slightly more leeway, insofar as they can – on some versions of the app – see different passengers' average ratings, thus for example avoiding low-rated passengers who might be more problematic customers.[76]

On the other hand, drivers' actual choice is severely limited, by at least two factors: first, the need to maintain an average acceptance rate of around 80 per cent of offers received while the driver's app is activated, as well as strict limitations on

---

72 <https://get.uber.com/drive/> accessed 13 February 2017.

73 <https://newsroom.uber.com/australia/ubersafeau/> accessed 13 February 2017.

74 <www.ridesharingdriver.com/fired-uber-drivers-get-deactivated-and-reactivated/> accessed 13 February 2017.

75 <http://observer.com/2015/02/uber-drivers-the-punishment-for-bad-ratings-is-costly-training-courses/> accessed 13 February 2017.

76 <www.npr.org/sections/alltechconsidered/2015/07/18/423549092/what-does-your-uber-driver-think-of-you> accessed 13 February 2017.

how many rides can be cancelled.[77] Second, drivers will usually not know what an individual passenger's destination is, unless they have contacted the customer immediately upon acceptance to determine where they are headed.

4.2.2 Receiving Labour and its Fruits

Uber similarly exercises the second employer function, as it is the direct recipient of the fruits of a driver's labour: payment is taken automatically from the customer by the platform. Uber also handles all aspects of invoicing, claim reconciliation, and complaints; the entire system is designed to avoid any direct financial interaction between passengers and drivers – up to and including a prohibition on tipping.[78]

4.2.3 Providing Work and Pay

As regards the provision of work, first, the key tool here is an Uber-provided smartphone app which allows drivers access to its network of customers. Drivers are never paid directly: out of the sums charged to customers, Uber takes a commission between 20 and 30 per cent,[79] before depositing the money in drivers' accounts – usually with at least a week's delay. The platform continues to experiment with varying the amount of commission payable, which is particularly harmful to part-time workers, as the percentage retained falls with the number of trips offered. Another common tactic is for Uber to offer reasonably generous rates when it first enters a new city or territory; a rate which is subsequently lowered both through a reduction in fares, and an increase in Uber's commission. As a Dallas driver notes, 'They started to tighten the rope. Gradually, we can't breathe anymore.'[80]

4.2.4 Managing the Enterprise-Internal Market

Under the fourth function, the employer enjoys coordination through control over all factors of production, up to and including the power to require both how and what is to be done. Through a combination of technology and human factors,

---

77 <www.ridesharingdriver.com/fired-uber-drivers-get-deactivated-and-reactivated/> accessed 13 February 2017.

78 This and the following information derive from the Uber help page <https://help.uber.com> accessed 13 February 2017.

79 <www.cnet.com/news/uber-tests-30-commission-for-new-drivers-in-san-francisco/> accessed 13 February 2017.

80 <www.nytimes.com/2016/02/03/business/uber-drivers-and-others-in-the-gig-economy-take-a-stand.html> accessed 13 February 2017.

Uber enjoys extremely tight control over all aspects of how a ride is provided: once the request has been accepted by a driver, for example, he or she will be directed to the passenger and onwards to the required destination, through the driver's version of the Uber app; customers can complain if a different route was chosen and they feel disadvantaged as a consequence.[81]

As has already been discussed, Uber also has tight control over the car types drivers may use,[82] occasionally inspecting them for everything from cleanliness to scratches. Control over the enterprise-internal market extends as far as the music to be played during the ride: through corporate partnerships, drivers must enable passengers to use music apps to set their own background music.[83]

In addition to technology-based control, notably GPS locators, Uber relies on star-based ratings to exert close control over its workforce. Customers and drivers rate each other anonymously following each journey; the resulting scores are displayed to passengers and operators respectively before the next trip commences. As Ben Sachs has noted:

> [T]he firms are (1) soliciting customer feedback, (2) setting relevant performance levels, and then (3) making termination decisions when the customer feedback reveals that drivers are not meeting the performance levels set by the firms. This is what *employers* do.[84]

4.2.5 Managing the Enterprise-External Market

Uber is equally exercising the final employer function: it is the entity undertaking economic activity in return for potential profit, whilst also being exposed to any losses that may result from the enterprise. At first glance, that assertion is once more counterintuitive, as the risks and income levels appear to depend on each individual driver's actions: if he or she drives more, their income will be higher. A recent US Department of Labor guidance recalls, however, that 'the worker's ability to work more hours and the amount of work available from the employer have nothing to do with the worker's managerial skill'.[85]

---

81 <https://help.uber.com> accessed 13 February 2017.

82 <www.uber.com/driver-jobs> accessed 13 February 2017.

83 <https://newsroom.uber.com/uber-spotify-music-for-your-ride/> accessed 13 February 2017.

84 <http://onlabor.org/2015/05/20/uber-and-lyft-customer-reviews-and-the-right-to-control/> accessed 13 February 2017.

85 <www.dol.gov/whd/workers/misclassification/AI-2015_1.htm> accessed 13 February 2017, section II.B.

The most important indicator of driver's earning ability, on the other hand, is Uber's dynamic pricing algorithm, which determines remuneration for distance and time on the basis of factors such as individual city pricing levels, or even demands specific to a particular location and time through so-called surge pricing.[86] The platform is, finally, also in full control of branding, thus providing a global service under a unified mantle.[87]

As even a brief overview of Uber's business model has thus shown, the platform very clearly exercises the full range of employer functions: analysed thus, despite its strong reliance on modern technology, it is little different from a traditional, unitary employer – with its drivers to be classified as employees. Given the range of functions exercised, the platform should therefore be responsible for the full suite of employment rights in each jurisdiction it operates: from minimum wage and working time laws to collective bargaining.

5. A Multiplicity of Employers

As the previous section has demonstrated, Uber's business model is surprisingly close to the traditional assumption that all employer functions will be exercised by a single entity (the platform), which should therefore be characterised as the employer counterparty to a worker's contract of service.[88] Our brief overview of the operation of crowdwork platforms in section I has highlighted, however, that a multiplicity of parties might often be involved in the organisation and execution of crowdwork. It is thus not possible to focus on a single entity exercising all employer functions as the only case regulatory models need to be capable of addressing.

Instead, functions may sometimes be jointly exercised by platforms, customers, and potentially even crowdworkers themselves. The shared exercise between two or more entities, or one where functions are parcelled out between different parties, arises where platform work arrangements lead to a fragmented exercise of employer functions – it is in those scenarios that the functional model of the employer will now be put to the test: there may be elements of genuine self-employment, platforms performing employer roles, and even customers could potentially become subject to regulatory obligations.

---

86 <http://abovethecrowd.com/2014/03/11/a-deeper-look-at-ubers-dynamic-pricing-model/> accessed 13 February 2017.

87 <www.wired.com/2016/02/the-inside-story-behind-ubers-colorful-redesign/> accessed 13 February 2017.

88 Prassl, *The Concept of the Employer* (n 8) 16–23.

5.1. Shared Exercise of Functions

The platform under scrutiny for this purpose is TaskRabbit, 'a web and mobile marketplace that safely and reliably connects people and businesses with fully vetted people in their community to get everyday and skilled tasks done.'[89] As the service's Terms & Conditions explain:

> Clients are individuals and/or businesses seeking to obtain task services ("Tasks") from Taskers and are therefore clients of Taskers, and Taskers are individuals and/or businesses seeking to perform Tasks ("Taskers") for Clients. Clients and Taskers together are hereinafter referred to as "Users." The Service is a platform for enabling connections between Users for the fulfilment of Tasks.[90]

TaskRabbit consequently denies any employer role, whilst at the same time leaving the question of employer status between clients and taskers as an open question.[91] Returning once more to the list of established employer functions, however, it becomes clear that TaskRabbit's self-classification as a 'platform for enabling connections' might not be the full extent of the story.

5.1.1 Inception and Termination of the Contract of Employment

The existence of an overarching relationship is primarily in the hands of the platform: TaskRabbit vets individual workers' credentials before activating their accounts,[92] and will terminate taskers for violations of its usage terms – including on occasion complaints about specific clients.[93] In contrast to other crowdwork providers, however, taskers' accounts are not terminated when their rating falls below a pre-set level. Instead, they find themselves subject to a series of 'performance standard probations',[94] and may be confined to low-value tasks,[95]

89 TaskRabbit, *The TaskRabbit Handbook* ('Handbook', electronic copy on file with the authors) 12.

90 TaskRabbit Terms of Service <www.taskrabbit.com/terms> (excerpts from clauses 1 and 2).

91 ibid clause 12.

92 <http://loneplacebo.com/adventures-of-a-first-time-taskrabbit/> accessed 13 February 2017.

93 <www.businessinsider.com/confessions-of-a-task-rabbit-2011-12?IR=T&page=1> accessed 13 February 2017.

94 <https://support.taskrabbit.com/hc/en-us/articles/204409440-TaskRabbit-Community-Guidelines> accessed 13 February 2017.

95 <www.theverge.com/2015/10/28/9625968/rating-system-on-demand-economy-uber-olive-garden> accessed 13 February 2017.

with well-paid or otherwise attractive requests reserved for taskers with higher ratings.[96]

5.1.2 Receiving Labour and its Fruits

Similarly to the analysis of Uber in the previous section, it appears that in most scenarios, the platform will be the primary recipient of the fruits of taskers' labour: it organises the invoicing, and no money (save for tips) may change hands directly between clients and taskers. The crucial role taskers play for the platform is explicitly acknowledged by TaskRabbit. As a blog-post on the company's website notes, the taskers 'are the face of TaskRabbit and frankly, do all the work. (We [the headquarters staff] just sit in our fancy office and watch while they do all the heavy lifting… literally.)'[97]

Under certain circumstances, finally, taskers may also 'apply for the longer-term business tasks under the "Jobs" filter' – a scenario which appears to be strongly reminiscent of traditional agency work.[98]

5.1.3 Provision of Work and Pay

The division of this third employer function is amongst the more difficult to analyse, as it varies drastically across different tasks. Looking first at the provision of day-to-day work, clients will post their tasks – from cleaning and shopping to repair services – on TaskRabbit. The platform then plays an important role in matching clients and taskers: on occasion this process is automated through its algorithms; other tasks are offered and accepted through direct client-tasker interaction.

The provision of pay is organised similarly: taskers are paid by the platform on a weekly basis, either by cheque or via PayPal. If the former method is chosen, TaskRabbit will also comply with certain tax-related formalities.[99] The levels of remuneration vary dramatically, as the platform continues to experiment with different remuneration models: a notable shift in 2014 saw a move away from the original auction-style mechanisms, where taskers could specify their offers for any given task, to an algorithm matching clients with a selection of workers for a job,

---

96 On *TaskRabbit* 'points and levels', see Handbook (n 89) 9.

97 <https://blog.taskrabbit.com/2011/04/29/aprils-runner-of-the-month-is/> accessed 13 February 2017.

98 <https://blog.taskrabbit.com/2013/05/22/takin-care-of-business-tips-for-business-tasks/> accessed 13 February 2017.

99 Handbook (n 89) 8.

displaying their relevant hourly rates.[100] The platform is thus not directly involved in the setting of wage levels: indeed, there is evidence that at least some taskers are becoming increasingly savvy at developing appropriate pricing mechanisms.[101]

5.1.4 Managing the Enterprise-Internal Market

TaskRabbit carefully couches work in terms of 'micro-entrepreneurship', 'neighbo[u]rhood heroes', and 'entrepreneurs like you who can help [busy people] get things done'.[102] In reality, the fourth employer function will usually be exercised by a combination of the platform, the tasker, and the client.[103] As regards actual control over individual tasks, the already cited terms and conditions note that the 'Company is not responsible for the performance of Users, nor does it have control'.[104]

This does not mean that the platform does not exercise the fourth employer function at all: tasks deemed inappropriate (such as dangerous tasks, or those of an illegal / sexual nature), for example, will be deleted by the platform, and can also be reported by individual taskers.[105] TaskRabbit also operates a comprehensive insurance scheme for clients and taskers alike, covering property damage, theft, and bodily injury (of clients, taskers, or third parties) during the performance of a task.[106]

Even more important is the fact that TaskRabbit operates a strict obligation on taskers personally to provide services – the Tasker manual explicitly notes that 'TaskPosters want to see your smiling face, not anyone else's … so please don't send someone that hasn't gone through our vetting process.'[107]

100 <www.theverge.com/2014/6/17/5816254/taskrabbit-blows-up-its-auction-house-to-offer-services-on-demand> accessed 13 February 2017.

101 <//www.priceintelligently.com/blog/bid/192053/Lessons-Learned-from-Creating-My-TaskRabbit-Pricing-Strategy> accessed 13 February 2017.

102 Handbook (n 89) 2.

103 <www.businessinsider.com/confessions-of-a-task-rabbit-2011-12?IR=T&page=1> accessed 13 February 2017.

104 <www.taskrabbit.com/terms (accessed on 13.2.2017)> (excerpts from clauses 1 and 2).

105 <https://blog.taskrabbit.com/2011/12/08/taskrabbits-guiding-principles/> accessed 13 February 2017.

106 <https://support.taskrabbit.com/hc/en-us/articles/204411640-Does-my-Tasker-have-insurance> accessed 13 February 2017.

107 Handbook (n 89)15.

5.1.5 *Managing the Enterprise-External Market*

Undertaking economic activity in return for potential profit, whilst also being exposed to any losses that may result from the enterprise, is the final function to be surveyed. Traditionally, one of the key elements of this function was the provision of relevant tools and investment for the economic activity to take place. As with other functions, work organised with *TaskRabbit* is highly heterogeneous: Some clients provide tools and closely supervise the work, whereas others will expect taskers to bring their own cleaning products or use their vehicles for transport-related tasks.[108] The same is true for remuneration levels. Over the course of the platform's development, numerous models appear to have been tested:[109] from customers setting their 'optimum price', to taskers offering their rates (with the platform then charging an additional service fee), or even pre-set 'Quick Assign' tasks, where TaskRabbit's algorithm determines the wages received. As a result, some taskers may find themselves earning in excess of USD $ 1,000 per week – whereas others barely manage to earn a minimum wage.[110]

Another important element in exercising this function is the acquisition and retention of clients. On the one hand, the platform strongly encourages – and financially incentivises – taskers to advertise its services, both through physical coupons and online.[111] It also provides detailed social guidelines, encouraging workers to 'Tweet or post about your great @TaskRabbit experiences' – whilst at the same time prohibiting them from including an affiliation with the platform in their Twitter user name.[112] On the other, it has more recently introduced features to 'encourage loyalty' between individual clients and Taskers: if 'a TaskPoster shows you some love, let them know they can use the Direct Hire feature to request bids and accept your bids easily in the future. They can also opt to hire you for Recurring Tasks like weekly grocery shopping.'[113]

TaskRabbit's operation is thus a prime example of how different employer functions are exercised by more than one entity – whether platforms, clients, or even

108 <www.bloomberg.com/bw/articles/2012-09-13/my-life-as-a-taskrabbit#p1> accessed 13 February 2017.

109 <http://venturebeat.com/2014/07/10/taskrabbit-users-revolt-as-the-company-shuts-down-its-bidding-system/> accessed 13 February 2017.

110 Compare, e.g. the reports at <http://time.com/money/3714829/working-for-taskrabbit/> accessed 13 February 2017 with those at <www.bloomberg.com/bw/articles/2012-09-13/my-life-as-a-taskrabbit> accessed 13 February 2017.

111 Handbook (n 89) 11.

112 ibid 12.

113 ibid 11.

individual workers themselves. In order to accommodate these different work arrangements, the second sub-section suggests, employment law needs to build on the identification of different employer functions, and embrace an openly functional concept of the employer, where the exercise of one or more employer function triggers the concomitant regulatory responsibilities – regardless of the underlying contractual arrangement(s).

5.2 A Functional Concept of the Employer

In order to reconcile these contradictions, and ensure a consistent application of employment law in the face of factual complexity, our conceptualisation of the concept of the employer needs to move from the current rigidly formalistic approach to a flexible, *functional* concept. In more concrete terms, the following working definition has been offered by Prassl – our concept of the employer should come to mean:

> the entity, or combination of entities, playing a decisive role in the exercise of relational employing functions, and regulated or controlled as such in each particular domain of employment law.

Calling for a functional definition of the employer is not a completely novel approach to the problems arising from multilateral employment arrangements.[114]

In order to embrace a functional approach, however, the law's underlying methods of reasoning need to evolve in part. The present sub-section thus sets out to consider the meaning of 'functional' in the proposed functional concept on a more abstract level, in the hope that this will allow for a clearer account of that approach. It further aims to develop functional typology as a richer concept than that of a simple contrast to the perceived formalism of the current bilateral-contractual approach,[115] thus avoiding at least some of the dangers of the 'transcendental nonsense' which can result from the indiscriminate use of the 'functional approach'

---

114 J Fudge, 'Fragmenting Work and Fragmenting Organizations: the Contract of Employment and the Scope of Labour Regulation' (2006) 44 Osgoode Hall Law Journal 609, 636; See also S Deakin, 'The Changing Concept of the "Employer" in Labour Law' (2001) 30 ILJ 72, 79.

115 J Fudge, 'The Legal Boundaries of the Employer, Precarious Workers, and Labour Protection' in G Davidov and B Langile (eds), *Boundaries and Frontiers of Labour Law* (Hart 2006) 310–13.

as a panacea to various analytical problems, 'often [...] with as little meaning as any of the magical legal concepts against which it is directed.'[116]

The account of functionalism proposed for purposes of identifying and defining the employer builds on the sociological concept of functional typologies, relying on the exercise of particular functions to determine the status of potential counterparties.[117]

The key idea of this *functional approach* is to focus on the specific role different elements play in the relevant context, instead of looking at the mere absence or presence of predetermined factors.[118] The presence of a contract of employment (or other contract) can thus be an important indicator in particular fields (for example the obligation to pay wages), but it is by no means the only one. To adopt Nogler's language to the present proposal, a functional concept of the employer is one where the employing entity or entities are defined not via the absence or presence of a particular factor, but via the exercise of specific functions.[119]

Under a functional approach, the composition of the employer acquires a degree of context- or domain-specificity: depending on the regulatory context, different subsets of the five employer functions will be of particular significance in identifying the responsible counterparty or counterparties. Whilst differences (potential or actual) in the concept of the employer across areas such as tax, tort, vicarious liability and 'employment law proper' have long been the subject of academic and judicial discussion,[120] the proposed definition goes further: adopting a functional method allows for even more detailed differentiation within what may all too easily have become perceived as a single regulatory domain.[121]

In concluding this section, the implications of a functional concept of the employer in the crowdwork context can briefly be illustrated by reference to two (hypothetical) workers. A first possible scenario in the context of platform work arrangements such as TaskRabbit is a cleaner, who is new to the platform and relies on its price matching mechanism to find work as quickly as possible. This

116 F Cohen, 'Transcendental Nonsense and the Functional Approach' (1935) 35 Columbia Law Review 809, 822.

117 Nogler (n 65). The following paragraphs draw extensively on this article and related work.

118 ibid pt 3.

119 ibid 463.

120 See e.g. E McKendrick, 'Vicarious Liability and Independent Contractors: A Re-Examination' (1990) 53 MLR 770.

121 Though cf. a notable countermove: M Freedland and N Kountouris, *The Legal Construction of Personal Work Relations* (OUP 2011) 17, 25ff.

means that the platform effectively sets his hourly rate, billing it (in addition to a commission) directly to the client. The first flat to which the cleaner is dispatched to, however, is rather large, and it is physically impossible to complete the task in the planned time. As a result, his earnings fall considerably below minimum wage levels. In this scenario, the platform has clearly exercised the relevant employer function by determining the cleaner's remuneration, and should be held responsible for minimum wage law compliance accordingly. This, however, does not mean that it should be the employer for all purposes: if a customer specifies dangerous working conditions, such as the use of particularly harsh cleaning chemicals, health and safety liability will be imposed on her, as she was in charge of exercising control over how the work should be done.

A second illustration is the case of an IT specialist, offering help with the development of online shops for fashion start-ups. She has a long track record of successful freelance work and is a sought-after designer and programmer, who has recently begun to channel her work through a platform as a single online market place. Her work commands a significant premium, which she reflects by setting her own wage rates at a higher rate per task. In this scenario, even if a task were to overrun and thus result in a too-low hourly wage, neither platform nor customers would be responsible for minimum wage levels under a functional concept of the employer, as the relevant employer function was exercised by the worker who genuinely set her own rate of remuneration. Over time, however, she finds that her ratings never rise to the top, and that there are fewer and fewer good offers available to her in consequence. This is due to the rating mechanism used by the platform systematically discounting female programmers' work, as users' biases become aggregated without correction.[122] Even though control over the inception and termination of employment relationships is shared between the worker and the platform, responsibility under anti-discrimination norms here would fall on the platform, as the operation of the ratings' mechanism is solely under its control.

6. Conclusion

The need for coherent underlying norms in employment law cannot be understated. 'It is no exaggeration to think of the classification of work relationships as

122 This example is sadly less hypothetical than one might expect: <www.bostonglobe.com/news/science/2013/08/08/the-pitfalls-crowdsourcing-online-ratings-vulnerable-bias/> accessed 13 February 2017.

the central, defining operation of any labour law system.'[123] In this paper, we have shown that crowdwork is the most recent threat to emerge to this need for underlying coherence from dramatic changes in the labour market: online platforms or 'apps' act as intermediaries in a spot-market for labour, providing clients with workers for a wide range of jobs referred to as 'gigs', 'rides', or 'tasks'.

A detailed discussion of potential avenues to operationalise each of the options discussed is beyond the scope of this book chapter. We hope that the brief examples nonetheless demonstrate how the proposed reconceptualisation would allow for a more subtle approach to effective employment law enforcement. By looking at the full range of functions exercised across various relationships to determine actual responsibility, obligations are placed on the most relevant party, but not beyond it. Whilst under the traditional approach, privity (or at most a specific statutory extension) would select the employer from this array of entities potentially able to exercise employer functions, in the reconceptualised concept of the employer, this role is replaced by the exercise of various functions. As a result, different employers may bear (or share) a range of obligations, depending always on their specific roles.

Whilst the advantages of a functional approach have been discussed more extensively elsewhere,[124] suffice it to say at present that this conceptualisation allows for flexibility across different regulatory domains, and can thus deal with the complexities arising from the fact that there are multiple entities, and multiple modes in which these entities can share the exercise of employer functions. The successful identification of the relevant employer for each function would restore coherence to the scope of employment law, resolving questions as to employee (and indeed customer) status in its wake.

A first move in this direction can be seen in a recent (UK) Employment Tribunal ruling that Uber drivers were workers employed by the company and were thus entitled to minimum wage and other basic labour rights. In *Aslam v Uber BV*, the court focused on the 'practical reality' of the relationship between *Uber* and its drivers and showed that the drivers, regardless of contractual statements to the contrary, are to be qualified workers. The mechanisms designed by Uber to insist that its drivers were self-employed merited a high degree of 'scepticism': 'Armies of lawyers' could not help a business avoid employment liabilities, despite contractual 'fictions, twisted language and even brand new terminology'.[125]

123 S Deakin and F Wilkinson, *The Law of the Labour Market* (OUP 2005) 4.

124 Prassl, *The Concept of the Employer* (n 8) ch 5.

125 *Aslam v Uber BV* (not yet reported), at [87] and [96]. For comment, see R Hunter and J Prassl at <http://ohrh.law.ox.ac.uk/worker-status-for-app-drivers-uber-rated/> accessed 13 February 2017.

The employment tribunal's ruling was widely welcomed by commentators. The tribunal's focus on the reality of the relationship between the parties and its clear and accessible analysis of the law as well as Uber's business are a role model for similar cases pending in jurisdictions worldwide. The basic protection now afforded to drivers will overcome some of the worst problems– not least, because the tribunal (rightly) ruled that a driver is 'working' for the entire time that his (the vast majority being male, as noted in the decision) Uber drivers' app is switched on, and he is able and willing to accept rides. In the longer run, however, Uber drivers – even when classified as workers – will still face many of the problems encountered by zero-hours workers across the UK: from low income to struggling with unpredictable shifts due to a lack of guaranteed work. Restoring the scope of employment protection is but the first step on the road to decent work in the on-demand economy.

Darcy du Toit

Towards Fairness in the 'Sharing Economy'

1. Introduction

The basic theme of this article is not new. It supports the argument for a theory of labour law in a globalised context moving beyond the paradigm of 'employment' to the broader paradigm of 'work'.[1] At one level, this argument presents no great challenge to traditional labour law. For example, the idea of 'employment' has been broadened to include what has been termed 'employment-like relationships',[2] as well as work based on economic 'dependency'.[3] Calling this 'work' rather than 'employment' could simply be seen as a definitional adjustment.

The article argues that it should be more than this. Adopting a paradigm of 'work' rather than 'employment', it is suggested, moves the focus from a particular *relationship* between the parties to the *activity* forming the purpose of their relationship.[4] This, in turn, invites reassessment of the nature and purpose of the applicable law. The 'main object' of labour law in its Fordist heyday was described as providing 'a countervailing force to counteract the inequality of bargaining power which is inherent and must be inherent in the employment relationship'.[5]

---

1 As in the contractual paradigm, work done for purely personal ends cannot enter the ambit of labour law. Also in the present paradigm, it becomes 'work' only when it is done for others, giving it 'social value'. The term 'social labour' is also used.

2 See, e.g., J Riley, *Employee Protection at Common Law* (The Federation Press 2005) 33; see also M Weiss and M Schmidt, *Labour Law and Industrial Relations in Germany* (4th edn, Wolters Kluwer 2008) 47–49.

3 Thus, section 200A(e) of the South African Labour Relations Act 66 of 1995 (LRA) lists the fact of being 'economically dependent' on the person for whom work is done as one of the factors triggering a presumption that the worker is an employee. Cf Weiss and Schmidt, *Labour Law and Industrial Relations in Germany* (n 2) 45–47; article 7:610 para 1 of the Dutch Civil Code.

4 Contrast M Freedland and N Kountouris, *The Legal Construction of Personal Work Relations* (Oxford University Press 2011), discussed by J Fudge 'Challenging the Borders of Labour Rights' in R Blanpain, F Hendrickx (eds) and D du Toit (guest ed), *Labour Law and Social Progress: Holding the Line or Shifting the Boundaries?* (2016) 92 Bulletin for Comparative Labour 73 at 82–83. See also A Blackett, 'Decolonizing Labour Law: A Few Comments' (2016) 92 Bulletin for Comparative Labour 89 at 96–98.

5 P Davies and M Freedland, *Kahn-Freund's Labour and the Law* (3rd edn, Stevens 1983) 18.

This resonates with the economic and legal subordination which is implicit in the concept of 'dependent labour' as much as in the contract of employment. But it also points at the divergence between a concept of labour law premised on the inherent dependency of the worker and one premised on the labour or 'work' which he or she performs. Simply put, the 'countervailing' function does not self-evidently present itself as the 'main object' of the latter paradigm because 'work' in a social sense does not necessarily presuppose inequality and dependency in the way that employment does.

But, it might be asked, isn't this a mere quibble in modern sectors of the economy where labour law has always been rooted? Here 'employment' in one form or another accounts for the bulk of the 'work' that is performed. Will the counteraction of inequality between worker and employer not remain the *de facto* priority of labour law?

The practical part of this argument cannot be denied; to the extent that social labour remains dependent labour, worker protection must remain as central as ever. But should the concept of labour law be limited to this? Few would deny that labour law should move with the times. Historically, it can be argued, it has done so.[6] It is no accident that 'employment' emerged as the dominant form of work in industrialized societies, having much to do with the control it gave entrepreneurs over workers' labour.[7] But the legal construct was drawn from diverse historical origins, ranging from the political economy of slave society to the master-servant relationship which preceded modern wage labour, whereas today we are witnessing the proliferation of new forms of work. In short, employment has seen enormous transitions, both in its own form and in the fabric of the surrounding society, driven by economic as well as social imperatives, not least by workers' own struggles against their subordination.[8] Law has sought to keep pace with all this. Looking forward, we should at least question any supposition that the current model of employment (including its non-standard varieties) represents the last word in the evolution of social labour.

---

6 Cf A Blackett 'Emancipation in the Idea of Labour Law' in G Davidoff and B Langille (eds) *The Idea of Labour Law* (Oxford University Press 2011) 420.

7 RH Coase 'The nature of the firm' (1937) 4 Economica 386; S Deakin 'The Contribution of Labour Law to Economic Development and Growth' in (2016) 92 Bulletin for Comparative Labour 21–24, and Fudge 'Challenging the Borders of Labour Rights' (n 4) 77–79.

8 Blackett 'Emancipation in the Idea of Labour Law' (n 6).

There are also more specific reasons for doubting this. A century or two into the process of 'proletarianisation' described by Coase,[9] employers have discovered the advantages of having work done by workers other than 'employees'.[10] Some forms of non-standard *employment* that have emerged in the era of globalisation have partly transcended the personal relationship which employment is supposed to embody; for example, agency work and 'contracting out' or 'in' of labour. More recently we have seen the appearance of 'gig work' or the 'sharing economy', discussed more fully below, possibly transcending the model of employment itself.

Understandably, organised labour and labour lawyers have been concerned in the first place with the protection of workers who are denied the safeguards that go with employment status. But on which legal foundations can this be done? Can new work relationships merely be seen as the construction of ever more ingenious forms of disguised employment? If so, the solution lies in lifting the veil and bringing aberrant work relationships back into the protected zone of 'employment'.

Seeking to do this has been one response to the plight of *Uber* drivers. But is this the whole answer? It can equally be argued that the genie of having work done under contracts other than employment contracts is well and truly out of the bottle. Seeking to extend the rights of standard employees to all workers, regardless of their manner of work, cannot be effective in areas where the assumptions of labour law based on standard employment simply do not fit.[11] And tweaking the rules to accommodate fundamentally different relationships might simply result in a regulatory hodgepodge, rife with inconsistencies and so imprecisely formulated as to be ineffective.

The article examines these propositions with special reference to the so-called 'sharing economy'. Rather than seeking to extrapolate answers from the contractual model, it proposes to start from the realities of work processes, regardless

---

9 Of course, Coase was not the first to do so; among the pioneers was Karl Marx in *Capital* (vol I) (Lawrence and Wishart 1974).

10 As Marc Linder and Lawrence Zacharias put it: 'Workers are ripe for disintegrative exploitation to the extent that the value to an entrepreneur of proletarianizing them is spent (that is, the workforce has been sufficiently disciplined) and to the extent workers can be remarketized in ways that retain all the advantages of earlier proletarianization to their former employers': 'Opening Coase's Other Black Box: Why Workers Submit to Vertical Integration into Firms' (1993) 18 Journal of Corporation Law 371 375.

11 As, for example, with the extension of standard labour rights to domestic workers, in a sector where the conditions for their implementation hardly exist. See ILO Decent work for domestic workers Report IV(1), International Labour Conference, 99th Session, Geneva (2010); D du Toit (ed) *Exploited, Undervalued – and Essential: Domestic Workers and the Realisation of their Rights* (Pretoria University Law Press 2013).

of the legal relationships which they embody. This does not repudiate worker protection or the rights-based tradition that labour law has adopted; rather, it seeks to embed fundamental rights in the rules by which all forms of work are or might be governed. But it is the nature of the work relationship itself, and not the assumptions of a quasi-contractual template, that should determine the kind of protection which workers require in different contexts, as well as the most effective ways of regulating it. The aim would be to develop a comprehensive body of rules of individual and collective labour law, procedural as well as substantive, that will be appropriate in regulating different forms of work.

Such an exercise might also address some of the difficulties bound up with the traditional idea of labour law as a 'countervailing force' which, by definition, remains locked into conflict with entrepreneurial freedom. On the one hand, there is a strong case that respect for workers' rights goes hand in hand with entrepreneurial success. But this is so only up to a point. Even employers who seek to be good corporate citizens are ultimately driven by competitive interests.

The precarious nature of labour rights was masked in the industrialized world for much of the post-World War II period, not least by economic growth and the scope it afforded for compromise and concessions. But every compromise tends to unravel if its cost is seen as exceeding its benefits. This, it is submitted, broadly describes what has happened since the 1970s and, more emphatically, since the crisis of 2008.[12] With the intensification of competition and the power of organised labour eroded after decades of globalisation, proponents of greater regulatory freedom have sought to minimise the restrictions imposed by the labour law of the Fordist era.

This unravelling lies at the heart of the challenges that labour scholars have been grappling with for a generation, reflected in the ideological contest between 'neo-liberalism' versus 'fair globalisation' and in conflicts over the maintenance of traditional labour rights at the national level. Of course, the process has been uneven. For some trade unions in relatively strong bargaining positions and their employer counterparts, it might be business almost as usual. But on a broader stage, with the levers of economic power in the hands of transnational and corporate employers, labour law premised simply on worker protection must face an uncertain future.

12 For fuller discussion, see Davidov and Langille *The Idea of Labour Law* (n 6); A Bogg, C Costello, ACL Davies and J Prassl *The Autonomy of Labour Law* (Hart 2015); M Finkin and G Mundlak (eds) *Comparative Labor Law* (Edward Elgar 2015).

Refocusing labour law on the regulation of social labour could offer a stronger basis. From being marginalised as a perceived obstruction to economic growth, labour law could be systematically reconceptualised as a regulatory framework at the core of *sustainable* growth. Much theoretical groundwork has already been done in laying the foundations for such a development, based on the implementation of workers' rights in the workplace as a precondition for broader goals of social justice, as well as enterprise-specific goals of sustainable growth and conflict transformation. While worker protection against abuse is non-negotiable, it does not emerge as an objective in itself, but as part of the primary object of regulating work in socially acceptable ways, also by realising human potential. Simply put, fundamental rights should be embodied in, and permeate, the regulation of social labour in ways no longer predicated on moderating inequality, but positively concerned with overcoming it.[13]

The article starts by looking at instances where social labour has tested the limits of the employment model or gone beyond it, with uncertain results in the current regulatory framework. It then turns to the model of the 'sharing economy' and legal challenges faced by Uber in the United States (US). Finally, it tries to draw some practical conclusions.

2. Independent Contracting

Labour law applies to workers only if they are classified as 'employees'; 'independent contractors' are left to the mercy of contract law.[14] In principle, this 'binary model' may be sound – self-employed workers, after all, cannot be equated with employees. But it creates an incentive for employers, in some cases, to misclassify employees as independent contractors in order to evade their labour law

---

13 The premise is that the rights to dignity, equality and freedom form an imperative basis for labour law. It implies the performance of work under conditions of maximum freedom, as opposed to inequality and subordination which is inherent in employment, where the aim of labour law is not so much to regulate worker subordination as to define workers' and employers' freedoms in different contexts. This line of thought is developed more fully in D du Toit 'The Right to Equality versus Employer 'Control' and Employee 'Subordination': Are Some More Equal Than Others?' (2016) 37 Industrial Law Journal (SA) 1.

14 Though there are exceptions of workers who are neither; for example, members of the clergy are in many cases regarded as performing a personal mission, facilitated by a church or other religious institution.

obligations.[15] Internationally, such practices abound to a point where various states have introduced civil or criminal sanctions to discourage false labelling of employees.[16]

But the real problem may lie deeper, as was shown in the South African case of *Buti & others v Member of the Executive Committee, Gauteng Department of Health.*[17] In this case, a state department had secured the services of some 10,000 community health workers on fixed-term contracts to provide basic health services to households. The contracts stipulated that they were 'independent service providers' acting as 'volunteers'. Some 15 years on, five workers who were required to reapply for their positions at the end of a contractual period applied to the Labour Court for an order declaring them to be 'employees' in order to challenge non-renewal of their contracts as 'unfair dismissal'.

The facts showed that the department's actions were not unreasonable, but that was not the issue. The facts also showed that the 'volunteers' had fixed hours of work and duties which they performed under the department's control. By applying the standard test for distinguishing employees from independent contractors,[18] the court decided that they were employees.

However, this did not solve the workers' problem. At best, the judgment meant that they were temporary employees whose contracts were about to expire. As such, their position was little different from that of independent contractors, while their employer enjoyed almost the same flexibility in dispensing with their services.[19] To prove 'dismissal', they would have to prove that they had a 'reasonable

---

15 See, e.g., *Building Bargaining Council (Southern and Eastern Cape) v Melmons Cabinets CC and another* [2001] 3 BLLR 329 (LC) where an employer's scheme to persuade its employees to enter into new contracts whereby they became 'independent contractors' was described as 'a cruel hoax': para 21.

16 ILO/European Labour Law Network *Regulating the employment relationship in Europe: A guide to Recommendation No. 198* (ILO 2013).

17 Case no: J 352/16, 18 March 2016.

18 In South Africa, there are three 'primary' criteria: (a) whether the worker is subject to the alleged employer's supervision and control; (b) whether the worker forms an integral part of the alleged employer's organisation; and (c) the extent to which the worker is economically dependent on the alleged employer. See *State Information Technology Agency (SITA) (Pty) Ltd v CCMA and others* [2008] 7 BLLR 611 (LAC).

19 Legislation designed to prevent the abuse of fixed-term contracts, by keeping employees in the limbo of a 'permanent temporary' status, is not intended to obstruct employment that is genuinely of a temporary nature. Thus, section 198B of the Labour Relations Act (LRA) allows employers unlimited scope to enter into temporary contracts if there is any 'justifiable reason' for doing so.

expectation' of continued employment,[20] whereupon the employer would need to prove that the termination was 'fair'. But, in the present case, the employees might well have failed at the first hurdle. This again demonstrates the insecurity inherent in non-standard employment and the limitations of existing legal protection.

The binary model also implies the possibility of converting employment relationships into relationships genuinely based on independent service provision. This was illustrated in a recent South African case[21] where a major courier company, UTI, had introduced an empowerment scheme converting its drivers to independent contractors. This made them owners of their trucks, but who tendered their services to the company to do the same work as before. Given the nature of the work, their conduct as well as the condition of their vehicles were regulated by contract, subject to cancellation in the event of non-compliance.

The dispute arose when some 20 drivers or ex-drivers, who had been sanctioned for breach of contract, claimed that they were employees who had been subjected to unfair labour practices or unfairly dismissed. Both the arbitrator of first instance and the Labour Court, on review, found that they were not employees. The Labour Appeal Court agreed. Amongst other things, some drivers had created corporate entities through which they operated and employed their own employees to render services to UTI.[22] The proposition that they were genuinely providing independent services, the court found, was 'frankly unassailable', and the controls exercised by UTI over their work were no more than 'essential requirements of the contract intrinsic to the nature of the services to be performed by [UTI] to its clients'.[23]

It is difficult to fault the judgment in principle; the real questions lie elsewhere. The dispute was confined to the issue of jurisdiction (whether the drivers were 'employees') and thus their real claim – that they had been unfairly treated or unfairly dismissed – could not be heard. Had 'work' rather than 'employment' been the starting point, this would not have happened. The fact that the drivers were indisputably performing work for UTI would have given a labour tribunal jurisdiction to hear the dispute on its merits, regardless of the form of their contract.

If so, which legal rules would have applied? In the present case, the Labour Appeal Court found nothing exceptionable about the terms of the contracts. However, this might not always be so; and, even when it is, there is (as with

20 Section 186(1)(b), LRA.

21 *Phaka and others v Bracks and others* [2015] 5 BLLR 514 (LAC).

22 Some of these, the company testified, operated more than one route and made in excess of 100 000 South African Rand per month (equivalent to some 14 000 USD at the time).

23 Paras 32, 33.

every contract) no guarantee that it will be complied with. Thus, the drivers in the present case might have sued UTI for breach of contract, though they would probably not have succeeded. South African courts have little scope for interference with contractual terms in the absence of illegality. 'Illegality' may arise from conflict with public policy or any right guaranteed by the Constitution. But, since no right is absolute, the law of contract may justify the limitation of any basic right up to a point.[24] This could explain why the drivers sought to rely on the broad principle of 'fairness' to which employees are entitled in labour law rather than on their narrow contractual rights.

Having said that, how far could contracts for services infringe on workers' rights before the limits of constitutional justifiability are reached? In *Barkhuizen v. Napier*,[25] the Constitutional Court agreed with the court below that the Constitution should be applied:

> ...to achieve a balance that strikes down the unacceptable excesses of "freedom of contract", while seeking to permit individuals the dignity and autonomy of regulating their own lives. This is not to envisage an implausible contractual nirvana. It is to respect the complexity of the value system the Constitution creates. It is also to recognise that intruding on apparently voluntarily concluded arrangements is a step that judges should countenance with care, particularly when it requires them to impose their individual conceptions of fairness and justice on parties' individual arrangements.[26]

But the court below did accept that 'a factor of particular importance is the parties' relative bargaining positions; for it is here that the constitutional values of equality and dignity may prove decisive'.[27] Endorsing this,[28] the Constitutional Court went on to say that 'the proper approach' is one whereby courts may 'decline to enforce contractual terms that are in conflict with the constitutional values even though the parties may have consented to them.'[29]

---

24 Basic rights may be limited by law of general application 'to the extent that the limitation is reasonable and justifiable in an open and democratic society based on human dignity, equality and freedom', subject to criteria of proportionality: section 36(1), Constitution of the Republic of South Africa, 1996.

25 2007 (7) BCLR 691 (CC) paras 12–13, upholding the judgment of the Supreme Court of Appeal in *Napier v Barkhuizen* 2006 (9) BCLR 1011 (SCA). At issue in this case was a clause in an insurance contract placing a time limit on the lodging of claims, which was upheld.

26 Para 13.

27 Para 14.

28 '[T]he relative situation of the contracting parties is a relevant consideration in determining whether a contractual term is contrary to public policy': para 59.

29 Para 30.

In Europe, the Principles of European Contract Law similarly state that '[a] contract is of no effect to the extent that it is contrary to principles recognised as fundamental in the laws of the Member states of the European Union'.[30] Although criticised by some as being 'too general',[31] the Principles also accept that freedom of contract may not trespass on fundamental rights and values. This is indeed very general, lacking the specificity with which labour law limits the contract of employment, and leaves much to the discretion of judges.[32] But it calls for clarification of those limits rather than abandoning the field to market forces, subject only to broad prohibitions contained in civil and criminal law.

Turning back to contracts for services, the fact that a person is an independent contractor does not necessarily imply bargaining equality with clients or exclude the possibility of unconscionable terms. If all workers have the same fundamental rights,[33] it becomes a task of the legislature to define the rights of independent contractors in more specific terms, as in the case of employment.[34]

The growth of independent contracting at the expense of standard employment is more than simply a shift between the two legs of the binary model. Work can show combinations of contrasting features,[35] as employment itself is increasingly doing in its non-standard permutations. But similar processes may affect independent contracting. Although inherently more open-ended than employment, this relationship may also acquire 'non-standard' features, such as significant degrees of customer control resembling that of the employer or, more insidiously, a triangular dimension through the intercession of third parties between customer and contractor. Thus, while areas of relatively unadulterated employment and independent contracting relations will no doubt remain, there may also be a growing range of hybrid forms of work that are

30 Art 15:101. The Principles contain model rules that are not directly enforceable.

31 M Storme 'Freedom of Contract: Mandatory and Non-Mandatory Rules in European Contract Law' (2006) Juridica International 40.

32 Which may result in narrow interpretations and reluctance to grant remedies, precisely because it is seen as the role of the legislature to do so.

33 Which, in South Africa, is guaranteed by section 23(1) of the Constitution.

34 See, e.g., the Australian Independent Contractors Act of 2006 which states that a court may review a services contract on the ground that it is 'unfair' and/or 'harsh': sections 5, 12. 'Unfair' contracts include those that are 'against the public interest', as well as those providing 'for remuneration at a rate that is, or is likely to be, less than the rate of remuneration for an employee performing similar work': section 9(1).

35 Compare G. Davidov 'Re-Matching Labour Laws with Their Purposes' in Davidov and Langille *The Idea of Labour Law* (n 6) 185–186.

difficult to confine within either category and for which dedicated forms of regulation may be needed.

The so-called 'sharing economy' illustrates these questions more specifically.[36]

3. The 'Sharing Economy'

The term 'sharing economy', according to Uber,[37] refers to 'online software platforms that connect buyers with sellers, owners with renters, or … drivers with riders'.[38] An economist explains that '[t]he 'sharing economy' matches people who want to share assets online'.[39] An article in the *New York Times* adds:

> Just as Uber is doing for taxis, new technologies have the potential to chop up a broad array of traditional jobs into discrete tasks that can be assigned to people just when they're needed, with wages set by a dynamic measurement of supply and demand, and every worker's performance constantly tracked, reviewed and subject to the sometimes harsh light of customer satisfaction.[40]

Judy Fudge explains:

> [it] involves traditional forms of work such as transport, cleaning, and clerical work [being] channelled through apps managed by firms for a final client. Digital technology allows consumers, firms, and workers to reduce transaction costs in order to match the demand and supply of services at a high speed enabling just-in-time work. This way of organizing work also facilitates risk shifting to workers.[41]

---

36 The discussion that follows does not attempt any comprehensive analysis of this highly complex phenomenon; it is limited to its general features and a few significant episodes in its evolution.

37 Commonly described as an 'online transportation network company', Uber was formed in 2009. By 2015, it was worth an estimated $68 billion, a value that General Motors is said to have taken 100 years to reach.

38 *O'Connor and others v Uber Technologies, Inc.*: Petition for Permission to Appeal from the United States District Court for the Northern District of California No. 3:13-cv-03826-EMC (15 September 2015; hereafter 'Petition') 1. The petition was finally granted on 5 April 2016: L Chiem 'Uber Asks To Halt Driver Tips Trial Amid 9th Circ. Review' *Law360* 7 April 2016.

39 G Petropoulos 'Uber and the economic impact of sharing economy platforms' (*Bruegel* 22 February 2016) at <http://bruegel.org/2016/02/uber-and-the-economic-impact-of-sharing-economy-platforms/> accessed 7 March 2017.

40 F Manjoo 'Uber's Business Model Could Change Your Work' (*New York Times* 28 January 2015).

41 Fudge, 'Challenging the Borders of Labour Rights' (n 4) 79. In South Africa, e.g., two platforms have been created offering access to the services of domestic workers: see www.sweepsouth.com *and* www.domestly.com/.

Thus, the 'sharing economy' refers to work done by A (the worker) for others (B), where A contracts with B through a means of communication typically[42] provided by a third party, C, in return for a fee and subject to terms and conditions stipulated by C.[43] Importantly, it is A who is typically the owner of any equipment used in the performance of the work. It thus shows resemblances with agency work, in that C facilitates the assignment of A to B, as well as with independent contracting in that A does work for B without becoming B's employee.

However, it also differs from agency work. C plays no active part in bringing about the contract between A and B and does not 'place' A with B; and, while C collects a fee, it may be from A rather than B. At the same time, it differs from typical independent contracting in that A and B might not strike their own bargain but may do so on terms laid down by C. Thus, the exercise of designing worker protection does not fit easily into existing labour law discourse. Whereas with agency work, the argument is typically that B should be regarded as A's employer in cases of dispute, in litigation arising from the 'sharing economy' it has been C rather than B who was alleged to be the employer.

The significance of the 'sharing economy' as a form of social labour is not entirely clear.[44] It is in its early days, and the signals appear to be mixed. Uber's spectacular success and that of some other operators suggest that it may grow exponentially. But it has also been argued that growth potential is mainly limited to sectors where the factors that allowed Uber's expansion are most strongly present; in particular, 'vulnerable markets' and scope for individual operators to provide services more efficiently than existing providers.[45]

---

42 But not necessarily: workers themselves could also own the platform and thus eliminate C. This would move it closer to independent contracting in its classic form.

43 In South Africa, to 'partner' with Uber, 'drivers need a professional driver's permit and an additional background check. Drivers go through an interview to monitor their basic city knowledge and customer service capabilities. Vehicles need to be roadworthy and have commercial insurance, along with passenger and third party liability. Mechanical and optical checks are performed before the vehicles are allowed onto the platforms. In Johannesburg, the vehicles have to be 2012 models or newer.' See Minutes of Parliamentary Portfolio Committee on Transport, 1 September 2015.

44 For a challenging assessment, see P Mason *Postcapitalism: A guide to our future* (Penguin Books 2015).

45 F Manjoo 'The Uber Model, It Turns Out, Doesn't Translate' (*New York Times* 23 March 2016). The contrast between this article and that by the same author dated just over a year previously (see n 40) can be seen as an indicator of the volatility surrounding the prospects for the 'sharing economy'.

On the other hand, there is no reason to think that the 'sharing economy' will be any less dynamic than other sectors in responding to challenges through adaptations and innovations. It remains to be seen which forms these might take and what the results may be. 'Crowdsourcing', for example, has demonstrated that relatively complex operations, as well as specific services, can be facilitated by means of information technology.[46] Building on such developments, ongoing technical advances make it likely that the 'sharing economy' will expand rather than decline. If so, labour law should take it seriously.

What does this mean?

4. The Case of Uber

The contractual relationships defining the 'sharing economy' are specific. The contract between B (the client) and C (the platform owner) regulates B's access to C's platform and not the provision of A's services. This places it beyond the normal framework of triangular work.[47] A (the worker) also does not become the employee of B, for whom A may only perform a one-off service. Legally, this can only give rise to a contract for the performance of that particular service.

From the standpoint of traditional labour law, that leaves the relationship between A and C as the only possible point of connection. Within the binary model, A must be classified as C's employee in order to gain legal protection. Clearly mindful of this, the contract between Uber and its drivers states that:

> …the relationship between the parties under this Agreement is solely that of independent contracting parties. The parties expressly agree that … this Agreement is not an employment agreement, nor does it create an employment relationship, between Company and you.[48]

---

46 An example of this is Wikipedia which, according to its website, is written collaboratively 'by largely anonymous volunteers'. Studies have indicated that its accuracy is comparable with that of Encyclopaedia Britannica.

47 In the case of Uber, the standard contract with users of the platform (B) stipulates that it entitles the user 'to arrange and schedule transportation and/or logistics services with third party providers of such services', adding emphatically: 'YOU ACKNOWLEDGE THAT UBER DOES NOT PROVIDE TRANSPORTATION OR LOGISTICS SERVICES OR FUNCTION AS A TRANSPORTATION CARRIER': <www.uber.com/legal/terms/in> accessed 7 March 2017.

48 Clause 13.1 of Technology Services Agreement between Rasier, LLC (an Uber subsidiary) and 'independent providers of rideshare or peer-to-peer … passenger transportation services using the Uber Services' dated 11 December 2015 at <https://s3.amazonaws.com/uber-regulatory-documents/country/united_states/RASIER%20

However, contracts are not to be taken purely at face value. In the case of Uber, the depiction of its drivers as independent contractors has been challenged both in theory[49] and in a series of legal processes in California. At the time of writing, the California Labor Tribunal had held drivers to be employees,[50] but courts had yet to pronounce on the issue. The question was centrally posed in *O'Connor & others*[51] where, as in *Berwick*, the inquiry centred on the test for distinguishing an 'employee' from an 'independent' contractor and, specifically, the degree of control exercised by Uber over the driver. Even so, the context of the 'sharing economy' required a somewhat different application of the test. In deciding that an Uber driver was an 'employee', this was how the Labor Commissioner explained it:

> Plaintiff's car and her labor were her only assets. Plaintiff's work did not entail any 'managerial' skills that could affect profit or loss. Aside from her car, Plaintiff had no investment in the business. Defendants provided the iPhone application, which was essential to the work. But for Defendants' intellectual property, Plaintiff would not have been able to perform the work.[52]

In *O'Connor*, Uber argued that the 'widely varying relationships between drivers and Uber' make it impossible for these to be classified 'in one fell swoop' and that 'most drivers do not want and did not intend to be Uber's employees'.[53] 'Wide variations in workers' circumstances and schedules based on individual

---

Technology%20Services%20Agreement%20Decmeber%2010%202015.pdf> accessed 7 March 2017.

49 A Rosenblat 'The Truth About How Uber's App Manages Drivers', *Harvard Business Review* (6 April 2016); F Lubian *Uber and the Law* (Master Thesis, University of Fribourg, Academic Year 2014–2015).

50 *Berwick v. Uber Techs., Inc.*, No. 11–46739 EK (Labor Comm. June 3 2015); P Vasan 'California: Former Uber driver was an employee' *CNET* 10 September 2015. In the earlier case of *Alatraqchi v. Uber Techs., Inc.*, No. 11–42020 CT (Labor Comm. Aug. 1 2012) the driver was found to be an independent contractor: *O'Connor* Petition (n 38) 3. Uber has lodged an appeal against the order made in *Berwick*.

51 Petropoulos 'Uber and the economic impact of sharing economy platforms' (n 39).

52 Cited in *Uber Technologies, Inc., A Delaware Corporation vs. Barbara Berwick* (Case Number: CGC-15-546378, Superior Court of California, County of San Francisco, 16 June 2015) Notice of Appeal at 9.

53 *O'Connor* Petition (n 38) at 3, 6, 19. In rejecting Uber's latter argument, the court did so on technical grounds without addressing the principled question of the position the law should adopt if it were true: see *O'Connor and others v Uber Technologies Inc* Class Certification Order [N.D. Cal. Case No. 3:13-03826-EMC, Dkt. 341] appended to *O'Connor* Petition (n 38) 24–25.

discretion and desire', it concluded, 'are distinctive features of the new sharing economy'.[54]

The question of the drivers' employment status was temporarily laid to rest in this case with the settlement between Uber and the drivers that was announced on 21 April 2016.[55] It meant that the drivers would remain classified as 'independent contractors'. However, the settlement agreement was subject to court approval and, on 18 August 2016, it was rejected.[56] The question may therefore resurface in this and in other pending matters. But, even if it is ultimately decided that the drivers are employees, the question is how much this will help.

For a generation, the difficulty of protecting 'non-standard employees' has been a central problem of labour law. Adding Uber drivers to this troubled category might bring legal closure, but will not necessarily resolve their problems.[57] On the other hand, it may have an impact on the 'sharing economy' itself. No doubt predictably, Uber has claimed that transforming 'independent contractors' into 'employees' 'would be effectively killing the [sharing economy] business model'.[58] In a formal sense, this may be true. However, in the *O'Connor* certification order, the court went on to observe: 'Indeed, even if Uber loses this case, it will be free to restructure its relationship with its drivers in such a way that the drivers would actually be bona fide independent contractors'.[59]

This was illustrated by the *Phaka* case, discussed above:[60] it is possible to transform an employment relationship into an independent contracting relationship in ways that can withstand legal challenge.

If so, it will call for new legal responses. Interventions thus far have not moved much beyond the binary distinction between employment and independent contract. A more realistic starting point may be to accept that the model of work associated with the 'sharing economy' (in its present or possible future permutations)

---

54 ibid 20.

55 D MacMillan, L Weber and R E Silverman 'Uber Drivers Settle With Ride-Hailing Company in Labor Dispute' *Wall Street Journal* (21 April 2016). The settlement, involving some 385 000 drivers in California and Massachusetts, is discussed in part 5 of this article.

56 N 61 below, and see D Alba 'Judge Rejects Uber's $100 Million Settlement with Drivers' *Wired* Business 18 August 2016.

57 As was demonstrated in the case of *Buti* (n 17).

58 *O'Connor and others* Petition 3.

59 (n 53) at 25.

60 *Phaka and others* (n 21).

differs from employment, but also from traditional independent contracting and, to this extent, may call for a different form of regulation.

Against this background, the settlement agreement between Uber and its drivers, despite its demise, sheds some light on the prospects for a more appropriate regulatory model that might be in the making.[61]

5. Towards Regulation in the 'Sharing Economy'

The drivers' main claims against Uber were to be classified as 'employees' and for certain monetary payments. In essence, the claim for employee status was abandoned and an amount of $84 million, plus a contingency payment of $16 million, was accepted in settlement of the monetary claims.[62] However, there were also other grievances – in particular, Uber's right to 'deactivate' drivers (i.e. terminate their status) without warning – illustrating a range of issues that may call for regulation in the 'sharing economy'. Dealing with these, the settlement agreement included the following terms:[63]

1. Drivers may only be deactivated for 'sufficient cause', subject to prior warnings (except in cases involving safety, fraud, discrimination or illegal conduct) plus a written reason, and Uber will publish its 'deactivation guidelines'.
2. Drivers who are deactivated or threatened with deactivation for certain reasons may appeal to a Driver Appeal Panel, which will include fellow-drivers. Drivers deactivated for specified reasons will be given the opportunity to take a course and be reactivated.
3. Drivers may go to arbitration to challenge deactivation unless it is based on safety issues, discrimination and fraud or illegal conduct, and Uber will pay the arbitration fees. The arbitrator would be required 'to determine if the deactivation was for sufficient cause'.
4. Uber will provide information to drivers about their 'star ratings', rankings relative to other drivers and what customer ratings a driver must maintain.

---

61 The agreement is summed up in the Order Denying Plaintiffs' Motion For Preliminary Approval (Case No. CV 13-03826-EMC, US District Court Northern District of California), <www.cand.uscourts.gov/EMC/OConnorvUberTechnologies> accessed 7 March 2017 (hereafter 'Settlement Order'). The settlement was subject to court approval and was rejected on 18 August 2016 as being 'not fair, adequate, and reasonable': Settlement Order 2.

62 The court rejected the settlement amount as being grossly inadequate.

63 The information and quotations are from Settlement Motion (n 61) 8–10.

5. Uber will 'fund and facilitate the creation of a "Driver Association" in California and Massachusetts', enabling drivers to elect leaders to meet quarterly with Uber management. It will 'work in good faith with the Association's leaders, to address issues of concern facing drivers.'
6. While Uber will make it clear that 'tipping is neither expected nor required', drivers are not prohibited 'from putting up signs or requesting a tip'.

These arrangements show resemblances to employee protection, but also differences. First and foremost, there is an equivalent to protection against unfair dismissal, effectively providing for 'substantive fairness' as well as 'procedural fairness'. This protection is significantly greater than that enjoyed by most employees in California, Massachusetts and other states where the doctrine of 'employment at will' applies[64] and, as the Settlement Motion puts it, 'mimics the protection that is typically only available to unionized employees working under a collective bargaining agreement'.

At the same time, these protections are significantly less than those enjoyed by employees in most countries, other than the US, where labour rights are upheld. Drivers accused of contraventions involving safety, fraud, discrimination or illegal conduct may still be 'deactivated' without warning and are not entitled to seek arbitration. Even though such accusations may be as questionable as any others, Uber can terminate at will and drivers are left without recourse other than litigation at their own expense.

The establishment of a drivers' association can be seen as a major advance, but again there is a significant qualification. The fact that it is funded by Uber would have made the organisation a 'yellow union' in US terms or, internationally, constituted interference with workers' right to organise independently.[65] This rule, of course, applies to trade unions and not to organisations of 'independent contractors'. Yet the same fundamental problems arise in the case of any organisation which is dependent on an opposing contractual party's goodwill. Thus, for Uber drivers, the question of autonomous organisation remains unanswered.[66]

---

64 That is, entitling either party to terminate employment without notice or any reason or procedure, except where a collective agreement provides otherwise.

65 See art 2(2), ILO Right to Organise and Collective Bargaining Convention, 1949 (No. 98). In South Africa, a trade union must be free of control or influence of any kind from an employer to be able to register and enjoy statutory rights: see s 95, LRA.

66 Steps have been taken towards organisation of Uber and other 'ride-hail' workers by the Teamsters Union, among others, by offering advocacy and other services: see J Fitzgerald Rodriguez 'Teamsters recruiting Uber drivers after settlement of employee lawsuit' *San Francisco Examiner* (25 April 2016).

This question could be critical in the longer term. The consultative exercise with drivers that had to precede finalisation of the settlement agreement points at the importance of what has been termed 'responsive regulation'[67] in contrast to top-down law-making.[68] Unlike collective bargaining, it is not premised on the exercise of power, which workers in the 'sharing economy' may lack. In the case of Uber, it was the legal and political pressure exerted by well-publicised litigation which induced the settlement. However, this could be replicated by legislative requirements for similar forms of engagement in unregulated parts of the 'sharing economy' aimed at developing self-regulation consistent with basic rights and public policy.

But, for this to happen, the interests of each group needs to be articulated by authentic representatives, a process for which any legislative framework would need to make provision.

6. Conclusion

This article started from the proposition that labour law should be understood in terms of regulating the performance of socially valuable labour in all its forms within a matrix of basic rights, adapted to the realities of different sectors and contexts. The 'sharing economy' is one such context, presenting formidable challenges to the binary model of labour law. It may combine elements of employment, of agency work and of independent contracting, without coinciding sufficiently with any one of these to invite the simple extension of existing rules. In particular, the protection associated with 'employee' status which Uber drivers have sought to achieve, while offering important advantages, has generally not proved effective in the field of non-standard employment. Its efficacy in the hybrid field of the 'sharing economy' is even more questionable.[69]

---

67 That is, regulation that is 'responsive to industry structure in that different structures will be conducive to different degrees and forms of regulation': I Ayres and J Braithwaite *Responsive regulation: Transcending the deregulation debate* (Oxford University Press, 1992) 4.

68 B Hepple 'Negotiating social change in the shadow of the law' (2012) *SA Law Journal* 248, 254; see also D Ashiagbor 'Evaluating the Reflexive Turn in Labour Law' in Bogg et al. (eds), *The Autonomy of Labour Law* (n 12) 123–148.

69 See also the idea of 'functional employer', discussed by Prassl and Risak on page 97–126 in this volume. Though proceeding from the assumption of an 'employment relationship', albeit of a special kind, this approach likewise transcends the binary model and refines the analytical framework for determining the nature of work.

The settlement between Uber and its drivers illustrates a different type of regulation within the domain of freedom of contract. While it may be rudimentary compared with employment law, it addresses issues and creates rights falling beyond the typical scope of employee protection. It also regulates conditions under which independent contracts may be terminated and creates new rights and duties which the parties had not contemplated at the outset. And, crucially, it was negotiated on behalf of the parties themselves (albeit by attorneys seeking to settle a lawsuit), rather than imposed from above.

At the same time, the settlement agreement was only brought about through the intercession of public law. This underlines the scope for promoting responsive regulation in areas that are unreceptive to conventional regulation. There are many instances where national law requires parties to draw up rules within given legal frameworks as a condition for operating lawfully.[70] In the field of work, it could take many forms, involving different balances between prescriptive frameworks and scope for self-regulation.[71] But the point, as Fudge points out, is that legal frameworks need not serve to maintain centralised control at the expense of self-regulation; they can also serve as drivers of social justice.[72]

More work must be done, and is being done, in exploring these very broad propositions.[73] One interesting question is the possible articulation of the 'sharing economy' with workers' cooperatives, enabling workers to own the platforms through which their services are made available.[74] But there are many more. The changing world of work gives rise to new forms of social labour which need to

---

70 E.g., the constitutions of companies and trade unions.

71 See, for example, the Maharashtra Mathadi, Hamal and other Manual Workers (Regulation of Employment and Welfare) Act, 1969 for regulating casual day labour in the Indian state of Maharashtra; discussed by Fudge, 'Challenging the Borders of Labour Rights' (n 4) at 86–87. On the application of the 'Mathadi Act', see *Bhuwalka Steel Indus. Ltd. Vs. Bombay Iron and Steel Labour Bd. and Anr.* Supreme Court of India Civil Appeals Nos. 8452–8457 of 2009 (17.12.2009).

72 Fudge, 'Challenging the Borders of Labour Rights' (n 4) 85; see also W le Roux 'Advancing domestic workers' rights in a context of transformative constitutionalism' in du Toit (ed) *Exploited, Undervalued – and Essential* (n 11) 31 at 54–56.

73 See, for example, Z Dudas *Sharing Economy: Think Global, act local? The regulatory challenges of sharing economy* (LLM thesis Tilburg University 2016).

74 See, for example, C Quigley 'Co-ownership and the Sharing Economy' (*Grassroots Economic Organizing,* 2015) at <www.geo.coop/story/co-ownership-and-sharing-economy> accessed 8 March 2017. For discussion of the South African context, see D du Toit and T Galani 'Do Cooperatives Offer a Basis for Worker Organisation in the Domestic Sector? An Exploratory Study' (2015) 36 Industrial Law Journal 1677.

be matched by a corresponding evolution of labour law. Seeking to extrapolate answers from the employment model may do little more than reproduce the incoherence between labour law and practice which we know so well. The limitations of existing legal frameworks in meeting these challenges indicate a need for extending regulatory capacity to those who are better able to respond.

Juliet McMahon, Michelle O'Sullivan, Tom Turner,
Lorraine Ryan, Jonathan Lavelle, Caroline Murphy,
Mike O'Brien and Patrick Gunnigle

Zero Hours Work and the Role of the Law in Ireland

1. Introduction

In recent years, the landscape of employment status and working time arrangements has changed alongside a demand by employers for more flexibility with regard to employment, most notably in relation to numerical flexibility, i.e., the ability to increase/decrease workforce numbers in line with fluctuating demands. Thus, a wide range of contract types and categories of contractual status has developed over time. Zero hours contracts have come under political and public scrutiny in a number of countries, notably Ireland, the United Kingdom (UK), Finland and New Zealand. Trade unions have criticised their use by employers and have sought greater legal protection for people working on a zero hours basis.

Increased lobbying by trade unions in Ireland led to the government commissioning a study on the prevalence and implications of zero hours contracts and the study was subsequently undertaken by the authors in 2015. Ireland is an interesting case study on the effect of the law on atypical work. The Organisation of Working Time Act 1997 regulates zero hours contracts and this law has been considered as an example of regulation that could be adopted in other countries.[1] This chapter analyses the 1997 Act and argues that, rather than adequately addressing the issue of zero hours contracts, it was constructed in a narrow fashion and did not prevent or adequately regulate the full spectrum of zero hours arrangements.

The chapter is structured as follows. It begins with a contextual backdrop to the introduction of the zero hours regulation in the Organisation of Working Time Act. The methodology is outlined followed by an explanation of the relevant regulation in Section 18 of that Act. This is followed by a discussion on the differences between zero hours contracts as provided for in legislation and the reality of zero hours working arrangements, based on interviews with informed stakeholders.

---

1 S Deakin, 'New Forms of Employment, Implications for EU law, The Law as it Stands', (Keynote paper, European Labour Law Network-7th Annual Legal Seminar, New Forms of Employment and EU law, The Hague, Netherlands 27–28 November 2014)

We then discuss the critical issue of employment status in Irish law and review case law which highlights the lack of legal protections afforded to people on zero hours working arrangements. Lastly, we consider proposals from commentators on how to extend legal protections to people undertaking zero hours work.

2. The Background to Zero Hours Regulation

Issues surrounding the use and consequences of zero hours contracts have been raised in Ireland by trade unions in public and political arenas sporadically over the last 20 years. In the mid-1990s, the retail, bar and administrative workers' union, Mandate, lobbied the government to include employee protections relating to zero hours contracts during the drafting of the Organisation of Working Time Act 1997. This was in response to a lengthy dispute in one of Ireland's largest retailers, Dunnes Stores, over working conditions including the use of zero hours contracts. Following the introduction of the legislation, zero hours contracts were rarely in public debate, but were of concern to specific trade unions and occupations. For example, in 2004, the Services, Industrial and Professional Trade Union (SIPTU), Ireland's largest trade union, entered into a collective agreement with the Health Service Executive and it provided that zero hours contracts would be banned for 12,000 home care workers employed directly by the health service. However, SIPTU spent much of the next decade in dispute with the health service over the lack of implementation of the agreement. Since the onset of the economic recession in 2008 and recent indications of recovery, trade unions nationally have prioritised the pursuit of 'decent work' and zero hours contracts formed part of their political lobbying agenda, aided by the increasing attention to the topic in the UK. Unions applied pressure on the coalition government that was in place from 2011 to 2016, particularly on the minority partner, the Labour Party, to address the issue of zero hours and in 2014, the government committed to undertaking a study on zero hours contracts in its Statement of Priorities.

3. Methodology

The chapter is based on analysis of three sets of data. The first is from cases taken to the state dispute resolution body, the Labour Court, as well as the civil courts (High Court and Supreme Court) in which employment status was a critical issue for determination, and also cases taken under the Organisation of Working Time Act 1997. This data brings to light the limited protections available under the working time legislation and the complexity of determining employment status for people on zero hours arrangements. The second set of data is records of parliamentary debates and government committees from the 1990s which reveal the context and objectives behind the introduction of zero hours regulation in the working time legislation. The third source of data is from 35 interviews with informed stakeholder organisations undertaken in 2015 (13 employer/business representative organisations, eight trade unions, five government departments/agencies, one employment law association, and four non-governmental organisations representing women, youth, the unemployed and migrants). Stakeholders were asked for their understanding on the existence and prevalence of zero hours contracts as there is no national statistical data available on their use.

4. Zero Hours Contracts and Employment Law

The Organisation of Working Time Act 1997 was implemented as a result of Working Time Directive (93/104/EC). At the time of its drafting and introduction, Ireland had a system of social partnership between trade unions, employer organisations and government. The drafting of the working time legislation coincided with negotiations between social partners on a new national wage agreement in 1996 in which the Irish Congress of Trade Unions (ICTU) demanded that employment legislation be reviewed in light of the growth of atypical work. This demand was highlighted in the resultant social partnership agreement, Partnership 2000 (Department of Taoiseach, 1996). In response to unions' concerns, the Organisation of Working Time Act 1997 was drafted to include the following provision.

Section 18 (provision in relation to zero hours working practices) states:

> –(1) This section applies to an employee whose contract of employment operates to require the employee to make himself or herself available to work for the employer in a week–
> (a) a certain number of hours ("the contract hours"), or
> (b) as and when the employer requires him or her to do so, or
> (c) both a certain number of hours and otherwise as and when the employer requires him or her to do so.

Under Section 18, employees are entitled to compensation if the employer does not require them to work in a given week where they are required to be available. They are entitled to compensation amounting to 25 per cent of the time they were required to be available or 15 hours pay, whichever is the lesser. Significantly, Section 18 continues to state that the requirement of an employee to make him- or herself available to work:

> … is not one that is held to arise by virtue only of the fact, if such be the case, of the employer having engaged the employee to do work of a casual nature for him or her on occasions prior to the said week (whether or not the number of those occasions or the

> circumstances otherwise touching the said engagement of the employee are such as to give rise to a reasonable expectation on his or her part that he or she would be required by the employer to do work for the employer in the said week).

Analysis of historical records of parliamentary debates on the drafting of the working time legislation provides insight into the lobbying undertaken by union and employer organisations. The debates suggest that the employers' organisation, the Irish Hotels Federation, had sought the above clause so that the protections in Section 18 would not apply to casual workers. With the insertion of the clause, opposition party politicians expressed concerns that Section 18 would not provide the maximum amount of protection for vulnerable workers and the law would not make zero hours contracts illegal. The main opposition party, Fianna Fáil, proposed Section 18 be amended to provide for minimum working hours, specifically, that employers who required employees to be available for work should provide three continuous working hours or remuneration in lieu of those hours. However, this proposal was rejected by the then Minister of State for Enterprise and Employment, from the Labour Party, on the basis that it would negatively affect casual workers who may not want daily minimum hours. In addition, the Minister stated that Section 18 had been discussed and accepted by Mandate, the trade union for retail, bar and administrative workers. The then Minister argued that the legislation would 'effectively deal with the problem' of zero hours contracts.

Employees who come within the ambit of Section 18 are covered by other Irish employment legislation, most notably the unfair dismissals and the redundancy payments laws. There are also indications that such employees would be entitled to exercise rights under the Protection of Employees (Fixed-Term Work) Act 2003. Under this Act, employees who fulfil certain continuous length of service criteria may be entitled to a contract of indefinite duration. However, it would also seem to be open to the employer to give a contract of indefinite duration with no guaranteed hours, as per the terms of the employee's original contract. There is limited case law in this regard, but a case taken to the Labour Court would give some indication that the contract of indefinite duration would be based on the contracted hours which could be zero hours, even where the employee regularly works hours over and above the contracted hours.[2] There is thus a danger that people might get tied in to a zero or low hours contract of indefinite duration.

---

2 *Labour Court, HSE v 90 named complainants*. Determination no FTD0611. 16 January 2007. In this case, Ireland's Health Service Executive (HSE) had accepted that the complainants were employees. The issue in dispute was the hours on which the contracts of indefinite duration should be based.

5. The Law and the Reality of Zero Hours Work in Ireland

The purpose of Section 18 of the Organisation of Working Time Act was to address concerns surrounding zero hours contracts. However, interviews with stakeholders revealed varying interpretations about what constitutes a zero hours contract in the Irish context. The nub of the difference between stakeholders seems to centre around interpretations which restrict the label 'zero hours' to the narrow coverage of Section 18, or which view zero hours as a much wider spectrum of practices than those regulated by the Irish legislation. In general, employer representative organisations' definitions accorded to that contained in Section 18, which clearly indicates that coverage is restricted to a) employees employed under a contract of service and b) where there is an obligation on those employees to make themselves available. In Ireland, there is a legal distinction between the term 'contract *of* service', which is used to depict an employee/employer relationship, and a 'contract *for* service', which is used to depict the relationship between an employer and an independent contractor or some other arrangement. The interpretation of a zero hours contract by the largest employers' body, the Irish Business and Employers Confederation (IBEC), is 'a contract as it is set out in the legislation' and that a person on a zero hours contract 'has an obligation to be available'. The view of IBEC is that people on zero hours contracts are clearly employees and as such are covered by protective legislation, but that such contracts are 'are almost never used in Ireland'. Similarly, the Irish Hotels Federation believes that the hotel sector does 'not have zero hours contracts where someone has to be available and has to turn up but not get any work', thus indicating that this body also interprets zero hours contracts solely as those which come within the ambit of Section 18 of working time legislation. The Restaurants Association of Ireland notes that it had 'never heard of a zero hours contract' until the government commissioned the study, and that it never received queries from its members about them.

In contrast, worker representative bodies generally use definitions of zero hours work which are broader in scope and they do not necessarily make the distinction between someone who is required to be available for work and someone who is not. In general, they refer to a range of 'casual' practices including variable working hours and 'low' working hours. The ICTU for instance refuses to use the term zero hours contract and instead refers to zero hours practices which they describe as involving not knowing from week to week how many hours someone is going to work, not knowing when hours will be scheduled and being sent home from work. The Migrants Rights Centre of Ireland defines zero hours contracts as those involving variable hours. These varying perspectives of stakeholders raise a critical issue which reflects the problematic nature of defining zero hours in the Irish context. The view of the employee representative bodies as to what constitutes zero hours contracts/work is perhaps more reflective of the wider international definitions. Existing research recognises that zero hours work covers a far wider range of practices than that contained in the Organisation of Working Time Act.[3],[4] In the UK for example, a zero hours contract is generally understood to be a situation in which an individual is not guaranteed any hours of work and may not be required to make him-/herself available to an employer.

Notwithstanding the differences of opinion between the stakeholders in Ireland as to what constitutes a zero hours contract, we find that there is a wider range of zero hours type practices and contracts operational in Ireland than governed by the Organisation of Working Time Act. The most prevalent of these is what interviewees label as an 'if and when' contract. This is an employment contract which does not guarantee an individual any work, but the individual is not contractually required to be available to an employer. The employer is under no obligation to offer work to the individual at any time, and the individual can refuse or accept the work as it chooses. Such contracts usually stipulate the rate of pay that will apply when the individual does accept and perform the work, but do not guarantee any set number of hours or pay. The available work can vary from day-to-day, week-to-week and month-to-month, and the period between assignments can also vary. Interviewees suggest that these contracts are prevalent in accommodation and food, community care, and in second and third level education and vocational teaching. Individuals on these work arrangements fall foul of the exclusion clause in Section 18. IBEC, whilst acknowledging the prevalence of casual and as and when contracts, emphatically rejects these type of contracts being deemed zero hours contracts, indicating that the law clearly delineates between 'if and when' type contracts where there is no requirement to be available and zero hours contracts as defined under the working time legislation. IBEC also observes that for employers, the use of 'if and when contracts' represents a more rational decision as they are free to call on people when work is available, but those people are only paid for actual hours worked. It notes that there have been very few cases taken by employees against employers under Section 18 of the Working Time Act, and therefore, this is evidence that the legislation is effective and such practices are not an issue. In contrast, trade unions in Ireland argue that the lack of employment

3 Deakin, 'New Forms of Employment, Implications for EU law, The Law as it Stands' (n 1).

4 G Davidov, M Freedland, and N Kountouris, 'The Subjects of Labour Law: Employees and Other Workers' in M Finkin and G Mundlak (eds), *Research Handbook in Comparative Labor Law* (Edward Elgar 2015).

cases taken under Section 18 is because people on 'if and when' contracts are excluded from its scope. The exclusion of individuals on 'if and when' contracts from the working time protections is not the end of the legal issues associated with them. Indeed, zero hours *work* through 'if and when' contracts run to the heart of the debate on what constitutes an employment relationship. Before examining the employment status of people on 'if and when' contracts, the next section summarises the principles of employment status developed in Irish case law.

6. Employment Status in Irish Employment Law

The legal question of employment status has re-emerged as a problematic issue with respect to casual work arrangements and the emergence of zero hours contracts. In Ireland, as in other countries, a person may sign a contract stipulating that he or she is an independent contractor, or may be labelled as such by a contracting company or agency, but the reality of the situation may be that the individual is in fact very dependent upon work provided by a single employer. For example, the individual may in actuality work solely for that employer and may be economically dependent on that employer. There is a growing cohort of workers who fit this description in that they do not actually own a business, but are being classified as self-employed or contracting for services. The implication of such a situation is that such people sit outside the protection of much of the employment legislation. Commentators[5,6,7,8] and legal experts interviewed for this study have questioned the idea that such individuals genuinely fit the category of 'self-employed'. In many cases, they could not be said to be truly 'in business on their own account'. For example, they do not possess business assets, they work under the 'control' of the employer, and they may not send a substitute to replace them. In some cases, they are required to sign exclusivity clauses preventing them from working for other companies. Thus, the 'economic reality' is that they are in fact often very dependent upon the contracting employer. Indeed, the nomenclature of 'dependent entrepreneur' has been used to describe this category of workers. The European Commission has also recognised the issue as problematic, observing in the 2006 Green Paper on

5 H Collins, K D Ewing and A McColgan, *Labour Law* (Cambridge University Press 2012).

6 C Barnard, *EU Employment Law* (Oxford University Press 2012).

7 P Leighton and M Wynn, 'Classifying Employment Relationships—More Sliding Doors or a Better Regulatory Framework?' (2011) 40 Industrial law Journal, (1) 5–44.

8 E Albin, 'The Case of Quashie: Between the Legalisation of Sex Work and the Precariousness of Personal Service Work' (2013) 42 Industrial Law Journal, (2), 180–191.

modernising labour that 'the traditional binary distinction between 'employees' and the independent 'self-employed' is no longer an adequate depiction of the economic and social reality of work'.[9]

Problems arise when one of the contracting parties, or indeed a third party, disagrees with the ascribed employment status.[10] The question of employment status has been the focus of many long drawn out court cases in Ireland: for example, *Minister for Agriculture and Food vs Barry and Others*[11], and in the UK, for example, *Stack v Ajar-Tec Ltd.*[12] In dispute situations, courts have examined the reality of the relationship between the parties to determine status. There are a number of tests that have been developed over time through case law that are utilised in this regard and which are widely known, such as the control test, integration test, economic reality test, entrepreneur test and test of mutual obligation. The issue of employment status came to public policy attention in Ireland in the late 1990s and, under the social partnership agreement, the Programme for Prosperity and Fairness, an Employment Status Group was established and it developed a code of practice for determining the employment or self-employment status of individuals[13], which was subsequently updated in 2007 by the Hidden Economy Monitoring Group.

Case law in Ireland and other jurisdictions has established that each case must be considered in the light of its particular facts and that there is no 'one size fits all' test. However, recent court decisions have indicated that the mutuality of obligation test is critical to establishing the employment status of an individual, and if a case 'fails' the mutuality of obligation test, then no other test need to be looked at. The importance of mutuality of obligation was clearly highlighted in the 2008 case of *Minister for Agriculture and Food vs Barry and Others*[14], where Edwards J stated:

---

9 Commission of the EC, Green paper Modernising Labour Law to Meet the Challenges of the 21st Century COM (2006) 708 final.

10 Many cases have been initiated by the state tax authority, the Revenue Commissioners, or the government department responsible for social welfare so that employment status can be established for tax and social insurance purposes. See for instance *Henry Denny and Sons (Ireland) v Minister for Social Welfare* and *Castleisland Breeding Society Ltd v Minister for Social and Family Affairs.*

11 [2008] IEHC 216.

12 *Stack v Ajar-Tec Ltd* [2015] EWCA Civ 46.

13 Code of Practice for Determining the Employment or Self-Employment of Individuals <http://www.revenue.ie/en/practitioner/codes-practice.html> accessed 12 June 2015.

14 [2008] IEHC 216.

> The requirement of mutuality of obligation is the requirement that there must be mutual obligations on the employer to provide work for the employee and on the employee to perform work for the employer. If such mutuality is not present, then either there is no contract at all or whatever contract there is must be a contract for services or something else, but not a contract of service. It was characterised in Nethermere (St Neots) Ltd v Gardiner, [1984] ICR 612 as the "one sine qua non which can firmly be identified as an essential of the existence of a contract of service". Moreover, in Carmichael v. National Power PLC, [1999] ICR, 1226 at 1230 it was referred to as "that irreducible minimum of mutual obligation necessary to create a contract of service." Accordingly the mutuality of obligation test provides an important filter. Where one party to a work relationship contends that that relationship amounts to a contract of service, it is appropriate that the court or tribunal seized of that issue should in the first instance examine the relationship in question to determine if mutuality of obligation is a feature of it. If there is no mutuality of obligation it is not necessary to go further. Whatever the relationship is, it cannot amount to a contract of service. However, if mutuality of obligation is found to exist the mere fact of its existence is not, of itself, determinative of the nature of the relationship and it is necessary to examine the relationship further.

The decision reinforces the centrality of the mutuality test and it notably draws on key principles set down in two leading UK cases (the cases of *Nethermere* and *Carmichael*[15]). The fundamental importance of the principle of mutuality was reaffirmed in High Court cases such as *Murphy vs Grand Circle Travel 2014*[16] and *Brightwater Selection Ireland v Minister for Social and Family Affairs*[17] where Gilligan J. stated:

> The mutuality consideration is by no means a determinative test, but is an irreducible minimum of a contract of service. Although the existence of mutuality of obligation is not determinative, without mutuality no contract of service can exist. It would be logical, therefore, for a court or tribunal to begin their analysis of the employment relationship by determining whether such mutuality exists and then inquire further into the relationship.

The mutuality test has become fundamental to deciphering the employment status of workers on 'if and when' contracts (see for instance *Contract Personnel Marketing Ireland vs Marie Buckley*[18] and *Ticketline Trading as Ticketmaster v Sarah Mullen*[19]).

---

15 [1999] ICR 1226 (HL) and [1984] ICR 612.

16 *Murphy v Grand Circle Travel* [2014] IEHC 337.

17 *Brightwater Selection (Ireland) Limited v Minister for Social and Family Affairs* [2011] IEHC 510.

18 2011 *Contract Personnel Marketing Ireland v Marie Buckley* (DWT1145).

19 Labour Court, *Ticketline trading as Ticketmaster v Sarah Mullen* (DWT1434) 10 April 2014.

7. The Operation and Effect of 'If and When' Contracts

The ability to rely on Section 18 of the Organisation of Working Time Act hinges on a person being employed on a contract of service and a 'requirement' or obligation on the part of the employee to be available. It specifically excludes from its protection those who are contracted on a more casual basis. More specifically, it excludes casual workers even where there is a reasonable expectation that they would be required to work a given week. While Section 18 excludes work of a casual nature, interviews with legal experts suggest that casual work itself is not defined by the Act.[20] A casual observer of Section 18 might be forgiven for thinking that 'as and when' contracts are covered by the following:

> –(1) This section applies to an employee whose contract of employment operates to require the employee to make himself or herself available to work for the employer in a week–
> (a) a certain number of hours ("the contract hours"), or
> (b) as and when the employer requires him or her to do so.

However, the insertion of the word 'requires' reinforces the principle of obligation in pursuing a claim under the Act.

The difficulties experienced by individuals seeking protections under the Organisation of Working Time Act 1997 were illustrated in the 2011 case of *Contract Personnel Marketing Ireland vs Marie Buckley*.[21] In this case, Ms. Buckley sought to take a claim under Section 18 of the working time legislation and her trade union argued that, contrary to the Act, she was not paid for a period when she was required to be 'on call'. However, because of an 'if and when clause' in her contract, the Labour Court deemed her not to be an employee on a zero hours contract as defined by the working time legislation, but to be in 'casual employment'. She was deemed not to be covered by Section 18 of the legislation.

According to Grogan, because of the strict contractual requirements of Section 18, it is reasonably easy for an employer to avoid coming within its ambit entirely by the insertion of certain provisions (including an 'if and when' provision) into a contract. He argues:

> The basis of structuring matters is to provide a contract which provides for zero hours. The second is to provide that it will be a casual contract to work as and when required.

---

20 R Grogan, 'The Organisation of Working Time Act 1997, Legal Effect and Cases' (2016) <www.grogansolicitors.ie> accessed 1 October 2016.

21 2011 *Contract Personnel Marketing Ireland v Marie Buckley* (DWT1145).

> The third is to provide that the employee can refuse any work assignment or decline work for any reason and that there would be no disciplinary action as a result of doing so.[22]

Such a clause would probably fall within the concept of a 'boilerplate' clause. A 'boilerplate' clause is one which might be inserted in contracts with the intention of refuting any mutuality of obligation. Indicative of such clauses would be those which make it clear that the employer is under no obligation to provide work and the individual is under no obligation to accept.[23]

Traditionally in employment status cases in Ireland as in the UK, there has been evidence of willingness on the part of employment rights bodies and the civil courts to go behind the contractual terms and examine the reality of the relationship.[24] One of the few cases taken under Section 18 of the working time legislation is illustrative of this: In *Ticketline Trading as Ticketmaster v Sarah Mullen*[25]. The complainant, Sarah Mullen, commenced working for Ticketline Trading as Ticketmaster as a box office assistant in June 2012. She signed a contract stating that she was working under an 'if and when' contract. She continued working until January 2013 after which she was assigned no further work. The claimant appealed a Rights Commissioner decision to the Labour Court, and alleged that the respondent infringed Section 18 of the Organisation of Working Time Act 1997 in not giving her compensation for hours she maintained she was required to be available. She alleged that although there was no requirement to be available in her written contract, the actuality of the situation was that there was a verbal condition agreed between her and a Ms. Anderson that she was required to be available. She had records of correspondence between herself and the company in which she cited the alleged verbal agreement and in which she queried why work was not being provided to her. Ms. Anderson never replied. Instead, a Mr. Kavanagh replied and contradicted her assertion of a requirement to be available. At the Labour Court hearing, Ms. Anderson was not present. Mr. Kavanagh represented the company and contradicted the claimant's assertion of a verbal agreement that she was required to be available. In finding for the claimant, the Labour Court held that Mr. Kavanagh was not a party to the discussions between the claimant and Ms. Anderson and was therefore not in a position to give evidence contradicting

---

22 Grogan, 'The Organisation of Working Time Act 1997' (n 20) 50.

23 Z Adams and S Deakin, *Reregulating Zero Hours Contracts*, (The Institute of Employment Rights 2014).

24 *Electricity Supply Board v Minister for Social Community and Family Affairs and Others* [2006] IEHC 59, *Autoclenz v Belcher and Others* [2011] UKSC 41.

25 Labour Court, *Ticketline trading as Ticketmaster v Sarah Mullen* (DWT1434) 10 April 2014.

the claims. The Labour Court held that on the basis of uncontroverted evidence, it accepted that the claimant's contract was administered as though she was required to be available for work at all times, and therefore, she was covered by the Act. It must be asked however, if the outcome would have been different if Ms. Anderson had presented herself in the Labour Court.

8. Legal Options for Extending Rights to People on 'If and When' Contracts

The review above highlights the legally precarious position held by people doing zero hours work through 'if and when' contracts. Employment status problems for people engaged in zero hours practices are not confined to Ireland and commentators internationally have presented possible remedies to encapsulate a wider group within protective legislation. Some such as Davidov *et al.*[26] examine the possibility of an intermediate category. Keane[27] and Freedland[28] explore the possibility of re-conceptualising what constitutes a contract of employment, while Collins *et al.*[29] identify the possibility of regulatory changes limiting contractual freedom with respect to 'if and when'-type contracts. These are discussed briefly in the following sections.

8.1 An 'Intermediate Status'

In recent times, the 'blunt' or binary distinction between a person being deemed an independent contractor or an employee has been recognised as problematic.[30,31,32,33,34] One remedy to the binary distinction is to establish the

---

26 Davidov, Freedland and Kountouris, 'The Subjects of Labour Law: Employees and Other Workers' (n 4).

27 E Keane, 'Providing Access to Job Security Legislation for Intermittent Workers' (2014) Kings Law Journal (25) 332–339.

28 M Feedland, *The Personal Employment Contract* (Oxford University Press 2003).

29 Collins, Ewing and McColgan, *Labour Law* (n 5).

30 COM(2006) 708 final. (n 9).

31 A Adams, M Freedland and J Prassl, 'The "Zero-Hours Contract": Regulating Casual Work, or Legitimising Precarity' (ELLN Working Paper Series March 2015).

32 Davidov, Freedland and Kountouris, 'The Subjects of Labour Law: Employees and Other Workers' (n 4).

33 Leighton and Wynn, 'Classifying Employment Relationships—More Sliding Doors or a Better Regulatory Framework?' (n 7).

34 M Freedland, 'From the Contract of Employment to the Personal Work Nexus' (2006) 35 Industrial law Journal (1) 1–29.

category of a 'worker' that falls between employee and independent contractor. The European Commission in its Green Paper commented:

> The concept of 'economically dependent work' covers situations which fall between the two established concepts of subordinate employment and independent self-employment. These workers do not have a contract of employment. They may not be covered by labour law since they occupy a "grey area" between labour law and commercial law. Although formally 'self-employed', they remain economically dependent on a single principal or client/employer for their source of income.[35]

In Ireland, workers seeking protection under much of the existing employment legislation are still subjected to a binary interpretation of employment status. However, other countries have recognised an 'intermediate' category (to varying degrees) in national legislation. These include Germany, Italy, Canada, Spain and the UK. Davidov *et al.* comment:

> Instead of an 'all or nothing' approach, it is acknowledged in these legal systems that some workers present only some characteristics of 'employees' but not others, and that it is justified to apply only some labor laws to them.[36]

In the UK, for example, the concept of 'worker' is recognised though the Employment Rights Acts 1996. A worker in this instance is defined in Section 230(3) as:

> an individual who has entered into or works under (or, where employment has ceased, worked under)---
> (a) a contract of employment; or
> (b) any other contract whether express or implied and (if it is express) whether oral or in writing, whereby the individual undertakes to do or perform work personally any work or services for another party to the contract whose status is not by virtue of the contract that of a client or customer of any profession or undertaking carried on by the individual.

Individuals categorised as 'workers' in the UK are covered by limited aspects of protective employment legislation such as minimum wage and holidays, but are excluded from protection relating to unfair dismissals, redundancy and minimum notice. In Ireland, there is no specific 'intermediate' category and most employment law covers only employees under a contract of service. Thus, people on 'if and when' contracts will fall outside the remit of most protective legislation. However, it is interesting to note that some laws go beyond the 'binary' employment classification. The Employment Equality Acts 1998 to 2015, the National

35 COM(2006) 708 final. (n 9).

36 Davidov, Freedland and Kountouris, 'The Subjects of Labour Law: Employees and Other Workers' (n 4).

Minimum Wage Act 2000 and the Payment of Wages Act 1991 confer rights to a broader spectrum of individuals than just employees. For example, the Employment Equality Acts 1998 to 2015 cover contracts whereby an 'individual agrees with another person to personally execute any work or service for that person'.

It could be argued that in countries such as the UK that have adopted some form of intermediate status, there is an attempt to separate those 'dependant entrepreneurs' from genuinely self-employed workers, to recognise that the former may be more reliant on a particular employer and to confer them with a certain amount of rights. As the European Commission notes:

> The "targeted approach" adopted in the UK to establishing differing rights and responsibilities in employment law for "employees" and "workers" is an example of how categories of vulnerable workers involved in complex employment relationships have been given minimum rights without an extension of the full range of labour law entitlements associated with standard work contracts.[37]

However, other commentators have argued that such an approach could well render a vulnerable group more vulnerable in the long-term. By statutorily creating a separate group with fewer rights than those with 'employee' status, an incentive might be created for some employers to siphon recruits into this intermediate tier. Thus, a 'grey zone' in relation to employment rights would be copper-fastened.[38] A further criticism of such an approach would be that it could have the effect of rendering a complex area of law with even more complexity.[39]

8.2 Reconceptualising the Employment Relationship

Some commentators examine the possibility of redefining the legal tests used for determining status. Freedland presents the idea of simplifying the issue around a single concept such as a 'personal employment nexus' (such as that already used in Irish employment equality legislation).[40] Such commentators assert that while the category of 'worker' in the UK may have limited the size of this group, determining the difference between a genuinely independent contractor and a dependent entrepreneur remains difficult. They conclude that while the test of personal performance of work remains important, the issue of economic dependence on a

---

37 COM (2006) 708 final (n 9).

38 B Burchell, S Deakin and S Honey, *The Employment Status of Individuals in Non Standard Employment*, (Department of Trade and Industry 1999).

39 Collins, Ewing and McColgan, *Labour Law* (n 5).

40 Freedland, 'From the Contract of Employment to the Personal Work Nexus' (n 34).

single employer should also be regarded as 'critical'.[41] These authors also raise the question as to whether the solution is to abandon the concept of 'employee' and extend the scope of laws such as unfair dismissal to all 'workers'.

Keane suggests that a possible way forward is that evidence of a commitment to an ongoing relationship should be the key test rather than evidence of an express promise that underlies the test for mutuality.[42] He cites L. J. Stephenson in *Nethermere (St Neots) Ltd v Gardiner*:

> I cannot see why well founded expectations of continuing (work) should not be hardened or refined into enforceable contracts by regular giving or taking of work over periods of a year or more.[43]

In other words, where there is a realistic expectation based on a continuing and consistent ongoing situation over a period that work will be provided, and that work will not be refused, then this should be used as a test for an ongoing mutual understanding of commitment/expectation. This certainly would have implications for Section 18 of the Organisation of Working Time Act, whereby casual workers are excluded, regardless of situations where they have a reasonable expectation that they would be required to be available on an ongoing basis.

8.3 Limiting Contractual Freedom

A further option is for legislation to place contractual limits on the extent an individual or company can use zero hours work. Space restrictions limit a comparative review, but limitations exist in other European countries. They can be restrictions on the length of time someone may work on a zero hours contract, restrictions on the groups of workers who can be employed on zero hours work, or requirements for companies to justify the use of zero hours work.[44,45] Indeed, the main recommendation of the authors in the Irish study on zero hours contracts is that legislation should limit the time an employer can contractually engage someone

41 Collins, Ewing and McColgan, *Labour Law* (n 5).

42 Keane, 'Providing Access to Job Security Legislation for Intermittent Workers' (n 27).

43 *Nethermere (St Neots) Ltd v Gardiner* [1984] ICR 612,629 (CA).

44 O'Sullivan, Turner, McMahon, Ryan, Lavelle, Murphy, O'Brien and Gunnigle, *A Study of the Prevalence of Zero Hours Contracts among Irish Employers and its Impact on Employees* (Department of Jobs, Enterprise and Innovation, Dublin November 2015).

45 Eurofound, *Flexible Forms of Work: 'Very Atypical' Contractual Arrangements* (2010) <www.eurofound.europa.eu/observatories/eurwork/comparative-information/flexible-forms-of-work very-atypical-contractual-arrangements> accessed 3 January 2015.

on an 'if and when' basis to the first six months of employment after which they must offer minimum guaranteed hours.[46]

8.4 Widening the Scope of the Organisation of Working Time Act 1997

A key restriction of Section 18 of the working time legislation for claimants is the exclusion of those on casual work arrangements. Casual work is not defined for the purposes of the Act, but it would seem that inserting a clause into a contract stipulating the 'as and when' nature of the working arrangement plus stipulating that the worker is under no obligation to accept work will render the arrangement a casual one.

Grogan draws attention to another Irish Act: the Protection of Employees (Part-time Work) Act 2001.[47] This Act refers to a casual worker as someone who has been in continuous service of the employer for less than 13 weeks and whose work could not be regarded as regular or seasonal. He subsequently suggests that this definition of casual work should be inserted into Section 18 of the Organisation of Working Time Act. This may then serve to include those workers employed continuously and regularly on 'if and when' type arrangements under the ambit of the protections afforded by the Act:

> The only viable way to give some protection is to utilise the definition in the Protection of Employees (Part-Time Work) Act, 2001 or for the Labour Court to specify what type of arrangements are "casual" and when does "casual" working cease to be "casual".[48]

This view is supported by the state's primary dispute resolution body, the Labour Relations Commission, which argues that the term *casualisation* should be defined and used rather than the term zero hours and that zero hours contracts carry 'an ideological tag of a race to the bottom'.[49]

9. Conclusion

While employment status issues have not been tested extensively in Ireland specifically with respect to 'if and when' contracts, case law which has addressed

46 O'Sullivan *et al.*, *A Study of the Prevalence of Zero Hours Contracts among Irish Employers and its Impact on Employees* (n 44).

47 Grogan 'The Organisation of Working Time Act' (n 20).

48 ibid 53.

49 The Labour Relations Commission was reformed and renamed the Workplace Relations Commission in October 2015.

employment status issues has established the fundamental principles by which any contract is assessed. The principles suggest that an individual on an 'if and when' contract will fall short of fulfilling the mutuality of obligation test. The consequence of this is that many workers employed on a zero hours basis in Ireland fall outside the scope of the very legislation intended to address the issue of zero hours practices in the Irish context, for example the Organisation of Working Time Act, because the narrow provisions of the act exclude non-employees. They are also precluded from claiming protection under employment legislation such as unfair dismissals and redundancy payments. Indeed, the framing of the working time legislation with its narrow definition of zero hours contracts has incentivised employers to hire people on more precarious 'if and when' type contracts, leading Ireland's largest union to comment that such contracts are a legitimate casualisation of the workforce. On the other hand, the use of these contracts represents an economically rational decision for employers who can avoid the liability of paying employees some compensation for not working, which they would otherwise be obliged to do under the terms of the working time legislation. Instead, they offer contracts which do not explicitly require workers to be available and therefore are under no obligation to pay anything for hours not worked.

The focus on the test for mutuality in cases taken under Section 18 and where employment status is in dispute has highlighted the binary system in Ireland in this regard. The binary distinction between 'contracts of' and 'contracts for' appears to be inadequate in addressing the evolution of atypical employment forms. This has been recognised by the European Commission when it asserts that:

> …the emergence of diverse forms of non-standard work has made the boundaries between labour law and commercial law less clear. The traditional binary distinction between 'employees' and the independent 'self-employed' is no longer an adequate depiction of the economic and social reality of work.[50]

Collins *et al.*, in considering the question of status, conclude that there is a substantial group of people who work under contracts that transfer the economic risks to them and they accept the work because they are vulnerable and have no alternatives.[51] The issue for the Irish government is balancing the need to protect such workers against the demands for more flexible forms of work, but we conclude that Section 18 of the Organisation of Working Time Act in its present form has not achieved this balance.

---

50 COM(2006) 708 final (n 9).

51 Collins, Ewing and McColgan, *Labour Law* (n 5).

Isabelle van Hiel

Between Registered and Precarious: Priority of Engagement for Dockworkers in European and International Law

1. Introduction

With its decision in *Holship*, the EFTA court struck another blow to the regulated labour market scheme for dock work.[1] Such systems are common to many countries, are protected by an International Labour Organization (ILO) convention, and are designed to benefit both dockworkers and their employers. Nonetheless, they are often regarded as outdated, inefficient and contrary to European law. Although *Holship* was the first case on this issue before the EFTA Court, it marks an evolution towards a liberalisation of port work that started in the 1970s, and in which a leading part was played by the European Commission and the Court of Justice of the European Union (CJEU). Surprisingly or not, most of the case law was deliberately initiated by employers and employers' organisations refusing to honour long-term arrangements, as can be illustrated by the *Holship* case and the related collective complaint of Bedriftsforbundet against Norway before the European Committee on Social Rights (ECSR).

2. The Origins of the Pool System

In many ports in Europe, regulations and practices exist which restrict the loading and unloading of goods. Such regulations and practices can be found in a majority of European Union (EU) member states.[2] Often a pool is put into place which requires registration of the dockworkers and grants priority or even exclusivity of employment to registered dockworkers. Terminal operators in need of dock

---

1 E-14/15, *Holship Norge AS v Norsk Transportarbeiderforbund*, EFTA Court 20 April 2016.

2 16 out of 22 maritime member states or almost 75 per cent have a regulated port labour market. Among those 16 states, 13 make use of registers for dock work, while 11 also grant preferential rights to registered dockworkers, see E Van Hooydonck, 'Port Labour in the EU, Volume I – the EU Perspective' (study commissioned by the European Commission, Final Report, Portius 8 January 2013) 263–264.

work services have to hire dockworkers from the pool which is jointly organised by employers and trade unions.

The restricted access to dock work has been the response to the precarious situation of dockworkers. As the size of the ships and the frequency of their arrivals varied, dock work was usually carried out on a day-by-day basis. Therefore, in the early 20th century, pools of registered port workers were created by management and labour which had to ensure a steady availability to employers of experienced staff, as well as an elementary form of job security for registered workers.[3] After World War II, dockworkers gained more extensive income protection as employment and working practices were further regulated by law or on the basis of collective agreements. To give dockworkers sufficient guarantees of employment and income, the number of dockworkers had to be kept in line with the growth in port demand.[4] Only in case of a shortage in qualified dockworkers, were employers allowed to hire workers from outside the pool.

The system was beneficial for both employers and dockworkers: the employers could have recourse to a flexible, cheap and competent labour force, while the dockworkers enjoyed employment stability or at least income security, as differences in supply and demands were compensated by social security benefits. Furthermore, in several countries dockworkers were regarded as a specific category of workers. They were subject to separate health and safety regulations and were excluded from ordinary labour law.[5]

3. ILO Convention No. 137

Although the ILO conventions generally apply to dockworkers, the ILO dedicated a specific convention to the health and safety of dockworkers as early as 1929. Convention no. 28 on the protection against accidents of dockworkers was revisited in 1932 by Convention no. 32, and in 1979, it was replaced by Convention no. 152 on health and safety and Recommendation no. 160 which supplements it. In 1973, another specific convention was adopted. Convention no. 137, concerning the social repercussions of new cargo-handling methods in docks, consolidated the pool system, as Article 3 required the establishment and maintenance

3 T Notteboom, 'Dock labour and port-related employment in the European seaport system' (Report prepared for European Sea Ports Organisation (ESPO) ITMMA, 2010) 53.

4 I Katsarova, 'Liberalisation of EU port services: issues and consequences for dock workers' (Library Briefing, Library of the European Parliament, 20 March 2013) 3.

5 Van Hooydonck, 'Port Labour in the EU, Volume I' (n 2) 55.

of registers for dock work and imposed priority of engagement for registered dockworkers.

The convention was elaborated in a particular context: the introduction of cranes and containers reduced the number of dockworkers required to handle cargo, which resulted in large-scale redundancies of port labour and a steep decline in the amount of dockworkers in most European ports between the 1950s and the late 1970s.[6] In view of the casual nature of the work, the ILO felt the necessity to try to provide dockworkers with regular work, or at least to establish a system of allocating work that could give them sufficient guarantees of employment and income. For that purpose, the ILO considered it necessary to create a system for the registration of dockworkers and to control the flow of new entrants to the trade.[7]

Even though the convention and recommendation were adopted by a very large majority,[8] the convention was only ratified by 25 ILO member states.[9] Yet, among those 25 states, there were 10 European states.[10] Nowadays, the ILO considers the convention and recommendation as instruments with interim status which means that they are no longer fully up to date, but remain relevant in certain respects.[11] Attempts to revise the convention failed because of widely divergent opinions between the workers' and employers' representatives on the relevance of the convention. At the 1996 tripartite meeting, the workers' representatives insisted on the need to promote the ratification of the convention, while the employers' representatives expressed the view that it 'was obsolete as it did not respond to the modern needs of the port industry'.[12]

---

6 Notteboom, 'Dock labour and port-related employment in the European seaport system' (n 3) 33.

7 Report of the Committee of Experts on the Application of Conventions and Recommendations, Report III (Part 1B), General Survey of the reports concerning the Dock Work Convention (No. 137) and Recommendation (No. 145), 1973, International Labour Conference 90th Session 2002, 2.

8 ILC, 58th Session, 1973, Record of Proceedings 683 and 687–690.

9 www.ilo.org/dyn/normlex/en/f?p=1000:11300:0::NO:11300:P11300_INSTRUMENT_ID:312282 accessed 13 March 2017.

10 The ten states are Finland, France, Italy, the Netherlands (which denounced the convention in 2006), Norway, Poland, Portugal, Romania, Spain and Sweden.

11 Resolutions adopted by the International Labour Conference at its 97th Session, Geneva, June 2008, 22, footnote 1.

12 Tripartite Meeting on the Social and Labour Problems caused by Structural Adjustments in the Port Industry, Geneva, 20–24 May 1996, Note on the Proceedings, TMPI/1996/10, paras. 31–32.

4. Pool System Under Pressure

Since the 1970s, the technological innovation in cargo-handling has intensified. Containerization and an enhanced accuracy in ship sailing schedules reduced the use of casual work, while it urged the sector to become highly capital-intensive.[13] The explosive growth in containerized trade increased the demand for skilled dockworkers[14] and triggered a trend toward more permanent employment at container terminals.[15] From the 1980s on, the traditional system of dock work was challenged, as port services were liberalised to increase the efficiency and competiveness of the ports, the result being that sector-specific rules and regulations on recruitment, training and health and safety of port workers were reduced or abolished.[16]

Economic and efficiency arguments justified the decline in social protection. Pools were denounced because of their high direct costs and the rigidity of the supply caused by strict job demarcation, low labour mobility, and large overmanned gang sizes. They would restrict the freedom enjoyed by both employers and employees by introducing a bureaucracy and by limiting competition, which would lead to excessive wages. Finally, when dockworkers are registered centrally and switch from one employer to another, they may not develop loyalty towards one or more employers, which might form a breeding ground for social conflicts between unions and employers' organisations.[17]

The reforms were seldom the result of collective bargaining between management and labour. Predominantly, liberalisation was enforced by external interventions of the EU Court of Justice and the European Commission, or an 'exceptional vigorous national government policy'.[18] Moreover, most port reform and port

---

13 H E Haralambides, 'Port Structural Adjustment and Labour Reform' (Proceedings of the 7th World Conference on Transport Research, Sydney, Australia, 1995) 5–6.

14 Report of the Committee of Experts on the Application of Conventions and Recommendations, Report III (Part 1B), General Survey of the reports concerning the Dock Work Convention (No. 137) and Recommendation (No. 145), 1973 (n 7) 31.

15 Notteboom, 'Dock labour and port-related employment in the European seaport system' (n 2) 38.

16 Van Hooydonck, 'Port Labour in the EU, Volume I' (n 2) 35–43.

17 Notteboom, 'Dock labour and port-related employment in the European seaport system' (n 3) 55.

18 Italy and Spain were condemned by the Court of Justice, while Greece, Ireland, Malta and Portugal had to adapt their legislation by order of the European Commission. In the United Kingdom (UK) and France, the abolishment of the pool system was the outcome of a government policy by Margaret Thatcher and Nicolas Sarkozy, see

labour reform took place in periods where there was a strong economic downturn and there were serious problems with the competitiveness of individual ports or the (national) port system. In periods of recession, trade unions are weaker and employers are less likely to avoid disputes which could temporarily immobilise their resources.[19]

5. EU Maritime Transport Policy

The EU commenced to proceed relatively late in the domain of transport. For quite a long time, the commission lacked the necessary powers to implement competition law in the transport sector as the 1962 Council Regulation 141 stipulated that Regulation 17 implementing Articles 85 and 86 of the Treaty establishing the European Economic Community (TEEC) (now 101 and 102 of the Treaty on the Functioning of the European Union, TFEU) did not cover transport. Yet, in 1974, the Court of Justice decided that the same articles did apply to the transport sector.[20] The subsequent Council regulation 4056/86 provided the Commission with powers in the maritime transport sector.[21] From 1995 onwards, the Commission broadened the scope of Article 85 and 86 to non-maritime services of shipping companies, in particular to port and quayside services which had not been dealt with before.[22]

In its 1997 Green Paper, the European Commission announced its willingness to liberalize port services.[23] A first draft directive, known as the first port services package, was proposed in 2001.[24] The draft directive, which included the principle of self-handling, was opposed by the dockworkers' unions and consequently rejected by the European Parliament in 2003. A second draft directive, known

---

E van Hooydonck, "Het Spaanse Havenarbeidersarrest (C-576/13): doodsteek voor de klassieke havenpools", (2015) Tijdschrift Vervoer & Recht 2, 37.

19 Notteboom, 'Dock labour and port-related employment in the European seaport system' (n 3) 61.

20 Judgment of 4 April 1974, Commission v France, C-167/73, EU:C:1974:35, known as the *French Seamen Case.*

21 R Whish and D Bailey, *Competition Law* (7th edn, Oxford University Press 2012) 970–974.

22 L Ortiz Blanco and B Van Houtte, *EC Competition Law in the Transport Sector* (Clarendon Press 1996) 259.

23 Green Paper on sea ports and maritime infrastructure, Brussels, 10 December 1997, COM(97) 678 final.

24 Proposal for a Directive of the European Parliament and of the Council on Market Access to Port Services, COM(2001) 35 final.

as the second port services package, was introduced in 2004.[25] As it was only slightly adapted, it met the same fate in 2006.[26] In 2011, the Commission adopted a White Paper in which it indicated that market access to ports needed to be further improved.[27] However, a new strategy was developed. While the Commission formulated a new proposal for a regulation,[28] it also launched infringement procedures and imposed reform in the context of other EU policies.[29]

5.1 Competition Law

In the 1990s, employers' recourses to the EU Court of Justice have been successful in reshaping the Italian legislation on dock work. In *Merci*, it disapproved of the Italian legislation which reserved the performance of dock work in the port of Genova to companies wherein workers (also members of these companies) were required to be of Italian nationality.[30] Article 90(1) of the TEEC, in conjunction with Articles 30, 48 and 86 of the Treaty, precluded national rules which conferred on a local undertaking the exclusive right to organise dock work and require it for that purpose to have recourse to a dock work company formed exclusively of national workers. The Court also disaffirmed that a dock work undertaking could be regarded as being entrusted with the operation of services of general economic interest within the meaning of Article 90(2) of the TEEC.

In response to the judgement, the Italian legislation was modified, and henceforth, restricted the monopoly of the former dock work companies to the supply of temporary labour. Yet another case was brought before the Court. In *Raso*, about the port of La Spezia, the exclusive right to supply temporary labour granted to the former dock work companies was contested as they were also authorised to carry

25 Proposal for a Directive of the European Parliament and of the Council on market access to port services, COM(2004) 654 final.

26 Katsarova, 'Liberalisation of EU port services: issues and consequences for dock workers' (n 3) 5.

27 Roadmap to a Single European Transport Area – Towards a competitive and resource efficient transport system, COM(2011) 144 final.

28 Proposal for a Regulation of the European Parliament and of the Council establishing a framework on market access to port services and financial transparency of ports, Brussels, 23 May 2013, COM/2013/296 def.

29 This option was favoured as 'it would be more targeted and efficient than a legislative proposal which may again stir up controversy and social unrest', see Van Hooydonck, 'Port Labour in the EU, Volume I' (n 5) 314 and 328.

30 Judgment of 10 December 1991, *Merci Convenzionali Porto di Genova v Siderurgica Gabrielli*, C-179/90, EU:C:1991:464 (1991] ECR I-5889.

out dock work.[31] A conflict of interest was deemed to arise if former dock work companies had a statutory monopoly on the supply of temporary labour for dock work and competed with other undertakings in the market for dock work. The Court considered this to be contrary to Articles 86 and 90 of the TEEC, although the national court did not identify any particular case of abuse. The view that the grant of an exclusive right in itself should be considered as contrary to competition law was a reversal of the Court's original position which allowed for public monopolies.[32]

However, in 1999 in *Becu*, the application of competition law reached its limits.[33] Since the Belgian legislation merely recognises the occupation of dockworkers without conferring a monopoly on undertakings or on trade associations, the Belgian pool system could not be dealt with on the basis of Article 90(1) of the TEEC, read in conjunction with Articles 85 and 86 of the TEEC. The articles are only applicable on 'undertakings'. Recognised dockworkers in a port area did not in themselves constitute undertakings within the meaning of community competition law. Nor could they, even taken collectively, be regarded as constituting an undertaking. In the same year as *Becu* put an end to the evolution towards the complete liberalisation of port work,[34] three judgements of the Court conferred immunity from competition law to collective agreements.[35]

5.2 Freedom of Establishment

These evolutions might have persuaded the Commission to approach the Spanish pool system in a different way. In the case *Commission v Spain*, the Spanish law which obliged terminal operators to participate in a dock work company and prevented them from hiring their own staff was alleged to be an infringement on freedom of establishment of Article 49 of the TFEU.[36] The case basically concerned

31 Judgment of 12 February 1998, *Raso and others*, C-163/96, EU:C:1998:54 (1998] ECR I-533.

32 S Giubboni, *Social Rights and Market Freedom in the European Constitution* (Cambridge University Press 2006) 186–187 and 290.

33 Judgment of 16 September 1999, *Becu and others*, C-22/98, EU:C:1999:419 (1999] ECR I-5665.

34 M-Y Le Garrec, 'Observations' (2000) *Le droit maritime français* 601, 181.

35 Judgment of 21 September 1999, *Albany*, C-67/96, EU:C:1999:430 (1999] ECR I-5751; Judgment of 21 September 1999, *Brentjens', joined cases* C-115/97, C-116/97 and C-117/97, EU:C:1999:434 (1999] ECR I-6025; Judgment of 21 September 1999, *Drijvende bokken*, C-219/97, EU:C:1999:437 (1999] ECR I-6121.

36 Judgment of 11 December 2014, *Commission v Spain*, C-576/13, EU:C:2014:2430; for an extensive commentary on the case, see M I Ribes Moreno, 'La movimentazione

port services, but was presented under the pretext of freedom of establishment. Like competition law, freedom of establishment applies to transport, while for free movement of services to be applicable in the field of transport, a legislative initiative of the Council and the Parliament is required.[37] What is more, the case was considered as one that raised no new point of law, so it could be determined without a submission from the Advocate-General.[38] The Court found the restrictions not to be justified by imperative reasons of general interest. It stated that less restrictive measures existed to guarantee the same outcome with regard to the continuity, regularity and quality of the service, as well as the protection of the workers. Although in general the burden of proof rests with the Commission,[39] the Court imposed a severe burden of proof on the Spanish state. The ILO Convention no. 137 invoked by the Spanish government was not taken into consideration. As the Commission in 2004 called on the member states to ratify the convention,[40] it probably did not see an inconsistency between its interpretation of freedom of establishment and the ILO convention, being designed as a flexible instrument to establish minimum standards.[41] Accordingly, the Court deemed it possible to leave it up to the terminal operators to hire permanent or temporary workers, as well as to administer or make use of the services of temporary work agencies.

Meanwhile the Court of Justice acknowledged that the principle of freedom of establishment did apply on collective agreements,[42] which permitted the

---

delle merci nei porti in Spagna e il diritto dell'Unione Europea', (2015) *Diritti Lavori Mercati* III, 619–630.

37 Article 61 of the EC Treaty, now 90(2) TFEU; Judgment of 22 May 1985, *Parliament v Council*, C-13/83, :EU:C:1985:220, ECR 15/3 (1986), 1 CMLR 138; Ortiz Blanco and Van Houtte, *EC Competition Law in the Transport Sector* (n 22) 5; V Power, *EC Shipping Law* (2nd edn, Lloyd's of London Press, 1998) 100; Whish and Bailey, *Competition Law* (n 21) 968.

38 See Article 252 TFEU and Article 20 para 5, Statute of the Court; T Materne, *La Procédure en manquement d'état* (Larcier 2012) 172.

39 Materne, *La Procédure en manquement d'état* (n 38) 149.

40 COM/2004/0654, par. 2.3.

41 Report of the Committee of Experts on the Application of Conventions and Recommendations, Report III (Part 1B), General Survey of the reports concerning the Dock Work Convention (No. 137) and Recommendation (No. 145), 1973 (n 7) 7.

42 Judgment of 11 December 2007, *Viking*, C-438/05, EU:C:2007:772. (2007] ECR I-10779; Judgment of 15 July 2010, *Commission v Germany*, C-271/08, EU:C:2010:426 (2010] ECR I-7091.

Commission to tackle national systems that could not be contested earlier.[43] In 2014, Belgium received its first notice.[44] Negotiations with the Commission and the social partners took place to adapt the legislation and allow employers to progressively hire their own workers and organise their proper training.

6. The EFTA Case - *Holship*

In the 2016 EFTA decision, both competition law and freedom of establishment were at stake, on account of similar provisions in Articles 31, 53 and 54 of the Agreement on the European Economic Area (EEA Agreement). Different from previous cases before the EU Court of Justice, in Norway the priority of engagement for registered dockworkers is based on collective agreements. In the port of Drammen, the applicable collective agreement stipulated that dockworkers *have preferential rights to employment:* shipping companies have to hire registered dockworkers from a pool in the port, unless the dockworkers do not utilise their priority right. Therefore, an Administrative Office for Dock Work (AO) was established. It was administered by three employers' and two workers' representatives and employed dockworkers on a permanent basis. Holship, a Norwegian forwarding agent of a Danish company, active in the port of Drammen, hired its own workers, and applied a collective agreement covering cleaning work on them.[45] As Holship refused to employ registered dockworkers, the Norwegian transport union Norsk Transportarbeiderforbund (NTF) notified a boycott to compel it to do so. In view of the case law of the Court of Justice on *Viking* and *Laval*, it also asked the national courts whether such action was lawful, a procedure covered by the Norwegian Boycott Act. Before the Supreme Court referred the case to the EFTA Court, two national courts had declared the boycott lawful.

---

43 Like pool systems solely based on collective agreements, see with regard to the Netherlands: Rb. Rotterdam 28 januari 1999, 112155/KG ZA 99–119 (*Matrans Marine Services B.V. en Transcore Rotterdam B.V./FNV Bondgenoten*); Rb. Utrecht 24 juli 2009, ECLI:NL:RBUTR:2009:BJ3474.

44 Brief van de Europese Commissie aan België van 28 maart 2014, ref. 20104/2088, C/2014/1874 final.

45 Holship is neither a party to the collective agreement on dock work nor a member of the largest employers' organisation Næringslivets Hovedorganisasjon (NHO). In fact, Holship is a member of another employers' organisation for small and medium sized enterprises, *Bedriftsforbundet*.

In *Landsorganisasjonen i Norge*,[46] the EFTA Court exempted collective agreements from the scope of the EEA competition rules, as the EU Court of Justice did in *Albany*. However, in recent case law, the Court of Justice increasingly confines the exemption.[47] The EFTA Court applied the more rigid case law. Consequently, it ruled that the exemption does not cover the assessment of a priority of engagement rule, or a boycott against a port user in order to procure acceptance of a collective agreement which entails such a priority of engagement rule. Only a small margin of interpretation was left to the national courts as to the assessment of the AO system under Article 53 and 54 of the EEA. The Court observed that it appeared difficult to demonstrate the necessity and that no services of general economic interest were concerned.

Moreover, the Court stated that a boycott to procure acceptance of a collective agreement providing for a system which included a priority clause would be likely to discourage or even prevent the establishment of companies from other EEA states and thereby constituted a restriction on the freedom of establishment. No credit was given to the ILO Convention no. 137 as protocol 35 to the EEA Agreement stipulates that in case of a conflict between national law implementing EEA law and other national provisions not implementing EEA law, EFTA states should introduce a statutory provision to the effect that national law implementing EEA law prevails.[48]

It must be specified, however, that the decisions of the EFTA Court do not have the same binding nature as the rulings of the Court of Justice of the European Union. On account of Article 260 of the TFEU, the states are required to take the necessary measures to comply with the judgment of the Court.[49] Particularly in Norway, the Supreme Court held that the opinions of the EFTA Court are of an advisory character only and that it is for the Supreme Court to decide for itself

---

46 E-8/00, *Landsorganisasjonen i Norge with Norsk Kommuneforbund v Kommunenes Sentralforbund* (2002] EFTA Court Report 114.

47 Judgment of 3 March 2011, *AG2R Prévoyance*, C-437/09, EU:C:2011:112 (2011] ECR I-973.

48 E-14/15, *Holship Norge AS v Norsk Transportarbeiderforbund*, EFTA Court 20 April 2016.

49 K Lenaerts, D Aerts, I Masalis and R Bray (eds), *Procedural Law of the European Union* (Sweet & Maxwell 2006) 168, no 5–064 and 171, no 5–069; N Fenger, M Sánchez Rydelski, T van Stiphout, *European Free Trade Association (EFTA) and the European Economic Area (EEA)* (Kluwer Law International 2012) 157.

whether and to what extent they are to be applied.[50] Cases in which the Norwegian Supreme Court did depart from the judgement of the EFTA Court are rare.[51] Still, in *STX*,[52] a case similar to *Laval*, it refused to follow the EFTA Court's decision and decided that expenses for travel, board and lodging were covered by the term 'pay'.[53] As the decision of the Norwegian Supreme Court was highly debated, it was doubtful whether it would be repeated. Besides, if an EFTA Court's decision is not implemented, the EFTA Surveillance Authority may initiate an infringement procedure.[54] The Court of Justice is not bound by the case law of the EFTA Court, but in practice frequently refers to its judgements.[55] Eventually, the Norwegian Supreme Court applied the EFTA Court's decision and judged the boycott to procure acceptance of a collective agreement with preferential rights to be unlawful.[56]

7. The ECSR Case – *Bedriftsforbundet*

At the same time as the EFTA case, Bedriftsforbundet introduced a collective complaint against Norway before the European Committee on Social Rights (ECSR).[57] The employers' organisation for small and medium-sized enterprises to which Holship was affiliated, argued that contrary to Article 5 of the Charter, closed shop practices existed in the Norwegian dock sector. It stated that dockworkers

---

50 Norwegian Supreme Court, *Finanger*, Rt-2000, 1811; C Barnard, 'Reciprocity, Homogeneity and Loyal Cooperation: Dealing with Recalcitrant National Courts?' in EFTA Court (eds), *The EEA and the EFTA Court* (Hart Publishing 2014) 159.

51 T C Poulsen, 'Norwegian Courts' in C Baudenbacher (ed), *The Handbook of EEA Law* (Springer 2016) 267.

52 E-2/11, *STX Norway Offshore AS and Others v The Norwegian State, represented by the Tariff Board* (2012] EFTA Court Report 4.

53 Norwegian Supreme Court, judgement of 5 March 2013 in Case HR-2013-0496-A (case no. 2012/1447); C Barnard, 'Social Policy Law' in C Baudenbacher (ed), *The Handbook of EEA Law* (Springer 2016) 815; Barnard, 'Reciprocity, Homogeneity and Loyal Cooperation: Dealing with Recalcitrant National Courts?' (n 50) 160.

54 Baudenbacher, 'The EFTA Court: Structure and Tasks' in C Baudenbacher (ed), *The Handbook of EEA Law* (n 53) 161.

55 N Fenger, M Sánchez Rydelski, T van Stiphout, *European Free Trade Association (EFTA) and the European Economic Area (EEA)* (Kluwer Law International 2012) 75.

56 *Holship Norge AS v Norsk Transportarbeiderforbund*, Case No. 2014/2089, Judgment of Norwegian Supreme Court of 16 December 2016, HR-2016-2554-P, <www.domstol.no/globalassets/upload/hret/decisions-in-english-translation/case-2014-2089.pdf> accessed 20 March 2017.

57 Collective complaint no. 103/2013, *Bedriftsforbundet v Norway* (ECSR Decision on the merits 17 May 2016).

in Norwegian ports must be members of the dockworkers' union NTF in order to be recruited and to be continued to be employed, since Norwegian law allows the NTF to maintain lists of registered dockworkers with preferential rights to employment.

At the level of the Council of Europe, the pool system has been tackled twice in the context of the negative freedom of association. In the 1990s, the ECSR objected to the former pool system in France as it suspected the existence of closed shop practices. Before 1992, in order to be employed, dockworkers had to hold a licence, issued on the recommendation of a committee made up of an equal number of employers' and employees' representatives, which were all members of the Confédération Générale du Travail (CGT). Objections were made against the fact that only dockworkers belonging to the CGT were recruited.[58] In 1992, the licence requirement was abolished for the great majority of dockworkers, but the Committee still worried about the implementation.[59]

The Committee also made observations on the Belgian system. It noted that in certain economic sectors, recruitment quotas determined that workers be chosen from among the quotas allocated to various trade unions. The Committee raised questions concerning those closed shop practices and the protection afforded to non-unionized workers, and sought clarification.[60] The next report gave the example of the Port of Antwerp, where this system of recruitment should have operated jointly between trade unions and employers. Again, the Committee asked for clarification of the legal protection of non-unionized workers.[61] The subsequent report did not contain the information requested,[62] but in the next report, the Belgian state was happy to announce that the system of recruitment of dockworkers at Antwerp was fundamentally changed. The amendment enabled the Committee to consider the situation to be in conformity with the Charter in this respect.[63]

With regard to Norway, the Committee has previously found the situation to be in conformity with Article 5 of the Charter; in particular, in Conclusions 2006 and

58 L Hislaire, *Dockers, corporatisme et changement* (Transports Actualités Group Usine Nouvelle 1993) 25.

59 ECSR, *Conclusions* XIII-1, XIII-3, XIV-1 and XV-1.

60 ECSR, *Conclusions* XIII-2 and XIII-4.

61 ECSR, *Conclusions* XIV-1.

62 ECSR, *Conclusions* XV-1.

63 ECSR, *Conclusions* XVI-1.

2010, no comments on this issue were made.[64] In its assessment, the Committee firstly recalled that under Article 5, no worker may be forced to join or remain a member of a trade union and that clauses in collective agreements or legally authorised arrangements whereby jobs are reserved in practice for members of a specific trade union are in breach of the freedom guaranteed by Article 5.[65] However, the negative freedom of association is protected by Norwegian law and by consistent and clear case law emanating from the Norwegian superior courts. The relevant collective agreements covering dockworkers, providing for the registration of dockworkers with priority rights, contain no provisions requiring registered dockworkers to be members of the NTF or any other trade union.

As Norwegian law provides an adequate framework for the implementation of Article 5, the question to be resolved was then whether a closed shop arrangement exists in practice; i.e. whether there is a *de facto* requirement to be a member of the NTF. The Committee decided that the evidence at its disposal was not sufficient to prove the existence of such a closed shop in practice, because no case had been brought up of an individual worker complaining to the Ombudsman or before the Courts that he/she had been forced to join or remain in a trade union. The Committee also relied on the Norwegian Court of Appeal which already considered the situation in the port of Drammen and found no evidence of a closed shop practice.[66]

8. A Happy Ending …

Although favoured by an ILO convention, pool systems which provide for priority of engagement for registered dockworkers have already been subjected to pressure for decades. They have been tackled by national governments as well as at the European level. The maritime policy of the European Commission had a major influence, as well as the EU Court of Justice which interpreted the community's competences in this field broadly and allowed for an extensive application of competition law. The evolution took place noiselessly as labour law practitioners were not aware of the potential danger, while competition law experts mostly welcomed the liberalization of regulated markets. Yet, some objections were raised: exclusive rights were too easily equalized with a position of power, small ports

64 In *Conclusions* 2014, the ECSR referred to the collective complaint, but the situation was still considered to be in conformity with Article 5 of the Charter.

65 *Conclusions* XIX-3 (2010), Iceland.

66 Borgarting lagmannsrett, Judgment of 8 September 2014, *Holship Norge AS v. Norsk Transportarbeiderforbund*, 14-076577ASD-BORG/02.

were too easily considered as part of the common market, and in general, the Court was recommended to be more reticent.[67] Also, it was argued that since the cases related to port services, they should have been decided on the basis of the freedom of services. However, its application on maritime transport was uncertain and at the same time required for a foreign service provider.[68] Since 2002, the Commission continuously attempted to extend the freedom of services to port services. Facing two failures, it sought to implement its transport policy by way of infringement procedures. It resorted to the freedom of establishment as its application on maritime transport was unquestioned.

For quite a long time, the protective nature of the pool system was overlooked. In *Merci*, both the plaintiff and the defendant were companies, whereas in *Raso*, the argument was only put forward by the Italian and German governments at the hearing. The first reference to the ILO Convention no. 137 was made by the Spanish government in *Commission v Spain*. Nevertheless, in the Court's dictum, the Convention remained unmentioned. Unlike the EFTA Court, which simply gave precedence to the EEA Agreement, the EU Court of Justice did not deny the effect of the ILO conventions. Apparently, the Commission and the Court of Justice observed no discrepancy between the liberalizing of ports and the Convention.

The European Commission seems determined to liberalize port services, regardless of the social implications. During the hearing in *Holship*, it stated that its policy of '(e)nsuring the mobility of dockworkers within the EEA could provide a better solution for the fluctuating demand for stevedoring in ports of EEA States than "recruit-local" requirements.'[69] In *Commission v Spain*, it already spilled that its aim is to replace the pool systems by permanent or temporary staff hired by the terminal operators, or put at their disposal by private recruitment agencies.[70]

Although the ILO Convention no. 137 is presupposed to be a flexible instrument which entails only minimum standards, it is unlikely that a full-scale liberalization of port services corresponds to it. The registration of dockworkers is not merely a formality but a means to allocate the available dock work. The long-term

---

67 E H Pijnacker and N M P Smulders, 'Gecombineerde noot bij Macrotron, ERT en Porto di Genova' (1993) 3 *SEW* 406–407. Advocate General Fenelly preferred to apply the freedom of services of Article 59 of the TEEC in *Raso*, but was contradicted by the Court which only decided on the basis of Article 86 and 90 of the TEEC. After *Becu*, it was argued that pool systems could better be disputed on the basis of the freedom of services, see M-Y le Garrec, 'Observations' (n 33) 187.

68 Pijnacker and Smulders (n 57) 410.

69 *E-14/15* Report for the hearing, para 132.

70 *Commission v Spain*, para 42–43.

objective of the Convention was to guarantee dockworkers either permanent employment or, failing that, at least regularity of employment or stabilization of their earnings, and registration has been the primary means of identifying workers for that purpose.[71]

Moreover, another reason for registration was to ensure that adequate training in cargo handling is available to the workers as the use of modern equipment requires the employment of a skilled, trained and responsible workforce. The Committee of Experts stresses that systematic use of casual labour cannot offer the same guarantees.[72] However, although many employers pursue the reversal of decasualization schemes, they still wish for their casual dockworkers to enjoy appropriate training. But, contrary to the current situation, the training should be developed in-house or outsourced to professional training agencies.[73] If the Court of Justice and the EFTA Court continue to fully support the Commission's policy, the outcome will be a privatization of dock work and training. This occurs by bypassing the trade unions and the European Parliament which opposed similar legislative initiatives.

Therefore, the decision of the ECSR needs to be saluted. Although it was only a matter of facts as a closed shop could not be demonstrated, and even though it had no significant impact on the outcome of the Norwegian dockworkers' case in the Norwegian Supreme Court, the symbolic value of the decision may not be underestimated. The claim was an apparent attempt to destabilize the pool system and reduce dockworkers' rights. Having been rejected, it might dissuade others from trying to pursue political aims which enjoy no (or not enough) democratic support by way of complaint procedures, at least at the level of the Council of Europe.

71 Report of the Committee of Experts on the Application of Conventions and Recommendations, Report III (Part 1B), General Survey of the reports concerning the Dock Work Convention (No. 137) and Recommendation (No. 145), 1973 (n 7). 50.

72 Report of the Committee of Experts on the Application of Conventions and Recommendations, Report III (Part 1B), General Survey of the reports concerning the Dock Work Convention (No. 137) and Recommendation (No. 145), 1973 (n 7) 59.

73 Notteboom, 'Dock labour and port-related employment in the European seaport system' (n 3) 56; Van Hooydonck, 'Het Spaanse Havenarbeidersarrest (C-576/13)' (n 18) 37 and 48.

Joanna Unterschütz

Employment Model and Freedom of Association – The Case of Poland

1. Introduction

The aim of this chapter is to demonstrate how transformation in the employment market may influence the workers' right to create and join trade unions on the example of Poland, where labour law has undergone a deep change since the transformation in the 1990s.

Freedom of association – one of the fundamental human and workers' rights – is also one of the areas where individual and collective labour rights are strongly intertwined. In practice, it is the national labour law system that decides whether a person performing work for the benefit of another entity is given legal means to execute this freedom.

Despite a relatively good economic situation in Poland in recent years, the number of workers performing subordinated work on the basis of civil law contracts or as self-employed persons has increased significantly. In addition, the number of fixed-time employees reached the highest number in Europe. During the same period, trade union participation rate dropped slowly. Even though there are various reasons explaining this phenomenon, one of them may be the changing structure of the employment models, together with provisions of trade union law. The latter has provided for the right to create and join trade unions to be granted to certain groups of workers only, such as employees as defined by the Labour Code, members of agricultural co-operatives and persons working under agency contracts. A large and still growing group of atypical workers has been deprived of this right. This state of law was subject to proceeding before the International Labour Organization (ILO) Freedom of Association Committee, as well as the Polish Constitutional Court, which is bound to lead to substantial changes in legislation.

2. From State Protection to Flexibility

Polish labour law has gone a long way since the 1990s, when political and economic transformation has strongly influenced its shape. The change from a state protected labour law model to one oriented towards flexibility favoured by liberal economists has changed individual and collective labour law alike.

Until the 1990s, state legislation in the sphere of labour law was comparatively rigid and favourable for workers. Economic transformation beginning in the 1990s brought deep changes in employment structure and a few waves of unemployment. At the start, the economy was confronted with a significant overemployment reaching 20–30 per cent of the workforce.[1] Privatization and rationalization of the economy triggered a huge wave of dismissals. In only one year – 1990 – the number of unemployed grew more than ten-fold, reaching 1.2 million people.[2] Therefore, major amendments of the Labour Code undertaken in the 1990s and the beginning of the 2000s were not only a part of a European Union (EU) accession process, but were most of all aimed to facilitate cheaper, faster and less formal employment procedures.[3] The liberalisation of labour law was accompanied by measures introduced to activate dismissed workers and the unemployed. One example is the Act on employment of temporary workers of 2003, which provided a legal basis for this form of work, and at the same time contributed to its expansion. Since then, employment by temporary employment agencies is growing. The number of agency workers in Poland (full-time equivalent) in 2014 was over 56,000 – double in comparison with 2009.[4] Yet, only 46 per cent of temporary workers are employed on the basis of an employment contract.[5]

With a strong support of employers' organisations, labour law seems to promote employer flexibility and competition based on low employment costs, mainly through generous options for fixed-term employment contracts and the substitution of employment contracts by civil law contracts. Obviously, changes in the employment market are strongly connected to various civilisation factors, such as globalisation; as an example, Poland is becoming an important centre of business services.[6] Post Fordism does not mean that the problems of workers' representation

---

1 J Męcina, *Wpływ dialogu społecznego na kształtowanie się stosunków pracy w III Rzeczypospolitej* (Instytut Polityki Społecznej-Uniwersytet Warszawski 2010) 193.

2 Męcina, *Wpływ dialogu społecznego* (n 1) 194.

3 J Wratny, 'Granice liberalizacji prawa pracy' (2007) 1 Dialog 30.

4 Polskie Forum HR 'Rynek agencji zatrudnienia w 2014 roku' 16 <http://admin.polskieforumhr.pl/dir_upload/site/70c12353731d477c8cda0204c7564695/raport/RAPORT_2015.pdf> accessed 26 August 2016.

5 ibid 17.

6 A Patulski, 'Praca niepewna jako produkt zmian na współczesnym rynku pracy' in G Uscińska (ed), *Prawo pracy. Refleksje i poszukiwania. Księga jubileuszowa profesora Jerzego Wratnego* (IPiSS 2013) 73.

and protection of workers' rights disappear, but the conditions of functioning for trade unions and other workers' representatives change.[7]

3. Trade Union Erosion and Decline in Trade Union Membership Rate

Freedom of association without a doubt constitutes one of fundamental human and workers' rights enshrined in various international, European and national legal acts. It is granted to workers independently from the legal basis of their employment. Nevertheless, in practice it is the national labour law system that decides whether a person performing work for the benefit of another entity is given legal means to execute his or her freedom.

The beginning of the 1990s was also the time when the laws setting the framework for new industrial relations were enacted: trade union law, law on employers' organisations and the law of settling collective disputes. In the Act of 23 May 1991 on Trade Unions (referred to as 'trade union law'), the legislator defines a trade union as 'a voluntary and self-governing organisation of working people, founded to represent and defend their rights, as well as occupational and social interests' (Article 1). However, in fact, the personal scope of trade union freedom was limited to employees (i.e. workers employed on the basis of an employment contract, appointment, election, nomination, or a cooperative contract of employment), and to members of agricultural production, co-operatives and individuals who perform work on the basis of an agency contract, if they are not employers.

Obviously, other groups of workers employed on the basis of civil law contracts (who are in fact far more numerous than the ones on agency contracts), as well as self-employed persons, fall out of this scope. This decision of the legislator, however arbitrary, could be explained by the fact that, in that time, atypical forms of employment were less common in the labour market. As the transformation of the economy and labour market progresses, this could also, in the face of a growing number of atypical forms of employment, largely contribute to the weakening of trade unions, especially in small and micro enterprises. Until the recent judgment of the Constitutional Tribunal in case K 1/13 (presented below in more detail), a significant percentage of the workforce had not benefitted from the freedom of association and other fundamental rights that stem from it: the right to collective bargaining, collective dispute resolution and the right to strike.

7 J Jarosiński, 'Globalizacja a rynek pracy i stosunki pracy w Polsce' in M Bsoul and F Bylok (eds), *Zwiazki zawodowe w procesie przemian społeczno-gospodarczych w Polsce i w wybranych krajach Unii Europejskicj* (Śląsk 2013) 95.

It is also important to note that Polish labour law consists mainly of statutory legislation. Workplace regulations and collective agreements cover all employees regardless of their trade union status, but they play no significant role in the system. Even when present, they rarely modify the statutory provisions in any significant manner. This does not encourage workers to join trade unions in order to get access to better employment conditions.[8]

In Poland, the process of trade union erosion characterized by diminishing trade union membership and the number of companies covered by trade union activity, has taken place since the 1990s.[9] According to polls carried out on a regular basis by the public opinion Research Centre (CBOS) in 1991, 19 per cent of the population in the production age category declared trade union membership. This number lowered gradually, reaching 12 per cent in 1997, 7 per cent in 2001 and 2007, and 6 per cent in 2015.[10] In the group of employees, trade union membership was higher: 20 per cent in 1997, 18 per cent in 2001, 17.6 per cent in 2007 and 16 per cent in 2015.[11] Trade unions are strongest in traditional branches of industry such as shipyards and mines, as well as public institutions and state-owned enterprises, including privatized companies and companies where the state holds the majority of the shares. The lowest level of trade union membership is found in private companies, although trade unions claim successes in

---

8 J Gardawski, 'Ewolucja polskich związków zawodowych' in J Gardawski (ed), *Polacy pracujący a kryzys fordyzmu* (Wydawnictwo Naukowe Scholar 2009) 487; P Czarnecki, 'Bariery prawne w zakresie rokowań zbiorowych w sektorze prywatnym w Polsce' in J Czarzasty (ed), '*Rokowania zbiorowe w cieniu globalizacji. Rola i miejsce związków zawodowych w korporacjach ponadnarodowych*' (Wydawnictwo Naukowe Scholar 2014) 124.

9 J Wratny, 'Związki zawodowe. Znaczenie w życiu politycznym i społeczno-gospodarczy' in J Wratny and M Bednarski (eds), *Związki zawodowe a niezwiązkowe przedstawicielstwa pracownicze w gospodarce posttransformacyjnej* (IPiSS 2010) 40.

10 Wratny, Związki zawodowe (n 9) 41; CBOS '*Opinie o związkach zawodowych i protestach górników 2015*' <http://cbos.pl/SPISKOM.POL/2015/K_066_15.PDF> accessed 26 August 2016.

11 Trade union membership is more frequent than the average among older workers: from 45 to 54 years of age (18 per cent), and especially from 55 to 64 years of age (23 per cent). Furthermore, trade union membership rates for other groups include: those living in cities up to 20 000 of the population (18 per cent), those employed in state-owned enterprises and public institutions (22 per cent), representatives of associate professionals and technicians (24 per cent), as well as executives and professionals with higher education (15 per cent), source: CBOS, 'Opinie o związkach zawodowych' (n 10).

retail (especially in large supermarkets) and private security companies.[12] It is worthwhile mentioning here that the sectors where trade unions remain strong more often than other sectors rely on traditional forms of full-time open-ended employment contracts.

There are many reasons for this negative tendency. One of them is trade union pluralism. As a reaction to the policy of one official trade union during the time of socialist regime, the legislator decided that a group of only ten workers may create and register a trade union, and in some companies, the number of trade union organisations reached several dozen[13]. The model of conflicting pluralism prevented these organisations from preparing to respond to the challenges of the market economy, and benefit from positive examples of trade union organisations in other EU countries.[14] This in turn has largely contributed to trade union erosion and marginalization in the private sector. Before the transformation, 100 per cent of the workers in traditional state enterprises were unionized. The number was much lower in privatized state enterprises (63.6 per cent) and in new companies with foreign capital (30 per cent), while the lowest rate was found in newly established companies with Polish capital (5.4 per cent)[15]. In practice, pluralization also means that trade unions represent only particular groups of interests and not the majority of workers. On the other hand, large trade union organizations representative on a country level[16] tend to fulfil a role similar to political parties, and their activities do not always concentrate uniquely on the protection of workers' interests.[17]

In the survey carried out by CBOS in 2004, most workers declared that they were not members of trade unions because of a lack of trade union organization at their workplace, which is often a small enterprise (46.2 per cent). 28.3 per cent

---

12 Wratny, 'Związki zawodowe' (n 9) 41.

13 Wratny quotes an example of PKP Cargo (a large railway company) with 263 trade union organisations, in Wratny, 'Związki zawodowe' (n 9) 43.

14 J Gardawski, 'Polskie związki zawodowe w procesie transformacji' in K Żukrowska (ed), *Transformacja systemowa w Polsce* (Szkoła Główna Handlowa w Warszawie 2010) 183.

15 Gardawski, 'Ewolucja polskich związków zawodowych'(n 8) 486.

16 The three largest are Niezależny Samorządny Związek Zawodowy (NSZZ Solidarność), Ogólnopolskie Porozumienie Związków Zawodowych (OPZZ) and Forum Związków Zawodowych (FZZ).

17 M Rycak, 'Wpływ koncepcji flexicurity na przemiany stosunku pracy' in L Florek and Ł Pisarczyk (eds), *Współczesne problemy prawa pracy i ubezpieczeń społecznych* (Lexis-Nexis 2011) 220; Jarosiński, *Globalizacja a rynek pracy i stosunki pracy w Polsce* (n 7) 97–99.

declared no need to be a trade union member and 16.5 per cent were critical about trade union activity, doubting if this type of organisation really protects workers or fearing a negative reaction from the employer.[18] Workers who left trade unions most often indicated retirement (25.2 per cent) or unemployment (17.6 per cent) as a reason, but some had lost trust in them (5.6 per cent) because they were not provided the support they had been counting on. Also in later polls (2010), workers expressed only limited trust in trade unions' efficiency in protecting workers' rights.[19] Some declared losing trust in NSZZ Solidarność, which had once been a large social movement, but failed their members by becoming involved in politics and not sufficiently protecting workers' rights. Interestingly, two per cent of the surveyed declared that they left trade unions because they were once obliged to be members and now they are free to choose.[20]

The survey also explains the absence of trade unions in companies. 36.5 per cent of the respondents suggest that the enterprise is too small. 11.9 per cent believe that privatization is the reason, and about the same number believe that a trade union is not needed. 10.3 per cent claim that the workers themselves are not interested in creating trade unions and do not take initiative. 7.9 per cent state that a trade union does not exist because of the employer's hostility and workers fearing repercussions.[21]

The opinion on managerial staff's negative attitude towards trade unions is not unfounded, as Gardawski suggests. In the initial period of economic transformation, NSZZ Solidarność had a strong influence in the process of eliminating representatives of a socialist regime from privatized and restructured enterprises. Those who lost their positions often established their own enterprises in the private sector and shared their resentment towards trade unions among other company owners and managers.[22] Similarly, trade unionists often have negative perceptions

---

18 A Mokrzyszewski, 'Przyczyny niskiego uzwiązkowienia Polaków pracujących' in J Gardawski (ed) *Polacy pracujący a kryzys fordyzmu* (Wydawnictwo Naukowe Scholar 2009) 572–574.

19 14 per cent of the respondents expressed a positive opinion on trade union's efficiency, while 33 per cent claimed that they do not see any effects of their activity, and 44 per cent claimed that their endeavours do not bring effects. P Kikosicki 'Związki zawodowe w zakładach pracy w Polsce w świetle badań opinii społecznej' in Z. Hajn (ed), '*Związkowe przedstawicielstwo pracowników zakładu pracy*' (Lex Wolters Kluwer 2015) 6–61. See also J Gardawski, *Związki zawodowe na rozdrożu* (ISP 2001) 106–107.

20 Mokrzyszewski, '*Przyczyny niskiego uzwiązkowienia*' (n 18) 575–578.

21 Mokrzyszewski, *Przyczyny niskiego uzwiązkowienia* (n 18) 579.

22 Gardawski, *Ewolucja polskich związków zawodowych* (n 8) 481.

of employers' organisations, which only deepens mutual distrust.[23] Especially in small enterprises, an environment hostile to trade unions prevents workers from creating and joining trade union organizations.[24]

Economic transformation also has changed the picture of workers' participation. Apart from workers' representatives in the supervisory boards in privatised enterprises, new participation bodies like works councils and European works councils (EWCs) appeared. Decreasing trade union membership was one of the arguments for creating works councils independent from trade unions.[25] Still, the largest influence on the workers' situation in privatized and restructured companies is due to trade unions concluding agreements with the future employer, which at least for a short period of time guaranteed better employment conditions and limited dismissals.[26]

4. Spreading of Fixed-Term Employment Contracts

Weakening of trade unions' position is also, as mentioned earlier, strongly connected with the transformation of employment relations. Greater flexibility of employment, manifesting in atypical forms of Labour Code-based forms of employment such as fixed-term contracts, agency work and civil law contracts, is obviously not a uniquely Polish phenomenon. Similar changes can be observed in all countries where the economy is transforming from an industrial economy based on Taylorist and Fordist organisation of production to a post-industrial economy. This change means limiting co-operated work performed at the same time by a large number of workers in one establishment under the employer's supervision, and the spreading of more individualistic patterns of work.[27] Flexibility of employment is both

23 ibid 518.

24 J Wratny, *Partycypacja pracownicza Studium zagadnienia w warunkach transformacji gospodarczej* (IPiSS 2002) 174.

25 ibid 50.

26 J Wratny, 'Wpływ prywatyzacji na zbiorowe stosunku pracy. Podsumowanie' in J Wratny and M Bednarski (eds), *Wpływ prywatyzacji na zbiorowe stosunku pracy. Aspekty prawne i społeczno-ekonomiczne* (IPSiS 2005) 166–167; Wratny, *Partycypacja pracownicza* (n 24) 44–45.

27 J Męcina, 'Zatrudnienie niepracownicze Z perspektywy polityki społecznej i rynku pracy' in KW Baran (ed), *System prawa pracy. Tom VII Zatrudnienie niepracownicze* (Lex Wolters Kluwer 2015) 30; see also K Walczak, 'Wpływ globalizacji I ogólnoświatowego kryzysu na podstawy i warunki zatrudniania. Wyzwania dla polskiego prawa pracy' in L Florek and Ł Pisarczyk (eds), *Współczesne problemy prawa pracy i ubezpieczeń społecznych* (LexisNexis 2011) 81; Wratny, '*Związki zawodowe*' (n 9) 43.

needed and possible because of phenomena like decentralization and delocation of the production process, individualization of tasks given to employees, a different attitude to working time, and new technical possibilities of monitoring employees outside the employer's establishment. Real results of work become more important than staying at the disposal of the employer. Modern technologies both facilitate reconciliation of work and private life and, at the same time, contribute to dissolving borders between the two spheres[28].

In Poland, the number of fixed-term employees reached the highest number in Europe in recent years – about 28 per cent in the third quarter of 2015.[29] In addition, the number of workers performing subordinated work based on civil law contracts or as self-employed persons increased significantly. Employment on the basis of fixed-term employment contracts and, to a larger extent, civil law contracts, seems to contribute most to the segmentation of the employment market, deepening differences between insiders and outsiders even more.[30]

Given the high proportion of those less protected employees, EU legislation such as the Directive on fixed-term contracts has the potential to improve employment conditions. The non-compliance of Polish law on fixed-term contracts with the *acquis communautaire* had long been calling for an action, and in September 2012, the NSZZ Solidarność trade union filed a complaint to the European Commission concerning the failure to implement Directive 99/70/EC.[31] The Commission announced that a formal infringement procedure had been started.[32] In these proceedings, the European Commission considered the significant differences between fixed-term and open-ended contracts in terms of resolution of the contract, as well as an insufficient mechanism for limiting fixed-term employment.

In addition, the EU Council Country Specific Recommendation for the years 2014–2015 for Poland requires the correction of the segmentation of the labour

---

28 Męcina, 'Zatrudnienie niepracownicze' (n 27) 32.

29 Central Statistical Office, *Kwartalna informacja o rynku pracy*, <http://stat.gov.pl/obszary-tematyczne/rynek-pracy/pracujacy-bezrobotni-bierni-zawodowo-wg-bael/kwartalna-informacja-o-rynku-pracy-w-iii-kwartale-2015-r-,12,22.html> accessed 26 August 2016.

30 Walczak, 'Wpływ globalizacji' (n 26) 87.

31 <www.solidarnosc.org.pl/stara/uploads/oryginal/1/4/2b5f6_Skarga_calosc.pdf> accessed 26 August 2016.

32 Press release in Rzeczpospolita Daily Newspaper Website: 'Po skardze "S" interwencja KE ws. umów na czas określony w Polsce' <http://prawo.rp.pl/artykul/1074268.html> accessed 26 August 2016.

market, among others, by improving the transition from temporary employment to permanent employment.

Another important step towards changing the situation of workers on fixed-term contracts was the preliminary ruling of the Court of Justice of the European Union (CJEU) in *Nierodzik*. In January 2013, a labour court in Białystok turned to the CJEU for a preliminary ruling concerning the interpretation of clauses 1 and 4 of the Framework agreement on fixed-term work. The proceedings were initiated by a nursing assistant, whose fixed-term contract was terminated by her employer (Psychiatric Health Care Institution). In its judgment, the CJEU reminded that Clause 4(1) of the Framework Agreement lays down, in respect of employment conditions, a prohibition on treating fixed-term workers in a less favourable manner than comparable permanent workers, solely because they have a fixedterm contract or relation, unless different treatment is justified on objective grounds.[33] The CJEU also argued that the mere temporary nature of an employment relationship is not sufficient to justify such a difference, otherwise the objectives of Directive 1999/70 and the Framework Agreement would be negated[34].

It is interesting to note here that the Court does not compare employment conditions (which include also the notice period for the termination of fixed-term employment contracts) of two workers, but the conditions of one worker throughout his or her employment by the same employer.

In that case, the Court concluded that the notice period prior to the termination of the worker's employment contract was fixed (two weeks) without taking account of her length of service. However, if she had been employed under a contract of indefinite duration, that period, calculated in accordance with her length of service, would have been one month, that is twice as long. The only factor capable of distinguishing the worker's situation from that of a permanent worker seemed to be the temporary nature of the employment relationship. It followed from this that the application of notice periods of different length constituted different treatment in respect of employment conditions.[35]

The result of this judgment and the previous proceeding before the European Commission was an important amendment in the Polish Labour Code, changing the system of limitation of fixed-term employments. Since 21 February 2016, the Labour Code distinguishes only three types of employment contracts: contracts for an indefinite term, fixed-term contracts and contracts for a trial period.

---

33 Judgment of 13 March 2014, *Nierodzik,* C-38/13, EU:C:2014:152.

34 ibid para 38.

35 ibid paras 34–35.

For the first two contracts, the new law introduces a unified system of notice periods that become longer with seniority in the company regardless of the type of contract (two weeks' notice for less than six months seniority in the enterprise, one month's notice for seniority of six months to three years, and three months' notice for workers employed for at least three years).

There are also new mechanisms to limit temporary employment: the maximum period of employment on a fixed-term contract is 33 months, plus a trial period of a maximum of three months – a total of 36 months. At the same time, the number of fixed-term contracts with one employer remains limited to three. Another contract, or a contract concluded for a longer period than stipulated by the law, will transform *ex lege* into a contract for an indefinite period. Exceptions to these rules apply to cases such as replacement or seasonal work. The exception also includes the situation where the employer indicates objective reasons based on actual temporary demand for labour, if it is necessary in the light of all the circumstances of the contract. Such agreements must be reported to the labour inspector.

Workers employed on fixed-term contracts are less willing to join trade unions.[36] The same can be said about teleworkers and foreigners[37], even though there are no legal obstacles for atypical workers (as well as home workers) employed on labour contracts to join trade unions. Although agency workers are not exempted from these provisions, in reality, trade unions are not formed in the agencies. This is caused by the temporary character of their employment, the fact that their real interests (e.g. remuneration) are connected with the user employer rather than the agency,[38] and last but not least, that over 50 per cent of them are employed on the basis of civil contracts, as mentioned earlier.[39]

It can be generally stated that atypical employment forms do not favour workers' participation in representative bodies, be it trade unions or works councils.[40] A weak bond with the company discourages employees to participate in the

36 J Wratny and M Bednarski, *Wpływ prywatyzacji na zbiorowe stosunki pracy Aspekty prawne i społeczno – ekonomiczne* (IPSiS 2005) 175.

37 There are however some individual exceptions of foreigners declaring their interest to join trade unions.

38 J Wratny, 'Elastyczność z ludzka twarzą' (2007) 3 Dialog 28.

39 Ministerstwo Pracy i Polityki Społecznej – Departament Rynku Pracy 'Raport z działalności agencji zatrudnienia w 2006 r.' <www.zapt.pl/pdf/RAPORT_AGENCJE_-_2006_-_MPIPS.pdf> accessed 26 August 2016.

40 Wratny, *Partycypacja pracownicza* (n 24) 175.

management process, but also influences relations between employees.[41] All this makes it difficult to organise atypical workers in trade unions, which influences industrial relations in the establishment.[42]

5. Replacement of Employment Contracts by Civil-Law Contracts

Employment based on civil law contracts often replaces the traditional form of employment. This shift towards independent, non co-ordinated forms of employment also results in a growing number of workers who are not covered by any protective regulations (except from basic health and safety ones) stemming from the Labour Code.[43] Employers are very willing to apply civil law contracts instead of employment contracts, both for fiscal reasons (social security fees are lower) and because it offers greater flexibility regarding the organisation of work, as well as the resolution of the contract. The national statistics do not precisely reflect the number of independent workers, but they may constitute from almost seven per cent to 13 per cent of the workforce.[44] Unfortunately, this number includes both workers who indeed are independent entrepreneurs, and cases of 'hiding' employment relationships under bogus civil law contracts and self-employment. Statistics of the Labour Inspection reveal that the scale of such unlawful practice is growing each year. While in 2007 the labour inspectors found irregularities in concluding employment contracts in only four per cent of controlled enterprises, the number had grown to 18 per cent in 2013.[45]

Civil law contracts are often signed for only one month and many of them are not fully covered by social security. This form of employment is also a disadvantage for workers as bank clients; banks tend to be critical towards civil-law workers while assessing their credit rating. Because of all these circumstances, workers tend to perceive this form of employment as precarious.[46]

---

41 M Bednarski, *E- parca a zmiany w firmie* (2004) 2 Polityka społeczna.

42 Wartny and Bednarski, *Wpływ prywatyzacji na zbiorowe stosunki pracy* (n 37) 176.

43 Męcina, 'Zatrudnienie niepracownicze' (n 27) 27.

44 Męcina, 'Zatrudnienie niepracownicze' (n 27) 40; Central Statistical Office *'Pracujący w nietypowych formach zatrudnienia'* <http://stat.gov.pl/obszary-tematyczne/rynek-pracy/pracujacy-zatrudnieni-wynagrodzenia-koszty-pracy/pracujacy-w-nietypowych-formach-zatrudnienia,11,1.html> accessed 26 August 2016.

45 Męcina, *Zatrudnienie niepracownicze* (n 27) 40.

46 ibid 42.

Despite prohibition of such practice in the Labour Code, employers and employees often conclude several civil law contracts before the establishment of a fixed-term employment contract. Only after a longer duration of such contracts do employers decide to hire workers on an employment contract for a trial period and then on a chain of fixed-term contracts. Under civil law contracts, workers are deprived of protection guaranteed by the Labour Code in terms of working time, minimum wage, holidays and privileges for working parents. In many cases, the nature of the work performed does not change throughout the period of employment. This applies in particular to the nature of duties, the way they are performed and the subordination of the worker. According to the view expressed by the Supreme Court and supported by labour law scholars, the type of the contract may not be changed (from employment contract to civil law contract) without changing the nature of the work, its intensity and character. Otherwise, it is an abuse of the law which is not justified.[47] The means to protect workers against such forms of abuse are the definition of the employment contract in the Labour Code and the so-called 'soft' presumption of the existence of an employment contract, as well as a ban to conclude a civil law contract instead of an employment contract.[48] There is also a specific procedure available to establish the existence of an employment contract.

Apart from negative effects in the sphere of individual labour law (access to promotion, training, remuneration), employment on civil law contracts also has negative effects on collective labour law. Although even in the present legal situation, civil-contract workers may be covered by collective agreements since 1995, they may not participate in the negotiation process. In practice unfortunately, only a few collective agreements deal with the rights of workers employed on other bases than employment contracts, which means that this tool is not sufficiently

---

47 Article 58 of the Civil Code; Supreme Court judgment of 14.12.2009, I PK 108/09 (2010) MOPR. 7, 364; E Suknarowska-Drzewiecka in K Walczak (ed), *Kodeks pracy. Komentarz* (C.H. Beck 2013); G Goździewicz and T Zieliński underline the autonomy of the parties to transform an employment contract into a civil law contract or a civil law contract into an employment contract; however, this change should be accompanied by a change of the character of the work performed. G Goździewicz and T Zielinski in L Florek, (ed), *Kodeks pracy* (WoltersKluwer, 2011) 148; See also Gersdorf in M Gersdorf, K Rączka and M Jackowski (eds) *Kodeks pracy. Komentarz* (LexisNexis 2012) 119.

48 J Unterschütz, '*Ograniczenie w zakresie zawierania umów na czas określony a „miękkie" domniemanie istnienia stosunku pracy (uwagi na marginesie wyroku Sądu Najwyższego z dnia 14 czerwca 2012 r., I PK 222/11)*' (2013) 16 Rozprawy Naukowe i Zawodowe PWSZ w Elblągu 131.

used. One of the causes may be the lack of trade union representation of dependent workers who are not employees in the meaning of the Labour Code.

6. Proceedings before the ILO Freedom of Association Committee

The problem of limited access to trade unions for workers employed on civil law contracts and for the self-employed was subject to proceedings before the ILO Freedom of Association Committee (CFA), as well as before the Polish Constitutional Court. Concerns presented by academia[49] were confirmed by the recommendations in the 2012 report of the CFA, as a response to the complaint made by the NSZZ Solidarność.

The trade union considered that by using a narrow definition of the term 'employee' inspired by the Labour Code, the legislator denied freedom of association rights to persons employed on the basis of civil law contracts (contracts for service), self-employed persons, and other persons performing work. According to the complainant, the scope of the right to organise is therefore restricted only to selected categories of workers, and the choice seems to be arbitral and does not reflect the reality of the Polish labour market where persons employed on civil law contracts and self-employed persons constitute a significant share of the workforce.[50]

The problem is even more visible in the case of self-employed persons. According to Articles 1 and 2 of the Law on Employers' Organizations of 1991, such workers may not join employers' organisations as they do not employ anyone. As a consequence, they are not considered 'employers' in the sense of the definition provided for in Section 3 of the Labour Code. As mentioned earlier, trade union law also grants the right to establish and join trade unions to some categories of workers, but these do not include self-employed persons and the majority of

---

49 Z Hajn, 'Prawo zrzeszania sie w zwiazkach zawodowych – prawo pracowników czy prawo ludzi pracy?' in J Stelina, M Tomaszewska and A Wypych- Żywicka (eds), *Zbiorowe prawo pracy w XXI wieku* (Fundacja Rozwoju Uniwersytetu Gdańskiego 2010) 175–183; B Cudowski, 'Prawo do zrzeszania się, prowadzenia rokowań i sporów zbiorowych w Polsce a europejskie prawo pracy' in W Sanetra (ed), *Europeizacja polskiego prawa pracy* (Wydawnictwo Naukowe Scholar 2004) 49; J Unterschütz, 'Naczelne zasady zbiorowego prawa pracy w multicentrycznym porządku prawnym' (Wyższa szkoła Administracji i Biznesu i. E. Kwiatkowskiego w Gdyni 2016) 289–292.

50 ILO '363rd report of the committee on freedom of association 313th session Geneva, 15–30 March 2012' paragraph 1070 <www.ilo.org/wcmsp5/groups/public/@ed_norm/@relconf/documents/meetingdocument/wcms_176577.pdf> accessed 26 August 2016.

workers under civil law contracts. The right to join trade unions (without the right to establish them) is granted to homeworkers, pensioners and the unemployed. State officers of uniform service may associate with restrictions as defined by specific legislation.[51]

This is a violation of Convention No. 87 as it makes a distinction between the rights of specific categories of workers.[52] Trade union law is also in violation of Convention No. 135 under which the term 'workers representative' refers not only to trade union members, but also to other persons in accordance with national law. Trade union law grants the protection against dismissal, and the privilege to be released from work to carry out trade union duties is again given only to employees and not other categories of workers.[53]

In its conclusions, the ILO Committee requested that the Polish Government take the necessary measures in order to ensure that all workers, without distinction whatsoever, including self-employed workers and those employed under civil law contracts, enjoy the right to establish and join organisations of their own choosing within the meaning of Convention No. 87. In addition, it should amend the trade union law so as to ensure that home-based workers can establish and join organisations of their own choosing, and to ensure that all workers and their representatives enjoy adequate protection against acts of anti-union discrimination, regardless of whether or not they fall under the definition of an employee under the Labour Code.[54]

7. Constitutional Tribunal on Freedom of Association and Definition of Worker

Contrary to the content of its earlier judgements (and perhaps as a reaction to changing employment market), the Polish Constitutional Tribunal has also decided to search for a different 'constitutional' definition of a worker, based on European and international law. The Court's findings have led to conclusions that the current definition in the Labour Code cannot be applied in order to ensure workers their fundamental rights.

---

51 The extent of these restrictions is also questioned. See: Z Góral, 'Zbiorowa reprezentacja pracowników sfery publicznej' in: Stelina, Tomaszewska and Wypych-Zywicka (eds), *Zbiorowe prawo pracy XXI wieku* (n 49) 136–138.

52 ILO, '363rd Report of the Committee on Freedom of Association' (n 51) paragraph 1073.

53 ibid paragraph 1074.

54 ibid paragraph 1087.

In its judgment of 2 June 2015 in case K 1/13, the Constitutional Tribunal stated that the provisions of the trade union law in force in Poland are unconstitutional. The proceedings before the Constitutional Court were initiated by one of the largest unions, the Ogólnopolskie Porozumienie Związków Zawodowych (OPZZ). The applicant challenged the provisions of the trade union law that grant certain individuals the right to form and join trade unions. According to the OPZZ, persons performing paid work on a basis other than an employment relationship within the meaning of the Labour Code are deprived of trade union freedom. This becomes even more serious as an increasing number of people provide work on the basis of civil law contracts or as self-employed. Such a restriction is contrary to the constitutional guarantees of freedom of association in trade unions and the ILO Convention (No. 87), declaring freedom of association in trade unions for all workers, regardless of the legal basis on which work is performed.

The Court held that the personal scope of the statutory guarantee to organise in trade unions was too narrow in relation to the constitutional norms (Article 59 paragraph 1 of the Polish Constitution) and those arising from international agreements binding for Poland. The legislator applied a criterion of legal basis of employment for determining the group of entities entitled to organize in trade unions. This criterion is not a decisive element for the exercise of freedom of association, but its application led to the preclusion of a large group of workers from exercising freedom of association in trade unions. Instead, the Tribunal constructed a wider definition of employee than the one enshrined in the Labour Code. The freedom of association should be enjoyed by people fulfilling three conditions: 1) gainful employment, 2) remaining in a legal relationship with the entity for which the employee performs work, and 3) having such professional interests connected with the work that could be collectively protected. This conclusion was based *inter alia* on the case law of the CJEU.[55] The criteria, which determine the

55 The Constitutional Tribunal refers to the following CJEU cases: judgment of 4 december 2014, C-413/13, *FNV Kunsten Informatie en Media*, EU:C:2014:2411, paragraph 34; judgment of 10 April 2014, C-270/13, *Haralambidis*, EU:C:2014:2185, paragraph 28; judgment of 21 February. 2013, C-46/12, *L.N. v. Styrelsen for Videregående Uddannelser og Uddannelsesstøtte*, EU:C:2013:97, paragraph 40; judgment of 14 October 2010, C-345/09, van Delft and others, EU:C:2011:57, paragraph 89; judgment of 4 September 2009, C-22/08 and C-23/08, Vatsouras and Koupatantze, EU:C:2009:344, paragraph 26, OJ. 2009, p. I-04585. The notion of worker has also been shaped by the following CJEU cases: judgment of 3 July 1986, 66/85, *Lawrie-Blum*, EU:C:1986:284; judgment of 12 May 1998, C-85/96, *Martínez Sala*, EU:C:1998:217; judgment of 13 January 2004, C-256/01, *Allonby*, EU:C:2004:18.

existence of an employment relationship in the constitutional meaning, include: providing work for another person, performing work under the direction of an employer and the fees for the work, and genuine and effective paid employment and economic risk of the employer[56]. The type of legal relationship (or contract) between the employee and the employer bears no significance. Both 'European' and 'constitutional' definitions of an employee thus have a substantial and not a formal character, and it is not based solely on the type of contract between the employee and the person using his or her work.

Finally, the Tribunal concluded that the legislator should enable all those who, from a constitutional perspective, belong to the category of workers, to perform the freedom of association. The legislator should, however, choose the right legislative technique ensuring the implementation of the constitutional norm. As a result, the government presented a bill amending the trade union law in a way that it covered all categories of workers. Currently (March 2017), the bill is under consultation with social partners.

It is still too early to see if the judgment of the Constitutional Tribunal contributes to the increase of trade union members, especially those on civil law contracts and the self-employed, but it certainly removes a significant legal obstacle. The example illustrates relations between individual and collective labour rights, as well as the multi-level character of guarantees for collective workers' rights.

56 M Tomaszewska, *Prawo integracji stosunku pracy. Między jednością a różnorodnością* (Wydawnictwo Uniwersytetu Gdańskieg 2011) 290.

Eberhard Eichenhofer

Precarious Work – New Implications for Social Security

1. Introduction – International Commitments Under International Law

Even in highly formalized and prosperous countries, low payment and precarious work are widespread. In the developed, welfare-oriented world of today,[1] dependent and paid work and social protection are key components of work relations and social policy and, thus, go hand in hand.[2] Work should be adequate for and adapted to the needs of people and guarantee that humans live in dignity. Thus, in the phase of both active employment and when social contingencies verify, adequate and sufficient social protection should emerge out of all paid work. Under the Decent Work Agenda of the International Labour Organization (ILO),[3] the protection of work should be built upon three pillars. Firstly, workers are to be protected as human beings against the inherent physical and mental risks of the technical work environment; this is done by health and safety laws. Secondly, employees should have employment rights, i.e. a fair return for their work done for the employer and rights to exercise voice in the gesture of an enterprise. Finally, work gives and should give access to social security[4] to protect individuals against social risks: old age and disability, sickness, unemployment, work accidents, occupational – i.e. work related – diseases and family responsibilities.[5] The risks entailed in the labour market jeopardize the life, physical integrity and earning capacity of each individual. Social security is based on state legislation and administered by public bodies.

---

1 International Labour Organization *Social Security for social justice and a fair globalization* (International Labour Office 2011).

2 International Labour Organization *Social Security and the rule of law International Labour Conference 100th session* (International Labour Office 2011).

3 ILO Declaration on Social Justice for a Fair Globalization 2008.

4 A Nußberger, 'Interpretation of International Social Security Standards, Problems and Prospects' in F Pennings and L Bijleveld (eds), *International Social Security Standards. Current views and Interpretation Matters* (Intersentia 2007) 33.

5 As to the ILO Convention No. 102 J Van Langendonck (ed), *The Right to social security* (Intersentia 2007).

This protection must be given to the employees irrespective of their gender, age, health, citizenship, or work profile. Binding imperatives of international law impose countries worldwide to respect human rights on work[6] and social security.[7] There is a further fundamental social right – internationally acknowledged and to be safeguarded worldwide[8] – as to which work should bring about fair remuneration – substantial enough to meet the employee's basic needs. Thus, good – well-protected, paid and inclusive – work is a prerequisite for good protection in social security. In many circumstances, however, human work is not adequately paid. Low wages do not enable the wage earners to afford their living. In addition, self-employed persons do not always receive continuous and adequate income or sufficient protection in social security. Finally, persons are exposed to precarious work, which endanger them in their later life. This is also a risk for persons who performed unpaid family work: child rearing and long-term care for frail relatives, friends or neighbours. So, shortcomings and insufficiencies in social protection can stem from both legal and economic factors.

The impacts that precarious work has on social security are, therefore, to be examined. One has to discern between precarious paid work (2–4) and unpaid work (5). The latter is not only precarious as such, but also brings about insufficient social protection. As to paid work, special problems are to be solved regarding irregular work (2), insubstantial work, and as to the status of work as being a 'dependent or independent one' (3). Also, new forms of atypical work give cause to special social security law reflections – not primarily, however, as to their legal status, but also as to their economic consequences (4, 6).

---

6 Art. 23 of the General Declaration of the Human Rights, Art. 1 of the European Social Charter, Art. 6 and 7 of the International Covenant on Economic, Social and Cultural Rights. M Ssenyonjo, *Economic Social and Cultural Rights in international law* (Hart 2009); M Langford, *Social Rights Jurisprudence* (Cambridge University Press 2008).

7 Art. 22 of the General Declaration of Human Rights, Art. 9 International Covenant on Economic Social and Cultural Rights. Van Langendonck *The Right to social security* (n 5).

8 Art. 4 of the European Social Charter, Art. 23 of the General Declaration of Human Rights, Art. 7 of the International Declaration of Economic Social and Cultural Rights. M Mikkola, *Social human rights* (Legisactio Oy 2010); Council of Europe *Social Protection in the European Social Charter* (Council of Europe Publishing 1999).

2. What Jeopardises Social Security Protection for Precarious Work in General?

Social security protection – as a fundament of fair work – is jeopardised by different legal or economic reasons.[9] If the accessibility to the labour market is restricted by law, the basis for generating social security rights is eroded. Legal restrictions keep people off the labour market or the social security system; economic restrictions may bring about social exclusion due to the fact that the work done is inadequate for sufficient social protection.

Since the 1970s and during the last decades, European societies envisaged high unemployment rates; they still struggle with them today. As a reaction, fringe work became legal. This made fringe work common, differentiated and widespread more and more. Within the European Union (EU) today, only one in four workers are in standard employment relations. Driven by global competition and unbalanced labour markets within the countries, the employers define the targets and set the rules, whereas employees have lost the realistic choice to evade them. Therefore, a scary labour market has emerged and new forms of work arrangements gained ground: part-time work, volunteers, para-subordination, sheltered unemployment, workfare programmes, short- and fixed-term work, intermittent work, zero hours work and on-call work.

This development was ignited by a debate on whether labour and social security law should be regarded as institutional hindrances for new work opportunities. This view is based on a neo-liberal stance[10] in politics, and it gained ground in many countries. It epitomized the end of the classical concept of a standard labour contract as it emerged at the beginning of industrialism and upon which both labour and social security law are built. The new emerging types of work were regarded as instruments to give the employer more flexibility. This should meet the demands of the expanding service-oriented and global economy.

More flexibility for employers as to the rights of their employees might result in less social security for the latter. This would undermine the workers' rights, and this would be detrimental to all those who depend on their work to afford

---

9 G Schmid, 'Non-Standard Employment and the New Standard Employment Contract Reflections from a Transitional Labour Market Point of View' (Paper presented to the IIRA European congress in Copenhagen 28–30 June 2010) <www.guentherschmid.eu/pdf/2010/copenhagen-10.pdf> accessed 10 March 2017; M Wilson, 'Precarious Work The Need for a New Policy Framework' (Whitlam Institute within the University of Western Sydney, February 2013).

10 OECD Jobs Study 1994.

their living. So, what is the impact of more flexible work to social security? In order to wrap up the reform of labour law in the direction of more flexible work arrangements, it should be guaranteed that such a reform will not end in exploitive labour practices and social consequences which are to be borne by the public – above all in the form of burdens as to social assistance.[11] The emergence of new forms of work does help the employers to increase their flexibility; but this target cannot justify waiving social rights.

3. Work Arrangements on an Insufficient Legal Basis and Social Security

The first topic to be dealt with is to determine which social security consequences work has, and if it is unlawful under labour law. For many decades, there is an ongoing debate[12] about whether labour relations which lack formality should be dealt with as work, both in social security and labour law, as they give rise to entitlements if the work was correctly done by the worker. If both the employee and the employer do not respect the legal rules established for employment (e.g. in cases of forbidden child work; in the moonlight economy without taxes, contributions, or registrations; or in work done by a non-documented foreigner whose access to the state's labour market is not allowed), the question to be decided by both social security and labour law is whether any labour or social security right can ever mature out of such employment.

In civil law, contracts which do not correspond with the established rules are unlawful and, hence, void. As to this solution, illegal work could not get any legal protection. As labour was done on the basis of a void contract, this cannot be accepted as lawful employment and, therefore, does not bring about any substantial legal consequences. This reasoning, however, has been rebutted since both social security and labour law came into existence. Despite the fact that at first glance it seems to be convincing and 'logical', this approach ignores the fact that the

11 Wilson, 'Precarious Work' (n 9) 6.

12 M Fuchs and U Preis, Sozialversicherungsrecht (2nd edn, Schmidt 2009); '§ 12 Seewald § 7 SGB IV' in S Leitherer (ed), *Kasseler Kommentar Sozialversicherungsrecht* (C.H. Beck 2010) Rn. 15 f; W Gitter, 'Beschäftigungsverhältnis und Arbeitsverhältnis' in W Gitter, W Thieme and H F Zacher (eds) *Im Dienste des Sozialrechts. Festschrift für Georg Wannagat* (Heymanns 1981) 147; H Seiter, 'Sozialversicherungsrechtliches Beschäftigungsverhältnis und Arbeitsverhältnis' (1976) 4 Vierteljahresschrift für Sozialrecht 179.

work was effectively done, and it does not reflect the rationale of why the legal relationship is to be nullified.

If the law regards a contract of a minor as void, unless it does not have the approval of her/his parents or the minor is not the legal age for paid work, the legal consequence shall protect the autonomy and physical integrity of the minor. As labour and social security law are also to protect the workers in their physical integrity, it would be paradoxical to outlaw the protection intended by both labour and social security law in cases where the labour relation is not valid, because the worker should be protected by law. So, the 'logical' alternative would lead to the irritating result that the violation of the law would liberate the employer from the protection he/she owes to the employee. If social security and labour law are to protect workers against risks and disadvantages from employment, neither can the employee be abandoned from her/his protection, nor can the law serve to set employers free from the observation of the established rules, because the work is done on the basis of a void contract.

The joint agreement of the employer and the employee to become active in the moonlight economy instead of the formal one and to disregard social security and tax law should also not be sanctioned by making the work exchange unlawful. Because again it would lead to the paradoxical consequence, that the employer could draw the profit of unlawful work without any return to the worker.[13] So, the sanction of a void contract would be imposed on the worker unilaterally, and the advantage of the illegal work would fall on the employer. Again, this would end in the bizarre result contradicting the imperatives of labour and social security law. This solution also prevails if a worker does work without a work permit. The Courts held that the contract is not void, but that the worker is incapable to do her or his work – due to lacking permission.[14] This idea is not convincing. In addition, the undocumented workers do work – many of them very well. So, again, an adequate answer is to be given on the assumption that protection is given in labour as well as social security law without a lawful, formal work contract. So, in the debate the observation gained ground that for protecting persons in both labour and social security law, the work practically carried out gives rise to all the rights an employee can expect to receive. This doctrine is sometimes explicitly stated in the law. As to this provision, social security protection is based on factual

13 Ruling of the Federal Court Bundesgerichtshof in matters of civil law BGHZ 111, 303.
14 Ruling of the Federal Labour Court BAG AP Nr. 3/4 zu § 19 AFG.

employment, and not necessarily on a formal employment contract.[15] Thus, under social security law, all work is treated as work, irrespective of its formality or informality or a legal justification.

4. Incomplete Social Security Protection by Law

A genuine insufficiency of social security protection results from the law itself. As social security is organised as a protection embedded in an employment relationship, the economic or social character of the employment should be appropriate for sufficient protection. There are shortcomings in protection above all for those whose labour market participation is far below the average standard of regular work, and above all for those who do work as self-employed workers without their own employees. If they do not belong to a specific category of protected persons (e.g. craftsmen, peasants, artists, economically dependent self-employed persons or members of the liberal profession), their protection is quite often insufficient.

In the light of a strategy in which social security plays a pivotal role to safeguard social justice in the context of a fair globalisation,[16] social security is to be regarded and acknowledged as a basic human right, which does not jeopardise but substantially strengthens the economic potential. In this context, the extension of social protection to all persons doing paid work irrespective of if this work is to be characterised as dependent or independent is a key task for the legislator, as all endeavours are required to make social security sustainable to meet the needs of beneficiaries in the future. As long as formal and informal work ends in fundamental differences as to social security protection, measures have to be taken and a reform is urgent. If social security is a human right, both dependent and independent workers require protection. This mission is not adequately accomplished as long as the differences in the costs of protection are not equally distributed for employees and the self-employed. The latter are not adequately protected as long as they have to pay the employee's and the employer's half of the contributions to social security altogether, because this makes the protection for the self-employed too expensive.

15 A Marschner, '§ 7' in R Kreikebohm (ed), *SGB IV* (C.H. Beck 2008) Rn. 3; Dankelmann in E Eichenhofer and U Wenner (eds), *Kommentar zum Sozialgesetzbuch I IV X* (Luchterhand 2012) § 7 SGB IV Rn. 2 ff.

16 ILO, *Social Security for social justice and a fair globalization* (n 1); E Eichenhofer, *Sozialer Schutz unter den Bedingungen der Globalisierung* (Berliner Wissenschafts-Verlag 2009).

5. Social Security Problems Emerging from Multiple Work Relations

Precarious work quite often unleashes a working life built upon more than one employment relation. So, multiple work relations expand, and hand in hand with this expansion, precarious work also grows in economic life. This has substantial consequences for social security relations, as they are traditionally built upon the normal employment relation, which is implicitly conceived as single employment. The topic is dealt with specifically in EU social security law and it raises some unsolved problems in domestic law.

Article 13(1) (b) and 13(2) (b) of Regulation (EC) 883/2004 on the coordination of social security systems provides that if a person – employed or self-employed – is active at the same period of time in more than one – dependent or independent – employment, the law of the member state applies in which the employment of the higher economic importance is carried out. This rule, valid since 1 May 2010, replaces the previous rule as to which joint employments are covered by the law of the member state of the person's residence.

Also in domestic social security law, multiple work relations are palpable and showcase subtle legal questions which are not yet tackled in a very convincing manner. This can be illustrated by a series of German Federal Social Court judgments enacted in the last years, which make it difficult to identify a clear position. If a work accident happened in one employment and the injury hinders the worker to do her or his second employment as well, the question to be dealt with is which social insurances are competent to compensate the double loss of remuneration. As to the case law of the Federal Social Court, the work accidents scheme has to replace the loss of income in all respects, if the by-laws of the accidents insurance scheme have such a proviso[17]. If this is not the case, the work accident's scheme is restricted to compensating the loss of income in the work relation in which the work accident took place[18].

If this injury renders it difficult for a worker to do the second job, the compensation should be borne by the health insurance from the second employment, in the lack of by-laws. And finally, if the incapacity resulting from the work accident is restored by measures of rehabilitation and training, whereas the incapacity for doing the second job remains unchanged, it is up to the work accidents scheme to compensate this loss of income by a pension, because it is induced by the work

17 Bundessozialgericht (BSG) 14.12.1995 2 RU 2/95 4.12.1991 2RU 76/90.

18 BSG 4.12.2015 B 3 KR 3/15 R.

accident whilst doing the first employment.[19] So, the rules lack coherence and consistency. They are even more confusing and quite far from being sufficiently clear.

6. Social Protection for Low Paid Employees

6.1 Minimal Jobs

Employees who earn less than 450 euros a month in Germany before taxes and social security contributions, and who are active in the labour market for less than 15 hours a week, have no social security status under German law.[20] Nevertheless, the employee does have to pay contributions and taxes. The employer has to deduct 12 per cent of the salary which goes to health care insurance, and a further two per cent for taxes. Another 15 per cent can be paid to the pension insurance, if the employee would like this. Low salaries bring about low pension rights, as the amount of a pension right corresponds to the proportional share of the earned salary in relation to the average salary. This problem is also relevant for zero hours contracts and on-call work – if the latter is limited to its size – and the work done by volunteers. In all these circumstances, the question is whether sufficient social protection can mature on the basis of a meagre participation in paid work. It can be observed that a minimal job can be utilized with the consensus of both employer and employee to deprive the latter from basic social security protection.

The question whether these provisions concur with the EU rules on gender discrimination was tried before the Court of Justice of the European Union (CJEU). The Court held that an indirect discrimination based on gender could not be observed: Despite the fact that the provision affects more women than men, it can be objectively justified that less work participation comes with a lower inclusion in social protection schemes.[21] From a political point of view, the exemption can be criticised because it gives premiums for splitting normal workplaces into

19 BSG 23.7.2015 B 2 U 6/14 R.

20 Section 8 Social Code Book IV and section 5 Social Code Book VI; C Rolfs, R Giesen, R Kreikebohm, P Udsching (eds), *Sozialrecht sgb IV; X SGG: Schwerpunktkommentar Sozialrecht* (C.H. Beck 2007) § 8 SGB IV Rn. 3 ff; Critical from a political point of view G Bäcker, G Bosch, C Weinkopf, *Vorschläge zur künftigen Arbeitsmarktpolitik: integrativ – investiv – innovativ.* (Gutachten für das Thüringer Ministerium für Wirtschaft, Technologie und Arbeit, 2011); R Waltermann *Abschied vom Normalarbeitsverhältnis* (Gutachten B zum 68. Deutschen Juristentag C.H. Beck 2010) B 9 f, B 27 f, B 110 f, Thesen 3 and 4.

21 Judgment of 14 December 1995, *Megner and Scheffel*, C-444/93, EU:C:1995:442 (1995 ECR) I-4741.

minimal ones and, thus, dismantles the social protection of many workers. From this perspective, the omission of low paid workers is assumed to be paradoxical, because it denies social protection to the most vulnerable members of the workforce. On the other hand, the result is that a substantial protection under social security depends on any substantial labour market participation. Otherwise a free rider problem could emerge that workers could earn substantial protection in health insurance for a small contribution. If the latter is lacking, the first cannot be achieved. On the basis of this observation, special programmes are required for the social protection of those people who work in sheltered employment or in workfare programmes. If they do not substantially contribute to the primary labour market due to their disabilities, unemployment or other social risks, a specific social policy strategy in favour of them is needed in order to compensate their lack in work potential.

6.2 Social Protection for Self-Employed Persons

As the formative principles of social security date back to the late 19th century, its provisions were primarily addressed to the fully paid male dependent worker. Therefore, a reduced participation in the labour market results in social security shortcomings and deficits. This full-time workers' orientation also neglected the self-employed. They were conceived as self-reliant persons who do not depend on any social protection. This historic legacy of a dependent, working class oriented Bismarckian approach to social protection is still vivid in the second decade of the 21st century. So, since the very beginning, only a small and limited group of the self-employed (coastal fisher- or boatmen, teachers, midwives and subcontractors working in their own work environment) were formally integrated into the social security system. These groups were accepted as vulnerable as the dependent workers. The public employees with a life-time commitment and a specific employment status which incorporates social security protection by the employer, are abandoned from formal inclusion into the general social security system as well, due to their protection having been organised and safeguarded by the state in its role as employer.

In a later phase, independent craftsmen, peasants, artists and economically dependent self-employed persons were covered in the general social security system or, as peasants, in a special scheme. For all the members of the liberal professions – above all medical doctors, dentists, barristers, notaries and architects – specific systems of protection for disability, old age and survivors were put in place. They find their legal basis in the laws made by the professional chambers, to which the liberal professionals adhere on a mandatory basis. In these systems, the employed members of the professional chambers are also integrated.

This feature illustrates the profoundly conservative character of the continental social security system, according to which a highly different and stratified system of social protection emerged.[22] In such an environment, a series of loopholes in protection comes into existence. At the same time, the social security organised in the context of each social protection system is restricted to certain groups within the workforce, whereas other groups stand apart. The neglect of social protection becomes evident in respect of new types of self-employment, which do not fit in the traditional forms. So the outcome is a selective system of social protection – in which different circles and levels exist and stand together in a completely uncoordinated manner.

This view is embedded in a late 19th century perspective of the industrial work society, which is no longer adequate for the working life of the 21st century.[23] With the growing expansion of a service-oriented economy, self-employment fits more and more with the demands of such an economic environment. Independent, i.e. target-oriented work, replaces dependent work more and more, and at the same time, dependent work tends to be replaced by internet-based machines. In such a working life, independent work gains ground and leads to meagre returns and inadequate health and safety protection of the self-employed workers. This deficit is becoming a topic of growing interest.

A system based on profound distinctions between the self-employed and the dependent workers becomes inappropriate in a world of paid labour in which traditional borderlines blur and, at the same time, frequent transitions between different legal forms of work occur. Above all, para-subordination becomes widespread among the self-employed. Such an approach is therefore not only inconsistent and incoherent, but also highly fragmented. Above all, people who work as salesmen or -women or self-employed workers in a new post-craftsmanship profession, which is simultaneously not classified as a classical liberal profession, are quite often free of any social protection. They are self-reliant and look quite frequently for protection by private insurance schemes. But as this protection is voluntary, one can quite often note lacks and deficits in protection, due to the high costs of private insurance on the one hand, and low or instable incomes of the self-employed on the other hand. There is a political debate on whether the German

22 G Esping –Andersen, *The three worlds of welfare capitalism* (Princeton University Press 1990).

23 A Supiot, *L'esprit de Philadelphie. La justice sociale face au marché total* (Seuil 2010).

social insurance scheme should be expanded to all persons who are self-employed and who do not employ any employees themselves.[24] Within the German system of social insurance for independent artists (*Künstlersozialversicherung*), a specific approach can be identified to give the artists social protection on the same conditions as a worker, and replace the employers' share of the contribution for workers by a special contribution imposed on those who draw economically personal profit from the artist's work.

6.3 Evasion from Social Protection by Contracting Out

This debate touches a sensitive issue as there is a growing move to evade the status of employees by virtue of specific contracts and transform the worker into the status of an unprotected self-employed worker.[25] Efforts undertaken by the legislator to outlaw those contracts turned out to become both inefficient and insufficient. The orthodox approach is to identify a labour relation on the basis of the 'real nature' test. This turns out to become difficult in reality.[26] This is because the freedom of contract implies the right, and so allows the enshrined legal possibility, of bringing about dependent work contracts as well as contracts between two self-employed persons. It is not a necessity that work to be done by one person for another should find its basis in a work contract. Above all, in the service economy, the peculiar conditions in service providing allow the negotiating parties to merely agree on both dependent and independent service delivery – without any substantial outcome on the circumstances of service delivery. If the service provider has such a freedom to decide how to do his or her work, if – above all – the provision of the services is defined as a result to be brought about by the provider and not as an obligation to follow the instructions of the recipient of the service, it lies in the logic of the contract concluded to conceive the latter as a contract *for* services (meaning that the worker is self-employed) and no longer as a contract *of* service (meaning that he or she is an employee). As the determination of the legal character is to be made by the contracting parties alone, it is quite often also the joint intention of both the service recipient and the service provider to find an agreement on the basis of a contract for services. The service

---

24 F Ruland, 'Ausbau der Rentenversicherung zu einer allgemeinen Erwerbstätigenversicherung?' in U Becker, H G Hockerts, K Tenfelde and B Dietz (eds), *Sozialstaat Deutschland* (Dietz 2010) 297.

25 E Eichenhofer, 'Ist die Abgrenzung des versicherten Personenkreises im deutschen Sozialversicherungsrecht zeitgemäß?' (2009) 64 Deutsche Rentenversicherung 293.

26 Wilson, 'Precarious Work' (n 9) 4.

provider loses his or her protection, but both partners are free from the commitment to pay contributions. Finally, by choosing this type of contract, the service provider gains a much higher range of autonomy in his or her work. There is a rapid and growing tendency towards leaving contracts of service, which are made intentionally to get rid of the employer's commitment to pay social security contributions and, at the same time, to increase the autonomy of the employed. The proposal had been submitted in order to undermine those windfall profits by making appropriate contracts.[27] In the 1990s, Austria integrated self-employed persons without their own employees into social security on a mandatory basis. Such a strategy is needed to close coverage gaps, and reduces the incentive to formally opt out from the social security systems – an option that can undermine the legitimacy of the system as a whole.

7. Social Protection for New Forms of Paid Work

7.1 The Neutral and Open Notion of Employment in Social Security Law

Seen from a social security law perspective, the new forms of paid labour: part-time, short- or fixed-term contracts, intermittent, zero hours or on-call work, are to be conceived as employment. Thus, they constitute a sufficient basis for social security. Their deviations from standard labour contracts as to their workload, stability over time and split as to the employers' rights raise problems as to the protective stance of labour law. But when it comes to social security, the characteristics of 'atypical work' in the context of labour law do not make them 'atypical' under social security law, as the latter is in profound contrast to the first. It treats all types of substantial dependent labour alike.

27 H Rische, 'Weiterentwicklung der gesetzlichen Rentenversicherung zu einer Erwerbstätigenversicherung' (2009) 64 Deutsche Rentenversicherung 285; E Eichenhofer 'Ist die Abgrenzung des versicherten Personenkreises im deutschen Sozialversicherungsrecht zeitgemäß? (n 27) 293; D Döring, 'Versicherungspflichtregelung in der gesetzlichen Rentenversicherung und Erwerbstätigkeit' (2009) 64 Deutsche Rentenversicherung 309; H-J Reinhard, 'Modelle der Erwerbstätigensicherung in Europa' (2009) 64 Deutsche Rentenversicherung 319; A Wallrabenstein, 'Verfassungsrechtliche Aspekte einer Erwerbstätigenversicherung' (2009) 64 Deutsche Rentenversicherung 329; R Kreikebohm, 'Die Erwerbstätigenversicherung aus beitragsrechtlicher Sicht' (2009) 64 Deutsche Rentenversicherung 336.

7.2 Economic Implications of Precarious Work

Despite the fact that the social security concept of employment is broad and open enough to encompass all new forms of atypical substantial dependent paid work, the economic consequences of these new forms jeopardize social protection. Due to low, unsteady, or insubstantial work participation – all of which translates to shortcomings in protection above all in old age, disability, survivors' pensions, and also protection by benefits in cash for social risks such as sickness, motherhood or paternity, work accidents, professionally caused diseases or unemployment – precarious work as far as it is not enough to secure a living wage as a minimum of existence for the worker and her or his family in economic terms, is not an appropriate base for adequate social protection.

7.3 Effects of Low Payment to Social Assistance

Economically precarious work also has an impact on social assistance, as it also offers protection for persons able to work. If the remuneration of workers is below the threshold of social assistance payments to the able-bodied and their family members, low or disruptive wages are to be supplemented by additional social assistance payments to fill the gap between insufficient earnings acquired by precarious work and the social minimum, if the latter exceeds the income earned on the labour market. In this arrangement, the basic needs of the worker are met; not by a living wage, but by complementary social assistance payments. From a legal point of view, this consequence is, however, problematic. Those subsidies to the low paid workers also subsidise their employers. By avoiding the payment of sufficient salaries, the employers shift the financial load for an adequate living wage from themselves onto the public purse. In such an arrangement, low paying employers win to the detriment and expense of adequately paying employers. Social assistance benefits implicitly and supplement low wages, against their function. This is conceived as an unfair distortion of the labour market.

8. Social Protection for Non-Paid Family Work

Further shortcomings in social protection become visible in the work unilaterally done on the basis of family commitments. Both child rearing and the long-term care for frail and elderly parents or other relatives – mostly done by women – raise the question on how such work can be integrated into social security law – above all on how to give the service providers access to social security rights. The German legislation of the last decades emphasises family work as being equivalent to paid work as far as their social security effects are concerned.

So, child-rearing periods are acknowledged in the legal context of pension law.[28] Under these provisions, a parent, who raises a new born child for three years, is dealt with as if he or she worked for three years and earned the average income of all insured persons. If the parent combined child-rearing in the first three years of the child's life with paid work, the pension rights emerging from employment are added to those acquired by child-rearing. This credit is, according to the Federal Constitutional Court, also to be maintained untouched if a parent earns additional credits out of work.[29] The costs for this protection are borne by the federal budget, which pays a substantial share of subsidies to the pension insurance as financial compensation for the protection awarded to parents. Parents who are not actively employed because they are rearing a child or children below ten years of age, are treated as if they were employed for the calculation of the pension rights acquired by doing paid work during a whole life span.[30] In the context of long-term care insurance, not only persons in urgent need of care are covered, but also those who give care to needy others. As the latter are entitled to a benefit in cash, which is meant to be transferred to the caregiver, the first are to be insured by long-term care insurance for the risks of disability, old age and for survivors. The protection corresponds to the range of engagements the carer invests in the long-term care of the entitled needy person. The same type of protection is given in the context of work accident and unemployment insurance. In this respect, long-term care insurance is also a means to give the caregiver an accompanying social protection.

9. Conclusion

Precarious work has far-reaching consequences for social security protection. They require attention from a legal and an economic point of view. From a legal perspective, the exclusion of self-employment from protection under social security law is sensitive, and as it incorporates an opt-out potential within the system of social security, it might undermine the sustainability of the system in general and at large. So, to include both dependent and independent workers into the social security protection would not only close gaps in support, but would also stabilise the system as a whole.

From an economic point of view, growing disparities in remuneration and increasing inequalities in wages are translated into social security with divergent

28 Section 56 Social Code Book VI.

29 BVerfGE (decisions of the Federal Constitutional Court) 94, 241.

30 Berücksichtigungszeiten section 57 of Social Code Book VI.

benefits. Loopholes in protection stem from discontinuous labour relationships. Poverty in old age is the predictable outcome, if low wages are pervasive, and unemployed beneficiaries are not sufficiently protected against the social security outcomes of periods of life not spent in paid work. A diminishing protection under social security law leads, finally, to a non-intended increase of social assistance law.

The prospect, however, that social assistance would compensate the losses of protection under social security law might lead to the question of whether, from the perspective of fair competition, the public has to bear the social consequences of inadequate protection of work by labour and social security law. Since its very beginning, social security should provide people with better protection than they would get under social assistance. Precarious work substantially weakens this function of social security. If social security cannot find appropriate answers to this challenge, it will become difficult to uphold it at large. So, to also endow precarious workers with adequate protection requires rapid and solid answers and substantial and thought-through structural reforms of social security law.

III. New Forms of Labour Mobility

Judy Fudge

Domestic Work, Mobility and Labour Law: Challenging Borders

1. Introduction

Who do you see in your mind's eye when you conjure up an image of a worker? Our image reflects how work is understood and valued at a particular time and in a specific place. In advanced industrial countries, our normative worker will likely have shifted from a male manufacturing worker who predominated from the mid-1940s to the mid-1970s, to a female nurse or teacher in the 1980s and to the men and women who work today as call centre workers and delivery drivers. Who we consider to be a worker tends to map on to one of the key players in labour law – the employee. This congruence is because labour law tends to function as a cognitive map in identifying what work is economically valuable and deserving of protection.[1]

In 2011, the International Labour Conference disrupted the prevailing cognitive map of labour law by adopting a Convention and Recommendation concerning decent work for domestic workers that placed the regulation of paid employment within private household squarely into the domain of labour law.[2] The Convention recognizes 'the significant contribution of domestic workers to the global economy, which includes increasing paid job opportunities for women and men workers with family responsibilities, greater scope for caring for aging populations, children and persons with a disability, and substantial income transfers within and between countries'.[3] It also acknowledges 'domestic work continues to be undervalued and invisible and is mainly carried out by women and girls, many of whom are migrants or members of disadvantaged communities

---

1 J Fudge, 'Feminist Reflections on the Scope of Labour Law: Domestic Work, Social Reproduction, and Jurisdiction' (2014) 22 Feminist Legal Studies 1.

2 Domestic Workers Convention, 2011 (No. 189), Convention concerning decent work for domestic workers (Entry into force: 05 Sep 2013) Adoption: Geneva, 100th ILC session (16 Jun 2011); Domestic Workers Recommendation, 2011 (No. 201) Recommendation concerning Decent Work for Domestic Workers Adoption: Geneva, 100th ILC session (16 Jun 2011).

3 Convention 189, preamble.

and who are particularly vulnerable to discrimination in respect of conditions of employment and of work, and to other abuses of human rights'.[4]

That domestic work has for so long been considered to be at the periphery of labour law is remarkable in light of the fact of the sheer numbers of domestic workers who are employed around the globe. Domestic work is a large – and in some countries growing – sector of employment, especially for women. Using conservative measures, the International Labour Organization (ILO) estimates that the number of domestic workers increased from 33.2 million in 1995 to 52.6 million in 2010 – or 3.6 per cent of global wage employment.[5] In order to get a sense of just how big this sector is, consider that this figure is greater than the number of people employed in large countries such as Mexico or Nigeria. The ILO notes that 'if all domestic workers worked in one country, this country would be the tenth largest employer world wide'.[6]

This chapter focuses on migrant domestic workers in order to explore what they tell us about both the past and future of labour law. It unfolds in four parts, beginning with an explanation of how the terms domestic work and domestic workers are to be used. The second part draws on feminist labour law and political economy literature in order to establish that domestic work, whether paid or unpaid, performed for others in the household is not only valuable, but a critical component of labour markets and essential to sustaining society itself.[7] In the third part, migrant domestic workers are used to illustrate how immigration law regulates labour markets in a globalized market economy. By focusing on migrant status and cross-border mobility, I want to emphasize both the differential inclusion of workers into citizenship regimes, understood broadly as assemblages of social and political rights and entitlements, on the basis of gender, race, and ethnicity, and the problem of regarding the authority of labour law as coterminous with the nation state. The implications of recognizing migrant domestic workers as a central subject of labour law are considered in the fourth part. My argument is that if we treat migrant domestic workers as central protagonists in labour law rather than as shadowy figures on its margins, we need to re-evaluate the foundations of labour law.

---

4 ibid.

5 ILO, *Domestic Workers Across the World: Global and regional statistics and the extent of legal protection* (International Labour Office 2013) 19.

6 ibid.

7 N Busby, *The Right to Care: Unpaid Care Work in European Employment Law* (Oxford University Press 2011).

2. Defining Domestic Work and Identifying Domestic Workers

Nomenclature is important when it comes to identifying and defining domestic work, which is replete with racial and class hierarchies.[8] Domestic work has been used to denote menial work, such as cleaning and housekeeping, whereas care work has been valorised as affective or 'mother's' work.[9] However, within feminist political economy literature, care is broadly defined to include 'nuturant care and other social reproduction activities', which also includes 'forms of household and domestic labour'.[10] Evelyn Nakano Glenn describes caring labour as involving 'three kinds of intertwined activities': direct caring for the person, 'maintaining the immediate physical surroundings/milieu in which people live', and 'fostering people's relationships and social connection'.[11] She explains that these different activities can be organized in a myriad of different ways; they can be performed for money, love or duty; by strangers, family members or friends; in the household or in institutions; and as a public service or for private profit.[12]

Although domestic work is often regarded as a subset of the broader category of care work, legal scholar Adelle Blackett treats the two terms as equivalents in order to contest both the radicalized hierarchies associated with, and the relative skill levels attributed to, domestic and care work. Similarly, the definition of domestic workers in the ILO Convention on Domestic Workers does not define domestic work in terms of the specific tasks or services performed by domestic workers. Instead, it focuses on the institutional setting in which the work is performed, the private household, and the nature of the arrangement, an employment relationship, under which the work is performed.[13] This industry-based definition is narrower in scope than an activity-based definition, as it excludes workers who provide care services in institutions such as orphanages, kindergartens, hospitals and old-age retirement homes, which are part of the broader care economy. It also excludes domestic workers who are not employed directly by the household,

---

8 A Blackett, 'Introduction: Regulating Decent Work for Domestic Workers' (2011) 23 Canadian Journal of Women and the Law 1, 3, 14.

9 ibid 1 referring to D Roberts, 'Spiritual and Menial Housework' (1997) 9 Yale Journal of Law and Feminism 51.

10 R Mahon and F Robinson (eds), *Feminist Ethics and Social Policy: Towards a New Global Political Economy of Care* (UBC Press 2011) 1.

11 E Nakano Glenn, *Forced to Care: Coercion and Caregiving in America* (Harvard University Press 2010) 5.

12 ibid.

13 ILO Convention 189 (n 2) Article 1.

but instead have a contract of employment with a service agency.[14] Because it emphasizes the existence of an employment relationship, the ILO definition also excludes family members who provide the same set of tasks for other members of the household without direct remuneration, as well as a 'person who performs domestic work only occasionally or sporadically and not on an occupational basis'.[15]

On the basis of this definition, the ILO found that domestic work is a large – and in some countries growing – sector of employment, especially for women. Women accounted for about 83 per cent of counted domestic workers in 2010.[16] Most strikingly, domestic work accounts for 7.5 per cent of women's wage employment worldwide, and a far greater share in some regions. In the Middle East, one out of three female waged employees is a domestic worker, and in Latin America and the Caribbean the figure is one in four.[17]

These figures raise the question of why it is that women and not men perform the overwhelming bulk of domestic work. Many factors lead women to enter domestic work. Women from poor households or disadvantaged communities often have few employment opportunities, and may face discrimination based on gender, caste, race or ethnicity. Cleaning, cooking, and caring for children and the elderly is almost universally regarded as women's work, so men rarely compete in this job market. Low levels of education and few marketable skills also play a role in explaining why women turn to domestic work, although some domestic workers who migrate from places such as the Philippines and Eastern Europe have medium or high levels of education.[18]

Domestic work is generally poorly paid, lacks clear boundaries that separate personal from working time, and falls outside the scope of labour law and social protection in many countries. Since domestic workers are employed in private homes rather than firms or enterprises, they tend to be invisible as workers and isolated from other workers in the sector. The widespread perception that labour standards cannot be enforced in the private home means many employers do not comply with and the government does not enforce labour laws regarding wages, benefits and working conditions. Domestic workers often have a personal, intimate knowledge of their employers, but the relationship is highly unequal, leaving many domestic workers vulnerable to verbal, physical, or sexual abuse.[19]

14 ILO, *Domestic Workers Across the World* (n 5) 10.
15 Convention 189 (n 2) Article 1.
16 ILO, *Domestic Workers Across the World* (n 5), 19.
17 ibid. 19, 21.
18 ILO, *Domestic Workers Across the World* (n 5) 21–24.
19 Blackett, 'Introduction: Regulating Decent Work for Domestic Workers' (n 8) 41.

Often differences in race, class and citizenship increase this inequality.[20] Moreover, domestic work's roots in coercive and status-based forms of labour, most notably chattel slavery and menial service, reinforce the view that domestic work is not employment.[21]

3. Social Reproduction and Labour Markets

Care and domestic work figure prominently in social reproduction, the term used by feminist political economists and labour lawyers to refer to the assemblage of processes supporting the daily and generational reproduction of human life. Social reproduction includes activities as diverse as domestic cleaning, family, health, sexual and religious care and education that is provided in a wide range of settings, such as the home, hospitals, hospices, churches, schools and brothels, across many different contexts, including individualized and private settings and institutionalized state and market locations. It comprises the human capacities available to create and maintain social bonds, which includes the work of socializing the young, building communities, and reproducing shared meanings, affective dispositions and horizons of value that underpin social cooperation, as well as the tasks of daily provisioning.[22]

Social reproduction provides what the social theorist Nancy Fraser calls the 'conditions of possibility' or the social basis upon which capitalism depends.[23] Like every social system, capitalism imposes a specific relationship between the production of goods and services and the social reproduction of the population. What distinguishes capitalism is the tendency towards the separation of the key site of social reproduction (the household) from productive relations (the workplace). This separation of production from reproduction gives rise to an essential contradiction in capitalist societies – the conflict between the standard of living of workers and the drive for accumulation, which is the need to make profits.[24]

20 Glenn, *Forced to Care* (n 11).

21 Blackett, 'Introduction: Regulating Decent Work for Domestic Workers' (n 8) 41; Glenn, *Forced to Care* (n 11).

22 J Fudge 'A New Vocabulary and Imaginary for Labour Law: Taking Legal Constitution, Gender, and Social Reproduction Seriously', in D Brodie, N Busby and R Zahn (eds), *The Future Regulation of Work: New Concepts, New Paradigms* (Palgrave 2016) 19–20.

23 N Fraser, 'Feminism's Home Front' (2016) 100 New Left Review 99, 100.

24 J Fudge and B Cossman, 'Privatization, Law and the Challenge to Feminism.' In B Cossman and J Fudge (eds) *Privatization, Law and the Challenge to Feminism* (University of Toronto Press 2002); A Piccho, *Social Reproduction: The Political Economy of the Labour Market* (Cambridge University Press 1992).

Moreover, since capitalism changes over time and across space, the boundaries between social reproduction and production, or more specifically between society and economy, work and family, are both contested and changing.[25] Fraser identifies at least three general regimes of 'social reproduction cum economic production in capitalism's history', and these are liberal competitive capitalism, state managed capitalism and globalized financial capitalism.[26] Each of these regimes institutionalizes a gender order.[27] Every gender order encompasses a gendered division of labour between social reproduction and production, which is sustained through gender norms and social arrangements that are achieved at particular times and in particular places. The gender order is stable to the extent that it has been institutionalized in certain key sites such as the family, labour market, firms, schools and state policies. For this to be achieved, there must be a set of shared understandings, practices and policies about the appropriate roles and expectations of men and women, as well as some fit, however temporary, fragile and incomplete, between the processes of reproduction and production.[28]

Prior to the development of markets for labour, the relationship of subordinated labour was treated as one of status in the United Kingdom. According to William Blackstone's authoritative 1765 treatise, *Commentaries on the Laws of England,* the relationship of master and servant, along with that of father and child and wife and husband, was marked not by equality and freedom, but by paternalism and dependence.[29] Throughout the history of the poor law, married women were treated as economically dependent upon their husbands, with little independent access to poor relief.[30]

Britain in the eighteenth and nineteenth centuries exemplified competitive liberal capitalism. With the advent of large-scale industrialization, master and servant status relations gradually (and incompletely) gave way to contract as the

25 See also D Alessandrini, *Value Making in International Law and Regulation: Alternative Possibilities* (Routledge 2016) 38–39.

26 Fraser 'Feminism's Home Front' (n 23) 104.

27 Gendering is a process in which social significance is attached to sexual difference which, in turn, structures organizations, affects social and political relationships, and becomes intrinsic to the construction of significant social categories and political identities. Fudge and Cossman, 'Privatization, Law and the Challenge to Feminism' (n 24).

28 ibid.

29 W Blackstone, *Commentaries on the Laws of England: A Facsimile of the First Edition of 1765–1769* (University of Chicago Press 1979).

30 S Deakin and F Wilkinson, *The Law of the Labour Market: Industrialization, Employment, and Legal Evolution* (Oxford University Press 2005) Ch 3; S Fredman, *Women and the Law* (Oxford University Press 1997) Chs 2 and 3.

predominant legal device for regulating the allocation and control of labour.[31] The household began to be separated from the worksite, and the wage became the key source of income for those who did not own property. This process of marketization simultaneously undermined older forms of protection and emancipated workers from paternalism.[32]

The concept of contract was crucial for the development of markets. The gradual extension of civil rights to property-less men in the eighteenth century enabled them to enter into contracts and to enforce their promises. The employment contract became the primary means for men to obtain access to the means of subsistence. However, married women were incapable of entering into contracts. The legal doctrine of coverture ensured that status and patriarchy continued as the form of regulation for the 'private, intimate and affective space of the home'.[33] Outside the household, on the market, the new legal taxonomy for 'productive work' – the employment contract – complemented and partially supplanted master and servant law. Unlike men, who as servants or employees surrendered their capacities only temporarily, married women were permanently dependents, as they were not considered to be 'proprietors of their own capacities' and therefore dependent upon the 'wills of others'.[34]

In the late nineteenth and early twentieth centuries, as men's wages improved through collective economic and political action, laws, regulations, and workplace practices excluded women from paid employment, confining them to the household, where they were responsible for domestic labour.[35] Moreover, 'as wages became the dominant mode of recognizing and rewarding labour, women's unpaid domestic contribution began to disappear as real work'.[36] Despite the abolition of coverture in the late nineteenth century, the embrace of more intensive production techniques along with 'Taylorist' organization of labour processes

---

31 Deakin and Wilkinson, *The Law of the Labour Market* (n 30) 107.

32 N Fraser, 'A Triple Movement? Parsing the Politics of Crisis after Polanyi' (2013) 81 New Left Review 119.

33 J Halley and K Rittich, 'Critical Directions in Comparative Family Law: Genealogies and Contemporary Studies of Family Law Exceptionalism' (2010) 58 The American Journal of Comparative Law 753, 757.

34 U Gerhard, T Knijn and J Lewis, 'Contractualization' in B Hobson, J Lewis and B Siim (eds) *Contested Concepts in Gender and Social Politics* (Edward Elgar 2002) 105, 108, quoting J Locke, *Two Treatises of Government* (first published 1690, Cambridge University Press, 1970) section 79, 337–8.

35 C Pateman, *The Sexual Contract* (Polity Press 1988) 2.

36 W Seccombe, *A Millennium of Family Change* (Verso 1992) 244.

made it increasingly difficult for women to combine childbearing with paid work. Middle-class norms of marriage, family and domesticity gained social currency. The family and household came to be associated with love, while the workplace was associated with money, obscuring the extent to which marriage and cohabitation with men was an economic necessity for most women and the degree to which legal inequality was inscribed within marriage and the family. The home and family were normatively, if not actually, constructed as a haven from work and the market, governed by affective relations.[37] The assumption, which was not necessarily borne out in practice, was that there was equal sharing within the household.[38] Androcentric views of work and contribution were entrenched in work and social security legislation.[39]

In the metropole, poor and working class women, unlike their middle class counterparts, could not rely on a male wage that could ensure the subsistence of economically dependent household members. They worked as servants or scraped an existence on the periphery of the labour market or as sex workers and prostitutes. In the periphery, colonialism subjugated indigenous populations, either destroying their social reproduction through the devastating 'Indian' wars of North and South America or incorporating social reproduction into the brutal North American slave trade. English settlers used various forms of coerced labour including African chattel slavery, white indentured servitude and convict labour, to develop the economy of pre-Revolutionary America.[40] Over the seventeenth century, the status of slaves and those of indentured servants were distinguished and radicalized, as slavery was limited to Black people and Native Americans while white indenture declined after the American revolution.[41] With the abolition of the slave trade, in 1807, control over the social reproduction of slaves became a paramount concern. An integral part of coercive labour was the appropriation of caring labour.[42] Poor, Black and immigrant women were coerced into care for others.

Liberal competitive capitalism collapsed in the first decades of the twentieth century in the face of inter-imperialist wars, economic depressions and

---

37 K Silbaugh, 'Turning Labor into Love: Housework and the Law' (1996) 91 North Western University Law Review 1.

38 G Becker, *The Economic Approach to Human Behavior* (University of Chicago Press 1976).

39 Fredman, *Women and the Law* (n 30).

40 Glenn, *Forced to Care* (n 11) 25.

41 ibid 26.

42 ibid 36.

international financial chaos.[43] After the crisis of World War II, state-managed capitalism resolved the contradiction between production and social reproduction by actively intervening in and supporting social reproduction. Most democratic capitalist countries adopted the Keynesian economic and welfarist social policies, which supported a stable and enduring gender order, composed of a male breadwinner and female housewife. This gender order depended upon providing high wages and secure employment to men. Tax, labour, family and social welfare law supported this arrangement, and trade barriers created protected enclaves for developed industrial economies. A virtuous circle of consumption and production was created as men's wages were linked to productivity increases. Fordist productive relations went hand in hand with social welfare, and industrial unions ensured that the social compact was respected. Collective bargaining was generally the preferred technique for limiting the commodification of labour.

Yet, despite the inclusion of male workers in the core and the expansion of citizenship rights to include a range of social benefits, state-managed capitalism differentially included other workers within the core from social protection while simultaneously excluding workers in the periphery. Married women's economic reliance on their husbands was actively constructed by law through a combination of carrots (the male breadwinner wage) and sticks (married women's disentitlement to unemployment insurance).[44] In the United States (US), racial hierarchies and exclusions further undermined social citizenship. Moreover, high tariff barriers and value extracted by foreign direct investment meant that the states of former colonies were not able to provide social protection to their populations.

In developed economies after World War II, employment and the family were sharply separated and regulated by their own distinctive technologies. The boundaries between home/market and public/private became deeply inscribed in contemporary legal doctrines, discourses and institutions such that the initial jurisdictional classification appeared natural and inevitable and not political and ideological. The background legal rules – tax, labour, tort, family, and welfare law – that shaped and maintained (constituted) specific family structures receded into the background, and the jurisdiction of family law came to be regarded as a uniquely appropriate way of dealing with the 'special' relations of family.[45] A particular form of the family (male breadwinner with a dependent housewife) was regarded as a natural artefact outside of law.

43 Fraser, 'Feminism's Home Front' (n 23) 108.

44 Fredman, *Women and the Law* (n 30); Deakin and Wilkinson, *The Law of the Labour Market* (n 30) 157 ff.

45 Halley and Rittich (n 33) 757.

Law operated as a gendering process, constituting 'male' and 'female' subject positions and contributing to identity formation. It is one of a range of practices, like education, 'through which gender is acquired, a process of which gender and gender differences are an effect'.[46] The terrain of work is legally constituted and regulated through the creation and deployment of distinctions such as public and private, work and family, and production and reproduction.[47] Once these distinctions are in place, the history of their active construction melts into air, and the legal institutions, such as the employment contract, which are central to constituting different forms of work, come to be seen as neutral devices that facilitate voluntary choices. Women are seen as choosing to assume domestic responsibilities as wives and mothers, rather than being channelled into these roles through the lack of alternative options. If women work for wages, employers are under no obligation to design employment arrangements to accommodate their 'private responsibilities'. Part-time and casual work enable married women to engage in waged employment, but these arrangements, which are often poorly paid and insecure, reinforce their economic dependence on men. The fundaments of the contract of employment are designed for workers who do not have to shoulder the bulk of care responsibilities, and the fact that women's employment arrangements deviate from the 'standard' employment contract is regarded as justifying their different, and detrimental, treatment.

State managed capitalism reached its apogee in the late 1970s when it was confronted with stagflation, a 'productivity' crisis, and declining profitability. Retreating from social protection, states in the advanced economies embraced marketization in the form of privatization and neo-liberal economic and social policies. During the 1970s, men's wages in the core capitalist countries no longer continued to increase as they had done since the end of World War II, and the participation of married women in paid employment began to rise dramatically, although there was no matching rise in men's participation in unpaid household work. The legacy of the unequal division of labour, which was shaped and channelled by legal and social institutions, continued to influence women's employment arrangements, as did the legacy of sex-based job segregation and pay scales.

Beginning in the 1980s, tariffs were reduced, capital was liberated from the control of the nation state, and a new era of globalized and financialized capitalism

---

46 J Conaghan, 'Reassessing the Feminist Theoretical Project in Law' (2000) 27 Journal of Law and Society 351.

47 J Conaghan and K Rittich, 'Introduction: Interrogating the Work/Family Divide' in J Conaghan and K Rittich (eds) *Labour Law, Work, and Family: Critical and Comparative Perspectives* (Oxford University Press 2005) 3.

was born. The economies of the core countries shifted from manufacturing to services. 'Debt', as Fraser explains, 'is the instrument by which global financial institutions pressure states to slash social spending, enforce austerity, and generally collude with investors in extracting value from defenceless populations'.[48] In the global South, International Monetary Fund structural adjustment policies limit the capacity of states to provide for their populations. The immediate interests of private investors have become paramount, with the result that the state no longer has the capacity to shore up social reproduction. In the global North, real wages have decreased and the hours of work of household members have increased. The dual-earner family has become the norm of the new gender order for globalized financial capitalism.

4. Migrant Domestic Workers and the Transnational Economy of Domestic Work

Historically, across a diverse range of countries, both developed and developing, women from disadvantaged racial and ethnic groups have tended to provide care and household services to meet the needs of more powerful social groups, with their own care needs being downplayed and neglected as they do so. Nowhere is this process of racialization and subordination more evident than when it comes to the globalization of domestic work in globalized and financialized capitalism.

In advanced industrialized economies, neo-liberal and austerity policies transfer the provision of care services from public services either to the market or to families in order to reduce costs borne by taxpayers. This privatization of social reproduction has been an important driver of the demand for migrant care and domestic workers, while structural adjustment policies imposed on the global South have, amongst other things, created a supply of women.

On the demand side, the feminization of migration is fuelled by the increase in women's labour force participation, falling fertility rates, increasing life expectancy, changes in family structure, shortages of public care, and the increasing privatization and marketization of care in developed economies. On the supply side, economic trends such as growing inequalities between high- and low-income countries, as well as insecurity, vulnerability, and instability due to economic crises combine with gender-related factors such as abuse, family conflict, and discrimination to increase the numbers of women who migrate in order to obtain paid work. Remittances are key for the survival of household, community, and country

48 Fraser 'Feminism's Home Front' (n 23) 112.

in a number of developing countries, given that exporting workers is one means by which governments cope with unemployment and foreign debt.[49]

In the global South, domestic and care work has been shaped by 'colonialization, income inequality within and between countries, and national policies concerning definitions of work'.[50] In Mexico and Brazil, for example, initially indigenous women were domestic workers for colonizers, and later rural women migrated to cities to become domestic workers. Increasingly, it is now women who cross contiguous national borders who are employed as domestic workers. In the Middle East and Gulf region, the demand for migrant domestic labour has been driven by both the increasing employment of women in the paid labour force and the desire to display emblems of middle class identity and privilege. In South Africa, the employment of large numbers of black domestic workers by white households was perpetuated by apartheid. However, in Central, Western and Eastern Africa, it is likely that there is a significant underreporting of domestic workers since most national labour force surveys do not consider care work in private homes to be work. Asia is both the largest source of migrant care workers, with the Philippines, Indonesia and Sri Lanka providing the greatest numbers of workers, and it also has the largest demand for care workers. However, the numbers of domestic workers in China and India are difficult to estimate.[51]

In 2013, the ILO estimated that there were 232 million international migrants, of which half were women and girls.[52] Domestic workers are an important part of this growing trend towards the feminization of migration. By the mid-2000s, around 6.3 million Asian migrants were legally living and working in the more developed Asian countries, with an estimated 1.2 million additional migrants with undocumented status in the region, many working as domestic workers. Arab countries employ millions of migrant domestic workers. In Saudi Arabia, there are approximately 1.5 million domestic workers and most come from Indonesia, the Philippines, and Sri Lanka. Women migrants from Mexico and other parts of Latin America make up most of the domestic workforce in the US. In

49 J Fudge 'Global Care Chains: Transnational Migrant Care Workers' (2012) 28 International Journal of Comparative Labour Law and Industrial Relations 63–70; Glenn, *Forced to Care* (n 11) 130.

50 M Romero, V Preston and W Giles, 'Care Work in a Globalizing World' in M Romero, V Preston and W Giles (eds) *When Care Work Goes Global: Locating the Social Relations of Domestic Work* (Ashgate 2014) 8.

51 ibid 9.

52 ILO, *Domestic Workers Across the World* (n 5) 19.

the European Union (EU), domestic work is performed both by EU citizens who come from recent accession member states and third country nationals.[53]

Many of the women who leave poorer less developed countries to work in richer countries are temporary migrant workers who do not enjoy either the right to become permanent residents in their host country or the right to circulate freely in the host country's labour market.[54] Others have an irregular migration status that makes it very difficult, if not impossible, either to exercise voice or to enforce any rights. Even migrant domestic workers that have labour market mobility face a range of social barriers, including language and limited options, that undermine their ability to insist on labour rights.

Immigration controls create a range of different migrant statuses – citizens, settled workers with permanent residence, workers with only a temporary right to work in the receiving country and undocumented workers – that are arranged hierarchically in terms of social and labour rights, supportive institutions and remedies.[55] These different statuses are often racialized and very precarious. In turn, migration statuses generate a differentiated supply of labour that produces precarious workers and precarious employment norms. Domestic work tends to be performed by migrant workers with precarious migrant status.

5. Labour Law and Migrant Domestic Workers

Paid domestic work performed in other people's homes troubles conventional legal categories. Whether this work is considered as a matter of the private sphere and family or related to the public sphere of work has long been contested. In order to bridge the gap between the valuable social and economic contribution that domestic workers make and the poor treatment that they receive, the ILO's Domestic Workers Convention placed the regulation of paid work within private households squarely into the domain of labour law. The Convention on Domestic Work establishes a number of labour standards for domestic workers. Essentially,

---

53 Women in Informal Employment: Globalizing and Organizing, Informal Workers in Focus: Domestic Workers <http://wiego.org/sites/wiego.org/files/resources/files/WIEGO_Domestic_Workers_0.pdf> accessed 11 October 2016.

54 Fudge 'Global Care Chains' (n 49).

55 B Anderson, 'What's in a Name? Immigration Controls and Subjectivities: The case of Au pairs and domestic worker visa holders in the UK' (2009) 29 Subjectivity 407; J Fudge, 'Precarious Migrant Status and Precarious Employment: The Paradox of International Rights for Migrant Workers' (2012) 34 Comparative Labor Law and Policy Journal 101.

the Convention treats domestic work like other forms of work by providing that the workers who perform it are entitled to the same rights as other workers. It also recognizes the distinctive problems faced by migrant domestic workers who work in private households. The Convention requires that domestic workers be given the right to privacy and the right, if they are migrants, to retain their travel documents, as well as the choice to live in their employer's home. It also stipulates that employment agencies that recruit migrant domestic workers should not charge fees or otherwise exploit domestic workers.[56]

When it comes to designing and establishing appropriate mechanisms and procedures for the supervision and enforcement of applicable laws with respect to domestic workers, there is no 'one-size-fits-all' approach. Although domestic workers should be entitled to the same labour and social protections as all workers, effective enforcement of domestic workers' rights needs to take into consideration the specific circumstances of such work. Since domestic workers toil in isolation in private households, it is also critical to develop innovative forms of collective representation and action.[57]

However, despite this international standard, nation states differ over where labour law draws the boundary between the private sphere of the household and the public sphere of employment when they explicitly interface. In England, the Working Time Regulations provide that domestic workers employed in a private household are not entitled to, among other standards, maximum weekly working time, limits on the length of night work, or a weekly rest period.[58] In Sweden, domestic workers who are employed by individuals to work in their private homes are not covered by collective agreements and there are no statutory minimum wages for them to rely upon.[59] In the US, live-in domestic workers are excluded

56 M Olez, 'The ILO's Domestic Workers Convention and Recommendation: A window of opportunity for social justice' (2014) 153 International Labour Review 143.

57 Blackett, 'Introduction: Regulating Decent Work for Domestic Workers' (n 8); J N Fish, 'Organizing through State Transitions and Global Institutions: Crafting Domestic Labour Policy in South Africa' in M Romero, V Preston and W Giles (eds) *When Care Work Goes Global: Locating the Social Relations of Domestic Work* (Ashgate 2014) 233; G Mundlak and H Shamir, 'Organizing Migrant Care workers in Israel: Industrial Citizenship and the Trade Union Option' (2014) 143 International Labour Review 93.

58 National Minimum Wage Regulations 1999, SI 1999/584, reg 2(2); Working Time Regulations 1998, SI 1998/1833, reg 19; Health and Safety Act 1974, s 51. J Fudge and S Fredman, 'The Contract of Employment and Gendered Work'. In M Freedland et al., (ed) *The Contract of Employment at* Work (Oxford University 2016) chapter 11.

59 C Calleman, 'Domestic Service in a "Land of Equality": The Case of Sweden' (2011) 23 Canadian Journal of Women and the Law 121.

from overtime provisions under federal law.[60] Across the globe there is continuing resistance to regulating work relations within the household.

However, labour law initiatives alone cannot address the problems experienced by migrant domestic workers. The Kafala system, which operates in many of the Gulf States, renders a migrant worker completely dependent on his or her sponsoring employer and creates conditions that are ripe for exploitation.[61] Temporary migration programs that require domestic workers to live in the employer's home and tie their migration status to an on-going employment relationship with a specific employer undermine their autonomy.[62] Undocumented migrants are particularly susceptible to abusive employment practices.[63] In many countries, they are simply unable to enforce any labour rights even if labour law covers domestic work.[64] Migrant workers are poorly served by labour laws, and migrant workers often need 'special' rather than 'equal' rights of national workers.[65]

Transnational migration also troubles the traditional ethical stance that the subject of labour law is the citizen worker. Privileging nation state waged work as the site for redistributive politics ignores and devalues the needs and concerns of the legions of migrant domestic workers who enable many citizens to work. Public policies in developed countries that emphasize increasing women's employment rates without simultaneously stressing the obligations of men to engage in care activities are likely to perpetuate the transfer of social reproduction across

---

60 *Fair Labor Standards Act*, 29 U.S.C. § 213(b)(21) (2005).

61 F T Malit, Jr. and G S Naufal, *Asymmetric Information under the Kafala Sponsorship System: Impacts on Foreign Domestic Workers' Income and Employment Status in the GCC Countries* (Bonn Institute for the Study of Labor 2016 Discussion Paper No. 9941 May 2016) <http://ftp.iza.org/dp9941.pdf> accessed 11 October 2016.

62 J Fudge and K Strauss, 'Migrants, Unfree Labour, and the Legal Construction of Domestic Servitude: Migrant Domestic Workers in the UK.' In C Costello and M Freedland (eds) *Migrants at Work* (Oxford University Press 2014) 160.

63 S Mullally and C Murphy, 'Migrant Domestic Workers in the UK: Enacting Exclusions, Exemptions and Rights' (2014) 36 Human Rights Quarterly 397.

64 For the United Kingdom, see *Hounga v Allen and Another* [2014] UKSC 47. For a discussion of other European countries, see V Pavlou, 'Migrant domestic labour, vulnerability and the law: immigration and employment laws in Cyprus and Spain' (2016) 7 Investigaciones Feministas 149.

65 P Herzfeld Olsson, 'Empowering temporary migrant workers in Sweden: A call for unequal treatment'. In J Howe and R Owens (eds) Temporary Labour Migration in the Global Era: The Regulatory Challenges (Hart Publishing 2016) 203.

national borders when women from poor countries migrate to richer countries to perform care work.[66]

Moreover, the transnationalization of social reproduction is not likely a sustainable solution to the growing tension and contradictions caused by the simultaneous privatization of social reproduction and austerity-driven public policies.[67] The employment of migrant women to perform domestic work in receiving countries is an individual fix for the broader problem of combining paid work with unpaid care work, a solution which is simply not an option for families who cannot afford it. In addition, the employment of migrant domestic workers from the South is likely to contribute to a vicious circle in the host country, in which private solutions delay collective efforts to search for appropriate public policies. This strategy for dealing with work-life conflict in developed countries also intensifies the burden on the individuals who assume the roles of the women in the family who have migrated for paid work. In the Philippines, for example, the export of women's labour results in a 'depletion of care resources'.[68] Since it is mostly women who assume the family care-giving roles of migrant women, there is a growing need for reconciliation and equality policies in the South.[69] While women's decisions to migrate can increase their financial autonomy and their financial contribution to their household through remittances, their absorption into the care markets of the North tends to reinforce the gendered nature of care as well as radicalized understandings of domestic work.[70]

Labour laws that are embedded in nation states are not particularly well-suited to addressing many of the challenges thrown up by the globalized market economy. Nor have traditional labour laws been particularly successful in valuing and regulating paid reproductive work that is typically performed by women. However, it is possible to lament the rapacious expansion of the market today without being wistful for the past. It is important to appreciate the extent to which the past was built on such institutionalized forms of subordination as patriarchy and colonialism. A return to the good old days is neither possible nor desirable. Nativism and parochialism are not the solutions for deciding the difficult questions of

---

66 L Benéria, 'The Crisis of Care, International Migration, and Public Policy' (2008) 14 Feminist Economics 1, 11.

67 Glenn, *Forced to Care* (n 11) ch 7.

68 R Salazar Parreñas, 'Gender Inequalities in the New Global Economy'. In A Fauve-Chamous (ed) *Domestic Service and the Formation of European Identity: Understanding the Globalization of Domestic Work, 16–21st Centuries* (Peter Lang 2005) 369.

69 Benéria, 'The Crisis of Care, International Migration, and Public Policy' (n 65) 11.

70 Fudge 'Global Care Chains' (n 49).

entry to and membership in a territory. Forging new foundations for labour law requires us to question and break down borders between production and social reproduction, the sexual division of labour and nation states, in order to develop new forms of and vehicles for solidarity, and to appreciate the need to emancipate, and not simply to protect, society from capitalism.

Mijke Houwerzijl

European Union Cross-Border Worker Mobility in Light of Digitalization of Labour – More Fragmentation Underway?

1. Setting the Scene

Over the last three decades, we have witnessed a profound change in the nature of free movement and cross-border mobility of workers within Europe. Whereas the founding fathers of the European Economic Community (EEC) focused on the free movement of full-time workers with an open-ended ('standard') employment contract, the current reality in EU labour markets is of a free labour mobility of all kinds of workers. Fixed-term contracts, part-time contracts, on-call contracts, zero hours contracts, contracts for workers hired through temporary employment agencies, freelance contracts etc. have become an established feature of European labour markets. These 'non-standard' contracts also left their mark on the case law of the Court of Justice of the European Union (hereinafter CJEU or Court). Starting with its judgments in *Lawrie-Blum* and *Levin* in the early 1980s, the Court established free movement of workers' rights also for the flexible workforce, as long as the work is of an economic nature and is not (too) marginal or ancillary. Nevertheless, until the beginning of the 21st century, cross-border labour mobility in the EU used to consist of a comparatively small group of migrant workers.[1] Hence, although fragmentation of production through outsourcing and relocation took place across borders, flexibilisation and hence fragmentation of labour occurred mainly within EU member states.

This picture changed dramatically after the enlargements of 2004 and 2007. Due to a change in economic drivers for geographical labour mobility, such as differences in wage-levels, living standards and employment opportunities across member states, a steady increase of intra-EU labour mobility from new to old member states was observed in the last decade. Transitional restrictions in place at the beginning of the 2004 enlargement diverted mobile workers away from traditional destinations – namely Germany – and towards the more easily

1 In 2002, only 600,000 people, or 0.4 per cent of the total employed population, worked in a country different from their country of residence. See Report 'The Social Situation in the European Union 2002' (European Commission 2002) 23.

accessible labour markets in the United Kingdom (UK) and Ireland.[2] Others went abroad through alternative legal routes, namely as posted workers or (bogus) self-employed workers.[3] In this process, flexibilisation of national labour markets and intra-EU labour mobility turned out to be each other's allies. Demand for cross-border labour was fuelled by legally permitted arrangements in the old member states, partly based on EU law, such as fixed-term contracts, (posted) temporary agency work, posting of workers in (sub)contracting processes and self-employment.[4] Hence, on top of the fragmentation of labour within national labour markets, a layer of cross-border fragmentation of labour within the EU arose.[5] This led to well-known challenges to the territorial application of labour law, to posting as a new business model based on 'regime competition'.

It is the influence of digitalization on cross-border fragmentation of labour processes which I will turn to in this contribution. Hybrid forms of cross-border labour mobility such as posting of workers[6] and 'Eurocommuting' are clearly

2 The research findings also suggest that, due to network effects, transitional arrangements can have permanent effects on the pattern of migration. See D Holland et al., *Labour mobility within the EU – The impact of enlargement and the functioning of the transitional arrangement* (National Institute of Economic and Social Research London 2011) <http://ec.europa.eu/social/main.jsp?langId=en&catId=89&newsId=1108&furtherNews=yes> accessed 15 March 2017.

3 See A van Hoek and M Houwerzijl, *Comparative study on the legal aspects of the posting of workers in the framework of the provision of services in the European Union* (Radboud University Nijmegen 2011), especially Annex I. <http://ec.europa.eu/social/BlobServlet?docId=6677&langId=en> accessed 16 March 2017. The choice for illegality or 'grey use' of routes for family migration or student mobility was also observed. See M Ruhs and B Anderson, 'Semi-compliance and illegality in migrant labour markets: an analysis of migrants, employers and the state in the UK' (2010) 16 Population, Space and Place 195–211.

4 M Kremer and E Schrijvers, 'Making Romanian and Bulgarian Migration Work in The Netherlands', WRR-Policy Brief no 1 January 2014 WRR. <http://test6.wrr.nl/fileadmin/en/publicaties/PDF-WRR-Policy_Briefs/2014-01_WRR_Policy_Brief_1_ENGELS_05.pdf> accessed 15 March 2017.

5 Also witnessed in other parts of the world. See the abundant literature on labour market flexibilisation and fragmentation, e.g. J Fudge, 'Fragmenting Work and Fragmenting Organisations: the Contract of Employment and the Scope of Labour Regulation' (2006) 44 Osgoode Hall L.J 609, 636; D Weil, *The Fissured Workplace: How Work Became So Bad for So Many and What Can be Done to Improve It* (Harvard University Press 2014).

6 See e.g. S Evju (ed), *Regulating Transnational Labour in Europe: The quandaries of multilevel governance* (Universitetet i Oslo 2014 Skriftserie nr. 196) 95–130. A digital version

facilitated by new technologies, in particular digitalization, since it is easier to maintain ties with the country of origin through the internet, smartphones and cheap flights. Moreover, new patterns of work organisation are on the rise, such as work-on-demand via apps, crowdwork and mobile work based in information and communication technology (ICT), where supply and demand for work is managed through online platforms and/or where workers can do their job from any place at any time with a connection through the internet and electronic tools.

Although the adaptation of forms of work to the 'gig-economy' is still in its infancy in most EU member states,[7] it already triggers fierce debates about its untapped opportunities for a global labour market on the one hand and its possibilities for further precarisation of working conditions on the other hand.[8] For instance, 'platform-work' makes the legal question of employment status re-emerge in an hitherto unknown context, as is acknowledged by the International Labour Organization (ILO) and the European Commission.[9] The first lawsuit in Europe where *Uber* drivers successfully claimed to be workers instead of independent contractors has been won in the UK,[10] and recently the European Parliament

is available at: <www.jus.uio.no/ifp/english/research/projects/freemov/publications/books/196.pdf> accessed 16 March 2017.

7 See estimates made by a team chaired by U Huws and S Joyce, *Crowd work in Europe – Preliminary results from a survey in the UK, Sweden, Germany, Austria and the Netherlands* (FEPS Studies December 2016). It is however difficult to measure the *size* of the 'gig economy'. One can adopt several perspectives, looking at the number of platforms, their economic significance, and the number of platform clients, workers or hours worked. Van Dijck however notices that assessments so far are not based on 'hard' statistical or empirical findings. As long as the growth signals are mainly based on trend reports and future outlooks, we should acknowledge them as 'weak signals' and focus on better methods to gather reliable data. See J. van Dijck, T. Poell and M. de Waal (2016), *De platformsamenleving: Strijd om publieke waarden in een online wereld* (Amsterdam University Press 2016) 15. <www.oapen.org/download?type=document&docid=618753> accessed 16 March 2017.

8 For a thorough examination of some key legal, economic, business, computer-science and sociological aspects of platform work, see special issue of the Comparative Labor Law & Policy Journal on 'Crowdsourcing, the Gig-economy and the Law' of May 2016, guest-edited by Valerio De Stefano.

9 See International Labour Office (ILO), *The future of work centenary initiative* Report of the Director-General, International Labour Conference, 104th Session, Geneva 2015; European Commission, *European Agenda for the Collaborative Economy* COM (2016) 356, 12–15.

10 Reserved Judgment of Employment Tribunals London Central of 28 October 2016, *Aslam and Farrar v Uber*, Case Nos 2202550/2015 & others, available at: <www.

adopted a report calling for social protections to be extended to new forms of employment, including work intermediated by digital platforms such as Uber.[11]

Clearly, the new ICT and platform-based patterns of work also pose new challenges to worker mobility law in the EU, and in particular to systems for determining applicable labour and social security law in cross-border situations. Therefore, the central issue addressed in this contribution is: How will new patterns of digitalized work affect intra-European labour mobility law?[12]

2. Defining and Distinguishing ICT-Based Mobile Work and Crowdwork

The focus of this contribution is on two topical manifestations of digitalisation of work: 1) 'ICT-based mobile working' remote from the employer's premises and 2) 'crowd work' facilitated by external digital platforms. Although I will explore these new forms of work separately in this paper, in reality they cannot be fully separated, but rather represent a continuum, ranging from partially to fully digitalized workplaces and employment relationships. I will use examples to enhance understanding and to identify and sketch some complex legal issues that may rise in a cross-border EU context.[13]

2.1 ICT-Based Mobile Work

So what is meant by ICT-based mobile work? As is already clear from the beginning of this century, digitalization sets in motion the erosion of the fixed, physical workplace. Ever more employees may work from everywhere, using virtual

judiciary.gov.uk/judgments/mr-y-aslam-mr-j-farrar-and-others-v-uber/> accessed 15 March 2017. Uber appealed the ruling.

11 Rapporteur: Maria João Rodrigues, Draft Report on A European Pillar of Social Rights, (2016/2095(INI) 13 September 2016, adopted by the EP on 19 January 2017.

12 A first draft of the analysis below is in my key note paper 'Digitalisation and free movement of workers/services', presented at the ELLN Conference Digitalisation and Labour Law in the Hague on 26–27 November 2015, and at a seminar on 15 February 2016 of the KU Leuven Institute for Labour Law on Digital labour markets, co-sourcing and worker mobility in the EU. Also, this final version benefited from comments and observations on my presentation about 'the internationalizing and fragmenting labour force' during the ReMarkLab Final Conference held in Stockholm on 19 and 20 May 2016, as well as from the discussion with participants in the workshop 'Precarious Work – the New Normative Model for Labour Law?' and others during this ReMarkLab Conference.

13 A thorough discussion of the issues identified lies beyond the scope of this paper.

collaboration tools such as e-mail, web-meeting software and file-sharing sites (e.g. *Skype, Google Docs, Dropbox, Slack)*. Some are real e-nomads, 'invisible workers working digitally from everywhere'.[14] According to Eurofound, 'ICT-based mobile working' refers to the possibility created by modern technology to work remotely from any location as effectively as from the employer's premises.[15] ICT-based mobile work may be labelled as a variation of teleworking. It comprises all kinds of work patterns, supported by electronic devices, that allow employees to operate from various possible locations outside the premises of their employer, for example, at home, at a client's premises or 'on the road'. It is characterised by the (partial or full) absence of a fixed workplace, internet-based processes, management support of mobility and a mobile working culture. Quoting from 2013 figures, Sassen draws attention to the fact that (already three years ago):

> In total, 30 million Americans work from home at least once each week, which will increase by 63% in the next five years. About 3 million Americans never go to an office and 54% are happier working from home than in an office. Furthermore, 70% of employees work from alternative locations (not just home) on a regular basis.[16]

While it is not easy to predict at what scale ICT-based mobile work will become manifest across borders within the EU, the potential impact is high, in particular in Euroregions such as SaarLorLux,[17] and as a tool to facilitate working from large distances.[18]

---

14 J. Popma, 'The Janus face of the "New Ways of Work". Rise, risks and regulation of nomadic work' (*ETUI Working Paper* 2013.07).

15 Eurofound, *New forms of Employment* (Publications Office of the European Union 2015) Ch 6, 72–81, 132.

16 S Sassen, 'Digitization And Work: Potentials and Challenges in Low-Wage Labor Market' (Position Paper Columbia University 2015) 3, citing 'One In Five Americans Work From Home, Numbers Seen Rising Over 60%', available at <www.forbes.com/sites/kenrapoza/2013/02/18/one-in-five-americans-work-from-home-numbers-seen-rising-over-60/#6fa66f7a4768> accessed 16 March 2017.

17 Comprised of five different regional authorities located in the French and German speaking parts of Belgium: Lorraine, a region of France; the French départements Moselle and Meurthe-et-Moselle; and the German federal states of Saarland and Rhineland-Palatinate.

18 For Norway, a country with low population density and long distances between communities, ICT-based mobile work in knowledge-intensive firms has been identified as a new potential driver for economic growth. It may offer workers who live far away from potential employers the chance to increase their employability without having to relocate. See Eurofound, *New forms of Employment* (n 15) 81.

How do we fit this (partially) digitalized mobile work into the acquis of EU freedom of movement for workers,[19] underpinned as it is by traditional notions of a fixed, physical workplace? Below (section 3–6), I will in particular explore the potential impact of the large-scale introduction of ICT-based work on deterritorialisation of applicable labour law and social security standards. How does digitalized mobile work impact on existing legal frameworks to coordinate and designate the applicable labour and social security law for cross-border workers?

2.2 'Crowdwork' and 'Work on Demand' via Apps

Crowdwork and work on demand via apps are the most recent and radical manifestations of digitalized work. These new forms of work are characterized by virtual platforms seeking to optimise on-demand access to paid and unpaid work.[20] The most famous example of the latter is *Wikipedia*, the most controversial example of the former is perhaps *Uber*. Limiting our analysis to paid work, a distinction must be made between platforms such as Uber, organising offline, physical work in local (labour) markets, and platform intermediaries such as *Amazon Mechanical Turk*, *Task Rabbit* or *Upwork*, purely organising work – for example, data entry and verification, copy-writing, programming and website design – which is done exclusively online. The term 'crowdwork' is mostly used to refer to the latter platforms, offering virtual and potentially global services, whereas the term 'work on demand via apps' is used to refer to the former platforms, offering physical, local services.[21]

As observed by Felstiner, due to platformisation, 'the traditional concept of a fixed workforce comprised of individually selected employees has begun to disintegrate.'[22] This is in particular true for platforms such as Amazon Mechanical

---

19 As confirmed in the Eurofound study (n 15), ICT-based mobile work is also taken up by self-employed persons. However, ICT-based mobile work among the self-employed is often linked to other new employment forms, such as crowdwork. Hence, for our purposes, it is more interesting to look at the employee-related impact of ICT-based mobile work, since the issues concerning qualification of ICT-based mobile work partly overlap with the issues raised in the context of crowdwork.

20 Facilitated not only by high-speed internet networks and the explosion of new forms of mobile devices, but also by 'Big Data': colossal masses of directly exploitable commercial, personal and geographic data merged by these online platforms.

21 See V de Stefano, *The rise of the 'just-in-time workforce: on-demand work, crowdwork and labour protection in the 'gig economy'* (ILO 2016) 7.

22 A Felstiner, 'Working the crowd: Employment and labor law in the crowdsourcing industry' (2011) 32 (1) Berkeley Journal of Employment & Labor Law 143–203; see

Turk, Upwork and also the German-based *Clickworker*. These platforms for online work replace stable workforces by networked 'crowds'. Howe defines this as 'taking a job traditionally performed by a designated agent (usually an employee) and outsourcing it to an undefined, generally large group of people in the form of an open call'.[23] Large business processes are broken into smaller specific tasks and distributed through internet platforms to crowdworkers regardless of geographic boundaries. For instance, in an example offered by Degryse, the 'search for a virtual assistant for administrative support, secretarial or data-entry work on the American site Upwork gives a result of 9088 candidates offering their services from 40 different countries.'[24]

Especially in the United States of America (USA), crowdwork and work on demand via apps has prompted a fierce debate and litigation on how the workers involved should be classified.[25] How do we deal with this issue in the EU-context? Below (section 7–9), I will focus on cross-border crowdworkers and explore whether they could be qualified as employees based on the case law of the CJEU in the framework of the free movement of workers. Included is a brief account of some jurisdictional questions arising before or concurrent with determining the employment status of the worker.

3. EU-Free Movement of ICT-Based Mobile Workers

Migrant EU workers have a right to equal wages and other working conditions given to national workers, including social advantages and social security benefits. This equal treatment principle is underpinned by the Regulations determining the applicable social security legislation (Regulation 883/04) and the objectively applicable labour law (Regulation 593/2008, 'Rome I'). The main principle underlying these rules has always been the law of the habitual place of work *(lex loci laboris)*.

---

also M Risak, 'Crowdworking: towards a "new" form of employment' (Working paper ELLN 2014).

23 J Howe, 'Crowdsourcing: A definition' (Crowdsourcing, 2 June 2006) <www.crowdsourcing.com> accessed 16 March 2017.

24 C Degryse, 'Digitalisation of the economy and its impact on labour markets' (*ETUI Working Paper* 2016.02) 32.

25 An account of American litigation is given by M Cherry, 'Beyond Misclassification: The Digital Transformation of Work' (2016) 37 *Comparative Labor Law & Policy Journal*. See also the overview in the report of C Codagnone, F Abadie and F Biagi, *The Future of Work in the 'Sharing Economy'. Market Efficiency and Equitable Opportunities or Unfair Precarisation?* (Institute for Prospective Technological Studies, JRC Science for Policy Report EUR 27913 EN 2016) 48–49.

The Treaty-provisions on free movement of workers and what are now Regulation 492/2011[26] and Regulation 883/04,[27] were designed with a 1960s version of migrant workers in mind: the full-time worker who relocates his or her (fixed) physical workplace and place of living (taking the family with him or her) to another member state. If migrant EU workers move both their physical place of work and living to another member state, the legal system runs smoothly. The right to equal treatment translates in full coverage of the migrant worker by the labour law and social security system of the receiving member state.

As explained above, ICT-based mobile workers do not fit into this archetype. They do not work at one fixed location, but work more flexibly, in various places or even on the road. In a Spanish case before the CJEU,[28] Advocate General Bot emphasised that such[29] workers are not able 'to choose to adjust their private life and their place of residence for the sake of proximity to their place of work, since that place varies daily' (point 21). So, translated to a cross-border (Euro)region, it might not make sense for workers without a fixed place of work to move their place of living to the member state of the employer's premises.

Interestingly, the fact that the workers in this Spanish case were without a fixed workplace and had to work ICT-based did not stem from the desire of the workers themselves, but from a decision of their employers to close down regional offices in order to cut costs. However, in several European countries, employees may request or even claim a right to (partially) perform work from their home and/or any location by means of ICT.[30] It is submitted that if undertakings allow for the ICT-based remote working of national workers, it would run counter to the equal treatment principle enshrined in Article 45 Treaty on the Functioning of the European Union (TFEU) and Article 7 Regulation 492/2011 to refuse such facilities to cross-border workers. One can imagine

---

26 On freedom of movement for workers within the Union, replacing the old Regulation 1612/68.

27 On the coordination of social security systems, replacing the old Regulation 1408/71.

28 Judgment of 10 September 2015, *Federación de Servicios Privados del sindicato Comisiones obreras*, C-266/14, EU:C:2015:578.

29 *In casu* the workers had the use of a company vehicle in which they had to drive every day to customers' premises in order to install equipment. They were provided with a mobile phone, and an application on their phones allowed the workers to receive daily a list with the various premises to visit that day, within their geographical area of working.

30 In the Netherlands, according to the Flexible Working Act, from 1 January 2016 on employees have the right to request more flexibility in respect of their place of work.

that ICT-based mobile working may even be more attractive in a transnational perspective, since it would greatly enhance the work-life balance of, for instance, frontier workers. From an EU-policy perspective, promoting this form of digitalisation may be helpful in realizing the goal of a 'genuine European labour market', since opportunities for ICT-based mobile working would certainly lower the barrier to accept a job (or a posting) with an employer based in another member state.

Unfortunately, it makes sense to discourage cross-border ICT-based mobile working from another perspective. At a large scale, it would have (too) far-reaching implications for the (predictability of the) applicable law and hence for labour costs and the administrative capacity of employers' human resources and payroll departments. In fact, experts in the field warn employers to be cautious.[31] From a member state perspective, it would not be applauded either; the sustainability of social security (and tax) systems and collectively agreed social funds may suffer from a large-scale adoption of ICT-based mobile working by employers.

4. A Hypothetical Example in a Euroregion

In a dramatized way, this point can be illustrated if we take the SaarLorLux region referred to above and assume that in company X, established in Luxembourg, 1000 employees are at work, 250 of them living in France, another 250 in Germany, and the other half in Luxembourg.[32] From 2016 on, company X would like to opt for ICT-based mobile work in order to cut costs. If all employees would spend 40 per cent of their working time in a remote ICT-based workplace (home, coffee shops, trains, friends' places and occasionally when travelling abroad), they can make attractive reductions in the office space they need. A point for consideration: What impact would this have on the applicable labour and social security law to the contracts with their cross-border workforce?

Currently, in accordance with the rules of Rome I and Regulation 883/04, company X applies Luxembourg labour and social security law (*lex loci laboris*) to their frontier workers. In case company X implements its plan, Regulation 883/04 would in most situations dictate a 'switch' of applicable social security law to the

31 See for instance S Nerinckx, 'International: Cross-border tele-working: beware!' (*fieldfisher* 27 June 2012) <www.fieldfisher.com/publications/2012/06/> accessed 15 March 2017.

32 In Luxembourg, cross-border workers account for approximately 45 per cent of the country's workforce.

country of residence, being France or Germany.[33] This would happen if employees would work at least 25 per cent of their working time away from the employer's premises, at – in these cases – French respectively German territory.[34]

Regarding the applicable labour law, the picture is less straightforward. This may or may not (partially) switch from Luxembourg to France/Germany, depending on several factors, such as the influence of a possible choice-of-law-clause[35] and the factual and for each employee's individual assessment of which country would objectively qualify as the country in which or, failing that, *from* which the employee habitually carries out his or her work in performance of the contract (Article 8(2) Rome I).[36]

If employees would work in such a mobile way across the SaarLorLux-region that no habitual country of work can be identified, the law of the place of establishment of the employer will have to be applied (Article 8(3) Rome I). However, the Court has interpreted this connecting factor as being strictly secondary to that of the habitual place of work. Therefore, it plays only a very subsidiary/ancillary role. If even international truck drivers are deemed to have a habitual country from which they carry out their work, this would not be different for our frontier workers of company X.

Finally, depending on the circumstances of the individual case, the law of a country of closer connection may trump the other two connecting factors. This

33 For part-time workers who may have another job with a different employer that is either or not based in Luxembourg or in the worker's country of residence, the coordination rules may work out differently.

34 In case of normally working in two or more member states, the rules laid down in Article 13 of Regulation 883/2004 apply. These point to the country of residence if a substantial part of a person's activity is pursued there. Pursuant to Art. 14 of Regulation 987/2009, 'substantial' would most often mean that at least 25 per cent of the person's working time is carried out in the member state of residence.

35 Rome I is based on party autonomy. Hence, the parties to the (employment) contract may designate the law applicable to the contract themselves. This chosen law will be the law governing the contract – the *lex causae*. However, in order to protect the employee, Article 8(1) limits the effect: a choice of law may not have the result of depriving the employee of the protection afforded to him or her by provisions that cannot be derogated from by agreement under the law applicable in absence of such a choice.

36 Even in the case of a truck driver working in international transport (Judgment of 15 March 2011, *Koelzsch*, C-29/10, EU:C:2011:151) or a sailor working on a seagoing vessel (Judgment of 15 December 2011, *Voogsgeerd*, C-384/10, EU:C:2011:842), the national court should try to establish whether, based on the circumstances as a whole, a country can be identified from which the work is actually performed.

could well make French or German law applicable, since factors taken into account pursuant to the *Schlecker*-judgment must include the country of social insurance coverage (which, as we saw, would switch to France/Germany).[37] However, many labour law rules, such as health and safety law and working time regulations, have an overriding mandatory character. Hence, Luxembourg labour law would probably still apply to some parts of the employment contracts (at least for the days that their cross-border workers have to work at the employer's premises in Luxembourg) and (partly) depending on the assessment of whether German or French law would not be more favourable for the workers concerned.[38]

5. If the Exception Becomes the Norm

Several variations could be added to this example, highlighting the almost prohibitive complexity of large-scale ICT-based remote working from an applicable law perspective. Within the limited scope of the present contribution, a reference to easily-available and accessibly-written practical guides on the applicable legislation[39] should suffice to underscore the main point to be made here: if ICT-based remote working would at any point in the future become regular HR-policy in large organisations (also) in cross-border regions, the systems for determining the applicable law might simply cease to function.

The time-consuming, unpractical need to make a close examination of each individual case (e.g. by examining perhaps frequently changing duty rosters or travel calendars or other information) in order to establish the time spent working in a particular state, would burden institutions and employers too much. Moreover, such individual assessment would also make other administrative and collective, modes of protection and enforcement more problematic. For instance, it might seriously hamper the possibility for the workers to protect their interests by way of collective negotiations. It also sits uneasy with the objective pursued by Articles 45–48 TFEU, namely of equal treatment, if the workers employed by a single

37 Judgment of 12 September 2013, *Schlecker*, C-64/12, EU:C:2013:551. In this Judgment, the CJEU clarified the scope of Article 8(4) Rome I.

38 Article 9(2) Rome I allows courts to apply domestic 'overriding mandatory' provisions (law of the forum), regardless of the (objectively) applicable law. As a result, Article 9 Rome I facilitates labour law systems which rely (sometimes heavily) on overriding mandatory law.

39 See for example European Commission, *Practical guide: The legislation that applies to workers in the European Union (EU), the European Economic Area (EEA) and in Switzerland* (European Commission 2012).

employer established in one member state (so not a multinational employer) would no longer as a default position be covered by the same law.

6. Is There a Way out of Complexity?

There is a need to tackle current impediments for large-scale ICT-based working across the EU. However, the heterogenic and individualistic nature of online working patterns makes it difficult to suggest adaptations to the systems for determining the applicable law which would suit all circumstances of transnationally working employees, their employers, and member states involved. A few building blocks can however be given.

- It is pertinent in all situations of cross-border ICT-based (highly) mobile working to avoid frequent changes in the applicable legislation.[40] This is in the interest of employees, employers and institutions alike. In principle, the applicable legislation should represent the place where the worker 'belongs'.[41] Ideally this means that the applicable law both indicates the closest connection with a state and ensures the most satisfactory protection of the weaker party in the contractual relationship (being the employee). In cases of doubt, the interpretation granting the employee the highest degree of social protection should be chosen.
- At least in the situation of cross-border telecommuting for only a part of the working time (as in the example of company X), it might be in the mutual interest of the employer, employees and competent state to create the legal fiction or rebuttable presumption that ICT-based mobile workers (virtually) perform their work in the country of the employer's premises.[42] ICT-based remote working relies on access to the employer's office and networks. Even

40 An example is: Article 14(10) of Regulation 987/2009 stipulating for flight or cabin crew that the applicable legislation is assessed on the basis of a projection of work for the following 12 calendar months, and should remain stable during that period (on the condition that there is no substantial change in the situation of the person concerned, but only a change in the usual work patterns).

41 See A van Hoek and M Houwerzijl, 'Where do, according to Rome I and the (E)PWD, EU mobile workers belong?' in H Verschueren (ed) *Where do I belong? EU law and adjudication on the link between individuals and Member States* (Intersentia Social Europe Series 36, 2016) 215–253.

42 It would in a sense 'codify' many company-practices where ICT-based working from home or elsewhere is only agreed upon informally and hence not reported to competent institutions for social security law. See Eurofound *New forms of Employment* (n 12) 75. See also Case C-570/15 (pending).

if equipment is not furnished (Bring Your Own Device, 'BYOD'), the workers must still log in to the online work environment of the employer in order to access company information and applications at any point and place.
- It would be interesting to explore sector-specificity of ICT-based mobile forms of cross-border work. Sector-specific aspects would allow for tailor-made solutions,[43] for instance in European sectoral social dialogue, and may include the modernization of the general EU Framework Agreement on Telework to sectoral needs.

7. Crowdwork in the EU-Context

As mentioned above, digitalisation not only boosts ICT-based remote and mobile working, but also the platformisation of labour. Whereas ICT-based mobile working as dealt with in the previous sections still presumes regular employer–employee relationships and physical employer premises in single countries, platformised labour allows the demand-side of labour to become 'place-unbound' as well. This enables even the smallest company or solo entrepreneur to become a 'micro-multinational' that sells and sources products, services and ideas across borders.

Online 'marketplaces for on-demand labour' such as *oDesk/Elance* (now merged and renamed Upwork) and Amazon Mechanical Turk bring virtual demand and supply together. They offer a virtual workforce of crowdsourced workers. Through such (mostly USA-based) platforms, work is outsourced to a crowd of people who work ICT-based remotely from anywhere in the world, when needed, on certain (micro)tasks or projects.[44] Hence, platformisation of labour is based on individual tasks or projects rather than on a continuous employment relationship.[45] According to Eurofound, crowd work is emerging in eleven member states, among a mix of large and small countries and geographic locations (Belgium, Czech Republic, Germany, Denmark, Spain, Greece, Italy, Latvia, Lithuania, Poland, UK).[46]

How does platformisation of labour (potentially) affect working across borders? So far, within the EU, no figures are available. To the extent that 'online platforms for work' may belong to what is called 'e-commerce', recent Eurobarometer

---

43 Including perhaps sector-specific Article 16 Agreements or the inclusion of extended collective agreements in the framework of Regulation 883/04 and collective-choice-of-law clauses in the framework of Rome I.

44 See Risak 'Crowdworking: towards a "new" form of employment' (n 22) 2.

45 This is also true for internet platforms offering on-demand labour that has to be performed offline, by 'Taskrabbits' or Uber-drivers.

46 Eurofound, *New forms of Employment* (n 15) Figure 15, 108.

data on e-commerce are relevant.[47] These data show that for companies that sell online, on average 85.4 per cent of their online sales in 2014 were from their own country. A further 10.3 per cent were from other EU countries, and 4.3 per cent were from outside of the EU. Hence, in contrast to the USA, a real EU digital single e-commerce market, let alone EU-wide platformisation of labour, is still in its childhood.

Regardless of its popularity in practice, the platformisation of labour has raised new and daunting questions concerning its classification. One-to-many relationships between employer and employees of an on-going nature are replaced by many-to-many relationships, of a very short duration, 'sometimes as little as a minute or two', facilitated through a standardized environment located in cyberspace.[48]

How do we qualify such crowdsourced work relationships in a cross-border EU context? Let's for example take a Polish crowdworker residing in Poland and performing cognitive digital piecework for on average of eight hours a week[49] on the German-based platform *Clickworker* for an unknown number of service recipients established in several EU countries.

8. E-Worker, E-Service Provider or even E-Consumer?

The CJEU has consistently held that the term 'worker' is an EU concept and may not be interpreted restrictively.[50] Case law clarified that the type of employment relationship, duration of employment, working hours, size, origin or type of remuneration,[51] and the need for income supplements, as well as the motive of the worker, are not criteria in themselves to assess who is regarded as a worker.[52]

---

47 Eurobarometer Flashreport 413 – February 2015.

48 Felstiner 'Working the crowd' (n 22) 146.

49 Felstiner reveals in his case study of Amazon Mechanical Turk that the average turker spends eight hours per week doing 'human intelligence tasks' (HITs), earning 1.25 USD per hour – well below the federal minimum wage (7.25 USD in 2011) Felstiner 'Working the crowd' (n 22) 167.

50 See Judgment of 19 March 1964, *Hoekstra*, C-75/63, EU:C:1964;19; Judgment of 23 March 1982, *Levin*, C-53/81, EU:C:1982:105; Judgment of 3 July 1986, *Lawrie-Blum*, C-66/85, EU:C:1986:284.

51 Here, the issue of virtual currencies and gamification of crowdwork in relation to the remuneration criterion rises. In the context of EU law, this may not cause insurmountable problems as only voluntary work without any form of remuneration seems to be excluded.

52 This was clarified and established by the CJEU in many cases dealing with atypical workers, such as part-time workers, fixed-term workers, short-term workers and

Accordingly, our Polish Clickworker may not be precluded from the scope on the sole basis of *the characteristics of his or her employment relationship*.

But what constitutes an employment relationship in the first place? In *Lawrie-Blum*, it was defined as 'the essential feature of an employment relationship [...] that for a certain period of time a person *performs services for* and *under the direction of another person* in return for which he receives *remuneration*.'[53] These indicators – 1) the obligation to personally carry out work, 2) in (organisational) subordination, and 3) in return for (periodical) payments – are used in most national labour law systems as well. Especially indicators 1 and 2 may prove difficult to apply to the radically flexible nature of crowd work. There are minimal commitments made with regard to who performs the tasks when and where. There is no need to give directions on how to do a certain microtask or small project.

And even if, in our example, subordination would be assumed, the question is to whom? Would our Polish crowdworker be subordinate to his or her service recipients (creating perhaps six 'employers' in the course of an hour) or to the German platform, which through its online environment exerts far-reaching control over the terms and conditions of work and has vested interests in the continued success of its business?

There are no clear-cut answers yet. However, as argued convincingly by Felstiner (for the USA), 'contrary to the expectations of vendors [platforms] and firms [service recipients], crowd workers claims to an employee status are neither presumptively barred nor inherently invalid'.[54] This is to some extent confirmed

on-call workers. See e.g. *Levin*, C-53/81, EU:C:1982:105; Judgment of 3 June 1986, *Kempf*, C-139/85, EU:C:1986:223; *Lawrie-Blum*, C-66/85, EU:C:1986:284; Judgment of 5 October 1988, *Steymann*, C-196/87, EU:C:1988:475; Judgment of 31 May 1989, *Bettray*, C-344/87, EU:C:1989:226; Judgment of 26 February 1992, *Bernini*, C-3/90, EU:C:1992:89; Judgment of 26 February 1992, *Raulin*, C-357/89, EU:C:1992:87; Judgment of 14 December 1995, *Megner and Scheffel*, C-444/93, EU:C:1995:442; Judgment of 6 November 2003, *Ninni-Orasche*, C-413/01, EU:C:2003:600; Judgment of 7 September 2004, *Trojani*, C-456/02, EU:C:2004:488; Judgment of 18 July 2007, *Geven*, C-213/05, EU:C:2007:438; Judgment of 4 June 2009, *Vatsouras and Koupatantze*, joined cases C-22/08 and C-23/08, EU:C:2009:344; Judgment of 4 February 2010, *Genc*, C-14/09, EU:C:2010:57.

53 Judgment of 3 July 1986, *Lawrie-Blum*, C-66/85, EU:C:1986:284, paras. 17 and 20.

54 Felstiner '*Working the crowd*' (n 22) 187. See also Cherry 'Beyond Misclassification' (n 25), who offers a comprehensive overview of relevant judicial cases, e.g. the landmark proceeding *O'Connor v. Uber*, which ended in a tentative settlement.

by analyses of Risak and Däubler/Klebe (for Germany).[55] Interestingly, the latter show that crowdwork neither fits easily into other concepts, such as the solo-entrepreneur and the *'Arbeitnehmerähnliche'*.[56] In their view, crowdworkers who only incidentally perform some work through an internet platform may classify as consumers.[57] This would render them (for example) protection against unfair standard contract terms by EU-consumer law.[58]

9. Real and Genuine Activities?

The surprising consumer option[59] also brings us to the key criterion for deciding whether a person is a worker, namely the nature of the work itself. The CJEU has consistently held that a person must pursue an activity of economic value which is effective and genuine, excluding activities on such a small scale as to be regarded as purely marginal and accessory.[60]

For our Polish crowdworker, who performs crowdwork for eight hours a week, this criterion is crucial indeed. The CJEU held that: 'Although the fact that a

---

55 Risak, 'Crowdworking: towards a "new" form of employment' (n 22); W Däubler and T Klebe, 'Crowdwork: Die neue Form der Arbeit – Arbeitgeber auf der Flucht?' (2015) *NZA* 1032.

56 Däubler and Klebe 'Crowdwork: Die neue Form der Arbeit' (n 55) Part III section 2 and 4.

57 According to Risak, crowdworkers can essentially be categorised into three groups: 1) those that have other sources of income and use crowdworking to earn a little extra (e.g. students, pensioners or homemakers); 2) those for whom crowdworking is the only – or at least the most significant – source of income (there are also differences here, namely between 2a) well-qualified people for whom crowdworking represents a temporary solution and 2b) people who work in this way on a permanent basis, as they would otherwise be at risk of long-term unemployment); and 3) those that are excluded from the regular employment market due to disabilities and social exclusion. Risak, 'Crowdworking: towards a "new" form of employment' (n 22) 2. For an empirical study see J Berg, 'Income security in the on-demand economy: Findings and policy lessons from a survey of crowdworkers' (2016) 37 Comparative Labor Law & Policy Journal. An early version of this article is available on SSRN at: <http://papers.ssrn.com/sol3/papers.cfm?abstract_id=2740940> accessed 16 March 2017.

58 Directive 93/13. See Däubler and Klebe 'Crowdwork: Die neue Form der Arbeit' (n 55), Part IV, who notice that more professional (and hence more dependent) crowdworkers would be left unprotected in case they are labelled as independent contractors.

59 Fitting in the notion of blurring lines between consumers and producers and the advent of so-called 'prosumers'.

60 COM (2010) 373 2, referring to *Levin* (C-53/81) paras. 16 and 17.

person works for only a very limited number of hours [...] may be an indication that the activities performed are marginal and ancillary [...], the fact remains that, independently of the limited amount of the remuneration for and the number of hours of the activity in question, the possibility cannot be ruled out that, following an overall assessment of the employment relationship in question, that activity may be considered by the national authorities to be real and genuine, thereby allowing its holder to be granted the status of "worker" within the meaning of [now Article 45 TFEU].'[61]

Even in the situation of an on-call worker who effectively worked only five hours a day over a period of 12 days, the CJEU confirmed that no threshold exists below which the economic activity performed may be regarded as purely marginal and ancillary.[62] The CJEU did however add that 'the national court may take account of the irregular nature and limited duration of the services actually performed under a contract for occasional employment.'[63] If we translate that to the relationship between our Polish crowdworker and his or her service recipients, it would be highly unlikely that such ultra-short-term and irregular relationships could qualify as employment relationships pursuant to EU law.[64]

Consequently, it only makes sense to invoke Art. 45 TFEU, if the platform may be deemed an employer.[65] This may be the case, if our Polish crowdworker keeps working eight hours a week or more and sticks to *Clickworker* long enough. As confirmed in *Genc*: 'Also, the total duration of a contractual relationship with the same undertaking must be taken into account and such [...] factors are capable

61 *Genc*, C-14/09, EU:C:2010:57, paras. 27 and 28.

62 See *Raulin*, C-357/89, EU:C:1992:87, para 13, and *Ninni-Orasche*, C-413/01, EU:C:2003:600, paras 25 and 32. See also COM (2010) 373 Part I, para 1.1.

63 *Raulin*, C-357/89, EU:C:1992:87, para 14. Emphasis added.

64 If a service recipient would frequently demand work and would choose again and again the same crowdworker, the situation might of course be different.

65 According to Risak 'Due to the strong influence of the crowdsourcing platform on these relationships, it is possible to classify this construction as a covert contractual relationship between the crowdworker and the platform.', Risak, 'Crowdworking: towards a "new" form of employment' (n 22) 3. See more extensively J Prassl and M Risak, 'Uber, Taskrabbit, & Co: Platforms as Employers? Rethinking the Labour Law of Crowdwork' in this volume. Also: M Risak and J Warter, '*Legal strategies towards fair conditions in the virtual sweatshop*' (paper presented at the IV Regulating for Decent Work Conference, ILO, Geneva, 8–10 July, 2015. <www.rdw2015.org/uploads/submission/full_paper/373/crowdwork_law_RisakWarter.pdf> accessed 16 March 2017.

of constituting an indication that the professional activity in question is real and genuine.'[66]

10. Cross-Border Link and Applicable Law

Suppose the Polish Clickworker would indeed meet the above definition of a worker, one crucial piece of the jigsaw puzzle is still missing. Our crowdworker must be a *migrant* worker in order to be covered by EU law. Hence, we need to establish the cross-border link. According to settled case law, EU rules apply when a person works in a member state other than his or her country of origin.[67]

However, the Polish clickworker does not physically (have to) exercise his or her right to free movement in order to work for the Clickworker platform based in Germany. As observed by Degryse, such platforms for online work might be considered to create a form of virtual immigration.[68] He quotes the American author Ford, who finds it 'somewhat ironic that many conservatives in the United States are adamant about securing the border against immigrants who will likely take jobs that few Americans want, while at the same time expressing little concern that the virtual border is left completely open to higher-skill workers who take jobs that Americans definitely do want.'[69] A very similar logic is at work on other platforms for middle and lower skilled work such as Amazon Mechanical Turk and Clickworker.

Hence, the situation of the Polish Clickworker prompts two questions: a) Can he or she be deemed a frontier worker, although he or she does not carry out work at the territory of another member state? and b) If so, what need or at least what incentive would there be for the Polish Clickworker to invoke Article 45 TFEU? Tentatively, these questions may be answered as follows:

a) So far, virtual movement has not been at issue in the context of Article 45 of the TFEU (see also section 3 above). Hypothetically, we might reason by analogy to the *Alpine Investment* judgment, where the CJEU decided already 20 years ago that (what is now) Article 56 of the TFEU applies to 'distance services' which a provider supplies without moving from the member state

66 *Genc*, C-14/09, EU:C:2010:57, paras 27 and 28.

67 See e.g. COM (2010) 373 7.

68 C Degryse 'Digitalisation of the economy' (n 24) 32.

69 M. Ford, *Rise of the robots: technology and the threat of a jobless future* (Basic Books 2015) 117.

in which he or she is established to recipients established in other member states.[70]

b) Currently, it is not clear *why* our Polish Clickworker would try to rely on Article 45 TFEU. He or she does not need the residence rights,[71] whereas the right to equal treatment with national workers regarding remuneration and other labour standards remains symbolic as long as national crowdworkers do not have a consolidated employee status. If this would be the case, the right to the statutory minimum wage in Germany could certainly be a trigger for invoking Article 45 TFEU. Otherwise, labour law entitlements would remain modest and crowdworkers would probably not be eligible for social insurance. In *Megner and Scheffel*, the CJEU upheld the exclusion of persons in minor employment from the German statutory social security schemes.[72] Such measures are common in other countries as well.

Last but not least, from an applicable law perspective, the Polish Clickworker would be confronted with similar problems of complexity concerning the applicability of German and/or Polish labour law and social security law, which depends on a close examination of his or her individual situation, as explored in section 4–5 above for ICT-based mobile frontier workers.[73] Contrary to such workers who work for only a part of the working time away from the employer's premises, crowdworkers have a fully virtualized workplace. In my opinion, this context makes it difficult to identify a common interest for all stakeholders involved (crowdworkers, platform-employer and competent state) in creating a

70 Judgment of 10 May 1995, *Alpine Investments*, Case C-384/93, EU:C:1995:126, paras 15 and 20–22. Distance selling – by mail, phone or internet – entails certain obligations (consumer protection) for the provider under Directive 2011/83.

71 Apart, perhaps, from rights for family members with a third country nationality (TCN) such as at stake in *Carpenter* (Case C-60/00) para 29: 'a significant proportion of Mr Carpenter's business consists of providing services, for remuneration, to advertisers established in other Member States. Such services come within the meaning of 'services' … in so far as he provides cross-border services without leaving the Member State in which he is established.'

72 Judgment of 14 December 1995, *Megner and Scheffel*, C-444/93, EU:C:1995:442, paras 26, 27, 28. Interestingly, in this judgment, the CJEU observed, referring to *Hoekstra* (case 75/3) that the concept of 'wage-earner or assimilated worker' in Regulation 3/1958 (predecessor of Regulation 883/04), had, like the term 'worker' in what are now Articles 45–48, a Community meaning. See *Megner and Scheffel* para 20.

73 Most often, as in the USA, crowdworkers have a full-time or part-time (regular) job next to their crowd work.

fiction or rebuttable presumption that crowdworkers (virtually) perform their work in the country of the platform's premises. A more thorough examination would be necessary.

11. Jurisdictional Issues

If anything is clear from the above, it is that many issues concerning cross-border crowdworkers remain to be clarified. Hence, to trigger some guidance, our hypothetical Polish crowdworker should in my view strongly be encouraged to invoke Article 45 TFEU before the court and claim his or her rights to mandatory statutory minimum wages under German law. In this section, some of the jurisdictional issues involved will be briefly addressed.

Pursuant to Article 21 of Regulation 1215/12 (Brussels I Recast), the Polish crowdworker may sue the German based platform (a) in the courts of the member state in which the platform is domiciled; or (b) in another member state, namely (i) in the courts of the habitual country of work; or (ii) if there would be no habitual country of work, in the courts of the country of engagement. Since the Polish crowdworker claims labour law protection under German law, it would be favourable for him or her to have proceedings before a German court and option (a) (the defendant's domicile) allows for that.

If the platform would challenge the jurisdiction of the German court (for instance alleging that our Polish crowdworker was an independent contractor who agreed with a choice-of-forum-clause stating that the courts of the American state Delaware have jurisdiction),[74] how would the Court proceed? We may look at the judgment in *Holterman*, where the CJEU had to rule in the reverse situation, of a defendant claiming employeeship, whereas the applicant had sued on the basis of the main jurisdiction rules for contracts.

The defendant (successfully) argued that the employment section of the Regulation trumps concurrent jurisdiction on the basis of contract. In its answer to the question of whether the defendant was to be classified as a worker under what is now Article 22 of Brussels I bis, the CJEU grasped the opportunity to expand its concept of a worker developed under Article 45 TFEU in the case *Lawrie-Blum*.[75] Above, in section 8 and 9 we looked at that definition and concluded that, depending on an overall assessment of the facts, our crowdworker may at least have a

---

74 In case the special jurisdiction rules for employees apply, such a clause would under Article 23 Brussels I Recast only be valid when entered into after the dispute has arisen. Under the main rules, the forum clause would be valid.

75 Judgment of 10 September 2015, *Holterman*, Case C-47/14, EU:C:2015:574, para 41.

chance to be classified as an employee. Thus, *Holterman* seems to have paved the ground for a crowdworker's case.

Interestingly, in the lawsuit where Uber-drivers in London successfully claimed to be workers instead of independent contractors, a conflict of laws aspect was involved as well.[76] According to the facts in this case, the legal rights to the app – the essential tool through which the Uber platform operates – are held by *Uber BV* (UBV), a Dutch corporation. This company acted as the defendant, together with its two UK based daughter companies (*ULL*). While ULL is responsible for making the invitations and acceptance of the bookings by passengers for a ride, the passenger pays the fare for the ride by his or her credit or debit card to UBV. The terms of reference stipulate that the drivers (sometimes referred to as 'customers') have a contractual relationship with UBV only, which renders payment to the drivers weekly.[77] In this agreement, a choice of law clause states that Dutch law is applicable. However, based on an assessment of the facts, the judge deems ULL the employment entity, since in reality ULL is the contact point between Uber and the drivers; 'It recruits, instructs, controls, disciplines and, where it sees fit, dismisses the drivers. It determines disputes affecting their interests.'[78] Only 'for what it is worth', the judge agrees that 'if the drivers were supplied by UBV to work for ULL, claims would lie against UBV'.[79] If that were the case, the judge concludes that the drivers could rely on Article 8 (or in the alternative Article 9) Rome I for their claims under English employment law.[80]

12. Concluding Remarks

What was once referred to as 'permanent' movement of migrant EU workers nowadays includes many cross-border movements very much of a temporary nature. After the enlargements of 2004 and 2007, a layer of cross-European fragmentation of labour was added to the fragmentation of labour *within* EU member states. While EU policy makers are currently in the middle of a debate on how to deal with the downsides of this development for host countries' systems of labour law and social welfare systems, new ICT-based and platformised fragmentation of jobs into micro-tasks seems to be underway. Clearly, ICT-based patterns of work,

76 Reserved Judgment of Employment Tribunals London Central of 28 October 2016 (n 10) paras 103–120.
77 ibid paras 15, 20–21.
78 ibid para 98.
79 ibid para 99.
80 ibid paras 103–120.

work on demand via apps, and crowd work pose new challenges to be faced and, in the coming years, to be met by social actors across the EU. In this contribution, some challenges of these new forms of work for EU free movement of workers' law have been explored, as well as those to systems for determining applicable labour and social security law in cross-border situations. One of the examples used was a case where employees are (fully or partly) tele-working at home, from different countries, for a business situated in an EU member state or in different countries. The question is whether EU free movement law applies and how this relates to principles of applicable (labour and social security) law. Regarding the other example of crowdworkers who perform tasks through a platform based in another member state, the question is not only if they are workers in the understanding of labour law, but also whether they are cross-border workers in the context of free movement of workers' principles.

Although the exercise above may have left the reader with more questions than answers, hopefully it did help to understand the far-reaching implications of cross-border ICT-based and platform work within the EU (let alone beyond). In my view, it is high time to examine these issues in a more in-depth way so that EU and national policymakers can act proactively in a period of time where these new forms of work are still largely in their childhood stage. Otherwise, it may prove difficult to prevent the dauntingly complex legal position of international transport workers from becoming the default for future generations of digital EU mobile workers.[81]

---

81 By way of illustration, see the pending joined cases *Nogueira and others* (C-168/16) and *Moreno Osacar* (C-169/16).

Petra Herzfeld Olsson

The Shortcomings of Equal Treatment for Temporary Labour Migrants

1. Introduction

The number of labour migrants present in the global labour market was estimated to be around 150 million people in 2013.[1] Demographics and the characteristics of globalization make it likely that many workers will continue to migrate for work.[2] However, safeguarding decent working conditions for these workers is particularly challenging. The problem is addressed by international organisations, politicians, and academic scholars, and the reasons identified behind this failure are many and complex.[3] One explanation highlighted in the international discussion is how immigration law can construct precarious workers.[4] For example, immigration law can have a detrimental effect on the application of labour law.[5] The aim of this chapter is to illustrate how well this explanation fits into the Swedish context.

As a rule, labour migrants shall be treated equally to domestic workers in Swedish law.[6] However, despite legal attempts to strengthen the position of labour migrants, abuse of their working conditions continues to occur.[7] In order to better

---

1 ILO, Global estimate on migrant workers (International Labour Organization 2015) 5.

2 J Howe and R Owens, 'Temporary Labour Migration in the Global Era – The Regulatory Challenges' in J Howe and R Owens (eds) *Temporary Labour Migration in the Global Era: The Regulatory Challenges* (Bloomsbury 2016) 10.

3 Howe and Owens, *Temporary Labour Migration* (n 1) 5.

4 B Anderson, 'Migration, Immigration Controls and the Fashioning of Precarious Workers' (2010) 24:2 Work, employment and society 301; J Fudge, 'Precarious Migrant Status and Precarious Employment – The Paradox of International Rights for Migrant Workers' (2012) 34 Comparative Labour Law & Policy Journal 96.

5 M Freedland and C Costello, 'Migrants at Work and the Division of Labour Law' in C Costello and M Freedland (eds) *Migrants at Work – Immigration and Vulnerability in Labour Law* (Oxford University Press 2014) 8.

6 See for example Government Bill 2012/13:148 Genomförande av blåkortsdirektivet, 99. This is however not the case for posted workers. See the Posted workers act (1999:678).

7 See examples in Commission of Inquiry SOU 2016: 91 Stärkt ställning för arbetskraftsinvandrare på arbetsmarknaden, 61; S Engblom 'Reconciling Openness and High Labour Standards? Sweden's attempts to Regulate Labour Migration and Trade

understand why, it is important to look at how the national labour law mechanisms establishing contractual equality between the worker and the employer play out if the worker is a labour migrant. In the following, I will illustrate how Swedish immigration law in some instances undermines such equalizing labour law mechanisms. Two particular aspects will be discussed – the conclusion of the employment contract and the law on dismissal.[8] The focus of the text will be on third country national labour migrants, meaning labour migrants coming to Sweden from non-European Union (EU)/European Economic Area (EEA) member states.

The chapter is structured in the following way. Section 2 introduces the international discussion on the interaction between immigration law and labour law. In section 3, some general characteristics of the Swedish labour law system will be presented. How the law is supposed to strengthen the worker's bargaining power when concluding the employment contract, and how the provisions on dismissal are constructed to protect the worker from arbitrary decisions will be explained in more detail in section 4. In section 5, the general characteristics of the Swedish labour migration regime will be described, and in section 6, I will explain how immigration law weakens the labour migrant's bargaining position. The chapter ends with some concluding remarks.

2. Background

The nation state guards the right to decide which persons shall be allowed to pass its borders and enter its territory. It is considered to be an important part of state sovereignty to be able to decide who to allow and not to allow into the country.[9] This assumption definitely applies for labour migrants. That is illustrated by the limited number of areas where free cross-border movements of workers

in Services' in Costello and Freedland, *Migrants at Work* (n 5) 354; P Herzfeld Olsson, 'Empowering Temporary Migrant Workers in Sweden – A Call for Unequal Treatment' in J Howe and R Owens (eds) *Temporary Labour Migration* (n 1) 211; C Woolfson, J Fudge and C Thörnqvist, 'Migrant Precarity and Future Challenges to Labour Standards in Sweden' (2014) 35(4) Economic and Industrial Democracy 704; C Calleman 'Domestic Services in a Land of Equality: The Case of Sweden' (2011) 23(1) Canadian Journal of Women and Law 121.

8 A Commission of Inquiry with the task to propose measures to strengthen the position of labour migrants on the Swedish labour market did not suggest that any changes would be done in this regard, SOU 2016:91 (n 7).

9 Catherine Dauvergne has summarised the situation in an elegant manner: 'in contemporary globalizing times, migration laws and their enforcement are increasingly

are guaranteed. International law to a very limited extent governs the right for persons to enter another state. The right of workers to cross-border movements within the EU is one of very few exceptions.[10] As a rule, it is the receiving state that regulates labour migration through immigration law.[11] This presumption is increasingly being questioned. Saskia Sassen, among others, argues that 'the regulatory role of the state and its capacity to manage migration are in the process of being altered through the changes engendered in the global economic system and other transformations'.[12] The state's capacity to control immigration may be incomplete.[13] But this starting point still governs the realities for many individuals every day. Through national labour migration schemes, work can be a qualifying factor for entrance and stay.

The focus in international law on labour migration is rather on the rights a migrant shall be guaranteed when present in the host country. The legal starting point is equal treatment with domestic workers with regard to employment and working conditions.[14] However, not even this principle is uncontroversial – the international legal framework contains a number of shortcomings with regard to equal treatment in particular for temporary labour migrants, and the ratification rates for the International Labour Organization (ILO) and United Nations (UN) Conventions regulating the rights of migrant workers are low.[15] In a European

understood as the last bastion of sovereignty' in *Making People Illegal: What Globalization Means for Migration and Law* (Cambridge University Press 2008) 2.

10 Article 45 Treaty on the Functioning of the EU.

11 Freedland and Costello, *Migrants at Work* (n 5) 3.

12 The citation is taken from C. Gabriel, 'Managed Migration and the Temporary Labour Fix' in L F Vosko, V Preston and R Lathman (eds) *Liberating temporariness? Migration, Work and Citizenship in an Age of Insecurity* (McGill-Queen's University Press 2014) 105. Gabriel refers to S Sassen, 'Regulating immigration in a Global Age. A new policy landscape' (2005)11(1) Parallax 35.

13 M Ruhs, The Price of Rights (Princeton University Press 2013) 33; S Castles, H de Haas and M J Miller, Age of Migration *International Population Movements in the Modern World* (5th edn, Palgrave Macmillan 2014) 324.

14 ILO Convention No. 97, Migration for Employment (Revised) 1949, article 6 and ILO Convention No. 143, (Migrant Workers (Supplementary Provisions) (1975), article 10; UN Convention on the Protection of the Rights of All Migrant Workers and Members of their Families (1990), art 25–27. See also B Friðriksdóttir, *What Happened to Equality? The Construction of the Right to Equal Treatment of Third-Country Nationals in European Union Law on Labour Migration* (dissertation Radboud University 2016) 37.

15 R Cholewinski, 'International Labour Law and the Protection of Migrant Workers – Revitalizing the Agenda in the Era of Globalization' in J D Craig and M Lynk (eds),

context the picture is a little bit different. Three EU-directives that regulate labour migration to the EU from third countries all include quite extensive, albeit fragmented and still incomplete, equal treatment provisions.[16] A crucial difference between the EU-directives and the ILO and UN Conventions is that the EU-directives *must* be implemented by the EU member states.[17]

The reasons for pursuing equal treatment for migrant workers are many. Some, such as ethics, dignity, prevention of exploitation and maximization of the development benefits of migration, are related to the worker, her family and home state. Others, such as prevention of unfair competition and segmentation, avoidance of outcompeting the national workforce and increased competitiveness, are in different ways related to the well-being of the host country.[18] However, there is also an ongoing discussion on trade-offs between rights and countries' openness to admitting migrant workers.[19] That discussion will not be explored further in this chapter.

But if the rights that are recognised in the law are made illusory, none of the goals aimed at will be upheld. The importance of effective enforcement is often

---

Globalization and the Future of Labour Law (Cambridge University Press 2006) 413; Fudge, *Precarious Migrant Status* (n 4) 128.

16 Directive (2011/98/EU) of the European Parliament and of the Council on a single application procedure for a single permit for third country nationals to re-side and work in the territory of a Member State and on a common set of rights for third country workers legally residing in a Member State [2011]: The Council Directive (2009/50/EC) on the conditions of entry and residence of third-country nationals for the purposes of highly qualified employment [2009]; Directive (2014/36/EU) of the European Parliament and of the Council of 26 February 2014 on the conditions of entry and stay of third-country nationals for the purpose of employment as seasonal workers [2014]. For a discussion on the shortcomings of the EU legal framework, see P Herzfeld Olsson, 'The Development of an EU Policy on Workers from Third Countries – Adding new Categories of Workers to the EU Labour Market Provided with new Combinations of Rights' in S Evju (ed) *Regulating Transnational Labour in Europe: The quandaries of multilevel governance*, (Department of Private Law, Skriftserie 196, University of Oslo 2014) 279; Friðriksdóttir, *What Happened to Equality?* (n 14) 37; E Guild, 'The EU's Internal Market and the Fragmentary Nature of EU Labour Migration'; in Costello and Freedland *Migrants at Work* (n 5) 98.

17 Article 288 Treaty on the Functioning of the EU.

18 International Labour Office, International Labour Migration: A rights based approach (2010) 189; 215: Ruhs, *The Price of Rights* (n 13) 188.

19 Ruhs, *The Price of Rights* (n 13) and M Ruhs, 'Protecting the Rights of Temporary Migrant Workers- Ideals versus Reality' in Howe and Owens *Temporary Labour Migration in the Global Era – The Regulatory Challenges* (n 2).

highlighted in this regard.[20] A right to equal treatment has no meaning if it cannot be upheld in practice. In order to safeguard equal treatment with regard to working conditions, it is therefore important to ensure that the mechanisms in the national labour law system ensuring decent working conditions for domestic workers can be adapted to labour migrants.

Labour law is built upon the assumption that the individual worker is in an inherently unequal or subordinated position in relation to the employer. And 'the struggle for contractual equality between the dependent or subordinated worker and the employer' has been an ongoing theme for labour law.[21] During the last decades, the foundations of labour law have been put under pressure through 'trends towards decentralization and disorganization in industrial relations and the economy'.[22] These trends have created new vulnerabilities affecting the working population[23] and increased tensions between different groups of workers including tensions between migrant and domestic workers.[24] How national labour law has been shaped to adapt to the trends of decentralization etc., is therefore also crucial for the position of migrant workers on the labour market. This connection can be articulated in different ways and one way of putting it is that the robustness of domestic labour law protection is decisive for ensuring that migrant workers are not outcompeting domestic workers because they are favoured by employers for their flexibility.[25]

Many national labour migration schemes only provide for temporary stays.[26] The fact that the right to stay and work in the host state is restricted in time can in itself weaken the labour migrant's bargaining power.[27] This is particularly the

20 ILO, *Promoting Fair Migration* General Survey concerning the migrant workers instruments (report of the ILO Committee of Experts on the Application of Conventions and Recommendations, International Labour Office 2016) 147.

21 B Hepple and B Veneziani, 'Introduction'. In B Hepple and B Veneziani (eds) *The Transformation of Labour Law in Europe* (Hart 2009) 5.

22 R Dukes, *The Labour Constitution The enduring idea of labour law* (Oxford University Press 2014) 9.

23 For an overview and analyses, see L Rodgers, *Labour Law, Vulnerability and the Regulation of Precarious Work* (Elgar 2016) 2.

24 Freedland and Costello, *Migrants at Work* (n 5) 8.

25 Freedland and Costello discussing Martin Ruhs contribution in *Migrants at work* (n 5) 13.

26 ILO, *Promoting Fair Migration* (n 20) 6 and 36.

27 Something that has been highlighted by a high number of scholars. See for example J Howe and R Owens *Temporary Labour Migration* (n 2) 32; Freedland and Costello, *Migrants at Work* (n 5) 8.

case if the employer can influence whether or not the labour migrant can stay in the territory.[28] Temporary migrant workers may, in practice, lack the ability to raise concerns about their working conditions.[29] This is particularly relevant in legal systems where enforcing employment rights may affect residence rights.[30] The reasons for moving temporarily to work in another country are complex. Escaping poverty and/or simply increasing income are important pull factors, but can also interact with other difficult circumstances in the home country.[31] The labour migrant's interest to stay in the host country can be stronger than the interest to enforce a specific level of working conditions.[32] Thus, immigration law may affect the bargaining power of the labour migrant in enforcing their rights[33] and in that sense 'structures demand for migrant labour, possibly leading to the erosion of terms and conditions in the particular sectors or segments concerned'.[34]

3. Some General Characteristics of Swedish Labour Law[35]

Some knowledge about the national labour law system is necessary to better understand how the national labour law mechanisms adopted to establish contractual equality between employees and employers play out for labour migrants. In this section, a few relevant parts of the Swedish labour law system will therefore be briefly introduced.

High trade union density has been described as a characteristic of the Nordic labour relations model.[36] In 1993, the level of unionisation was 85 per cent in

28 Anderson, *Migration* (n 4) 310.

29 ibid.

30 ILO, *Promoting Fair Migration* (n 20) 147.

31 S Castles et al., *Age of Migration* (n 13) 25; D S Massey, J Arango, G Hugo, A Kouaouci, A Pellegrino and J Edward Taylor, *Worlds in Motion Understanding International Migration at the end of the Millennium* (Clarendon Press 2008) 8, 15, 278.

32 M Ruhs, 'Immigration and Labour Market Protectionism – Protecting Local Workers' Preferential Access to the National Labour Market' in Costello and Freedland, *Migrants at Work* (n 5) 65.

33 Andersson, *Migration* (n 4) 306; Freedland and Costello, *Migrants at Work* (n 5) 8.

34 Ruhs cited in Freedland and Costello, *Migrants at Work* (n 5) 7.

35 This section is based on P Herzfeld Olsson and E Sjödin, 'The Fissured Workplace: Some responses to contemporary Challenges in Sweden' (the section The Swedish Model – Some Characteristics of the Swedish Labour Market) (2015) 37(143) Comparative Labour Law & Policy Journal 146–147.

36 N Bruun, B Flodgren, M Halvorsen, H Hydén and R Nielsen, *The Nordic Labour Relations Model* (Dartmouth 1992) 3.

Sweden. Since then, a decline of 15 per cent has taken place. From an international perspective, the level is still very high – but in some sectors the union density is much lower. This is the case for the hotel and restaurant and berry picking sectors, where the number of labour migrants is particularly high.[37]

Collective agreements are the most important sources of norms regulating wages and employment conditions in Swedish law. In 2014, 85 per cent of the labour force in the private sector was covered by collective agreements, and 100 per cent in the public sector.[38] This is explained by the high level of employer organisation. Organised employers employed 89 per cent of the labour force in 2014.[39] An employer who is a member of an employer organisation is automatically bound by the collective agreements that this organisation has concluded.

For a long time, the legislator has systematically promoted this development, to a large extent through non-intervention. In the 1970s, after a period of industrial unrest, the legislator decided to take a more active role and a number of important labour laws were adopted, such as the Employment Protection Act and the Co-Determination Act. The balance between collective agreements and legislation was altered.[40] All workers are nowadays entitled by law to employment protection, paid holiday, a regulated working time etc. But a large part of these provisions in law are semi-mandatory, meaning that it is possible for the trade unions and employers to deviate from them through collective agreements and thereby adapt the applicable provisions to the needs of the company or the sector.[41]

---

37 The Hotel and Restaurant Workers' Union organised 34 per cent of the workers in the sector 2015. A Kjellberg, 'Parternas organisationsgrad och kollektivavtalens utbredning' in I B Anderson (ed) Avtalsrörelsen och lönebildningen 2015 (Medlingsinstitutet 2016) 48. No similar figures are available for the berry picking sector but the Municipal Workers' Union which organises those workers indicate that the level of organisation is very low, see for example S Eriksson, 'Säsongsarbetaren från tredje land i dag och i framtiden, Examensarbete i arbetsrätt' (Juridiska insitutionen Uppsala universitet 2016) 32.

38 Kjellberg, 'Parternas organisationsgrad' (n 37) 43.

39 ibid 45.

40 K Ahlberg and N Bruun, 'Sweden: Transition through Collective Bargaining'. In T Blanke, R Blainpain, E Rose (eds) *Collective Bargaining and Wages in Comparative Perspective: Germany, France, the Netherlands, Sweden and the United Kingdom* (Kluwer Law International 2005) 117.

41 On this issue, see R Fahlbeck,'Derogation from Labour Law Statutes under Swedish Law' (2006) Juridisk Tidskrift 41.

Another important and crucial feature of the Swedish system is the absence of legislative provisions on minimum wages. The importance of the collective agreements when setting wages cannot be overestimated.

If an employer and a worker bound by a collective agreement conclude an employment contract with terms that are in conflict with the collective agreement, the terms are void.[42] The norms in collective agreements also play an important role for employers and employees not covered by them. It is, however, possible for such employers to conclude individual employment contracts with lower wages than those set by the collective agreements.[43]

An employer who is a member of an employer organisation is, as mentioned above, automatically bound by the collective agreements that the organisation has concluded. Unorganised employers can instead enter into a special type of collective agreements called accession agreements with a trade union.[44] However, there is no mechanism for extending the binding force of collective agreements to others than the signatory parties and their members, and give the collective agreements *erga omnes* effect.[45]

Collective autonomy and non-intervention by the state is still an essential feature when it comes to regulating the wages and working conditions of the Swedish labour market.[46] This is also evident when it comes to the responsibility for monitoring that the employment conditions in law and collective agreements are applied. This responsibility, with an important exception, is borne alone by the parties to the collective agreements, the trade union and the employer organisation or the employer. The Work Environment Authority monitors the application of the occupational health and safety provisions and the working time provisions, if the latter is not dealt with in a collective agreement.

42 Section 27 of the Co-Determination Act (1976:580).

43 J Malmberg, 'The Collective Agreement as an Instrument for Regulation of Wages and Employment Conditions' in P Wahlgren (ed) *Stability and Change in Nordic Labour Law* (Scandinavian Studies in Law vol 43 Stockholm Institute for Scandinavian Law 2002) 207.

44 ibid 196.

45 Ahlberg and Bruun, 'Sweden: Transition' (n 40) 122.

46 ibid 117.

4. Some Further Details about Two Particular Labour Law Aspects

4.1 Conclusion of the Employment Contract

From the above it can be concluded that when an employment contract shall be entered upon, the freedom of contract is to a great extent restricted in Swedish law. This restriction is governed by the interplay between law and collective agreements. As a rule, the law can only be deviated from through collective agreements. The content of the collective agreements restricts the scope for bargaining for employers and workers bound by them. The collective agreements play a particularly important role with regard to wages – as there is no minimum wage protected by the law.

On the other hand, if the employer is not bound by a collective agreement, the wages and other conditions not dealt with by mandatory provisions in legislation will be decided by the bargaining power of the individual worker and the employer. It is well known that some workers, as the so called Gold Collar Workers, can get a quite good output in such situation. For others, the outcome is more unclear.[47]

4.2 Employment Protection – Principles on Just Cause for Dismissals

In contrast to principles governing other contracts, the right for an employer to terminate a contract of employment is restricted in Swedish law.[48] According to the Employment Protection Act, a dismissal by the employer must be based on an objective just cause (objective grounds), otherwise the dismissal can be invalid and/or generate damages.[49] A just cause can be of two different kinds, either economic or individual. Economic reasons are related to the company and individual reasons are related to the individual employee's conduct, competence or other personal conditions. Sigeman summarizes the rules on dismissals on individual grounds in the following way:

> The rules presume that the conflicting interests of the two parties will be weighed against each other and allow a wide variety of circumstances to be taken into account. Generally speaking, dismissal is justifiable only if the employee has been guilty of a breach of or

47 On this theme, see for example Rodgers, *Vulnerability* (n 23) 142.

48 T Sigeman, 'Employment Protection in Scandinavian Law' in Wahlgren, *Stability and Change in Nordic Labour law* (n 43) 257.

49 Sections 7, 34 and 38–39 Employment Protection Act (1982:80).

> failure to fulfil a contractual obligation of material interest to the employer, and if the existence and importance of this obligation have been made known to the employee. The court's assessment is based not merely on the course of events leading to the dismissal but, more particularly, on the interferences that can be drawn from the situation regarding the employee's suitability for continued employment. Accordingly, isolated instances of misconduct, provided they do not involve gross negligence, have often been deemed as insufficient grounds for dismissal, whereas in cases of repeated offences the courts have not infrequently taken a sterner view, especially if the offender has earlier been reprimanded by the employer.[50]

The Employment Protection Act is also complemented by the Discrimination Act which prohibits dismissals related to discrimination on the grounds of sex, transgender identity or expression, ethnicity, religion or other belief, disability, sexual orientation or age.[51]

In contrast to the strict rules on dismissals for individual reasons, it is much easier for an employer to verify that a dismissal is based on an economic good cause. As Sigeman explains, Swedish law on 'redundancy is based on the principle that companies must be able to apply modern methods of efficiency in order to survive in the long run'.[52] A good economic cause can be the traditional shortage of work, but also the result of organisational changes which the employer is free to make. The employment protection in these situations is governed by the rules on selection for redundancy dismissal. A seniority rule related to the length of service applies – the last relevant worker employed should be the first one to go.[53] The seniority rules can only be deviated from in a collective agreement.[54]

The Swedish sanction system for dismissals without just cause is quite strict, and considered to be the strictest one in the four Scandinavian systems.[55] If the court finds that the employer lacks just cause for a dismissal on individual grounds, the employee can claim the dismissal to be invalid. In that case, the employer can chose either to accept the judgement and re-instate the worker or, as a last resort, to extricate itself from the employment by paying compensation ranging from six to 32 months' pay, depending on the employee's length of service.[56]

---

50 Sigeman, 'Employment Protection' (n 48) 264.

51 Chapter 2 section 1, Discrimination Act (2008:567).

52 Sigeman, 'Employment Protection' (n 48) 268.

53 Section 22 Employment protection Act (1982:80), Sigeman 'Employment Protection' (n 48) 269.

54 Section 2 Employment Protection Act (1982:80).

55 Sigeman, 'Employment Protection' (n 48) 267.

56 Sections 34 and 39 Employment Protection Act (1982:80) and Sigeman, 'Employment Protection' (n 48) 267.

Otherwise, damages can be awarded both for financial loss and for the non-material damage suffered.[57] If the employer violates the rules on seniority related to dismissals on economic grounds, damages can be brought, but not claims for the invalidity of the dismissal.[58]

The rules on dismissals in the Employment Protection Act apply for indefinite employment contracts. The rights apply from day one, if the employee is not employed on a trial basis.[59] In contrast, temporary employment contracts expire when the contracts end and can only be terminated in advance if the employee has committed a particularly serious breach of contract.[60] The possibility to use temporary employment contracts is to a certain extent restricted.[61]

5. The Swedish Regulation of Labour Migration[62]

In order to understand how the above described labour law provisions play out for labour migrants, some basic knowledge about the Swedish labour migration regime is necessary. Therefore, a short introduction to these rules will follow.

The Swedish regulation on labour migration is described as the most open one within the Organisation for Economic Co-operation and Development (OECD).[63] The labour migration scheme is purely employer demand-driven. No labour market tests are done, no skill preferences based in law or quotas apply, and the system is open to all sectors of the labour market.[64] The only requirement that could look like such restrictions is the demand that employers respect the principle of EU preference. In reality, that only means that the vacancy must have been published on the websites of the Swedish Public Employment Service and the European

57 Section 38 *Employment Protection* Act (1982:8), Sigeman, 'Employment Protection' (n 48) 267.

58 Section 34 Employment Protection Act (1982:80).

59 Section 6 Employment Protection Act (1982:80). A trial period can last for six months.

60 Sections 4 and 18–20 Employment Protection Act (1982:80).

61 Sections 5 and 6 Employment Protection Act (1982:80).

62 This section is based on P Herzfeld Olsson, 'Empowering Temporary Migrant Workers in Sweden' in Howe and Owens, *Temporary Labour Migration* (n 2).

63 OECD, 'Recruiting immigrant workers: Sweden' (OECD 2011).

64 The implementation of the EU directive on conditions of entry and residence of third-country nationals for the purposes of highly qualified employment (2009/50/EC) and the Directives on Seasonal employment (2014/36/EU) and Intra-corporate transferees (2014/66/EU) has and will to a certain extent modify this uniform approach (the Directives on Seasonal Employment and Intra-corporate transferees are not implemented in March 2017).

Employment Services for at least ten days.[65] Having done that, the employer is free to offer the job to anyone.

The individual employers decide whether they need to recruit workers from third countries (countries outside EU/EEA). This generous principle however has a strict frame. It is a crime for employers to employ foreigners without a legal right to be in Sweden or without the necessary work permit.[66] For foreigners obliged to have a work permit, it is also a crime to work without having obtained such a permit.[67]

In order to be granted a work permit, the migrant worker needs an offer of employment from the employer. To ensure that migrant workers will not replace domestic workers, the offered terms of employment must be similar to those domestic workers enjoy.[68] The law therefore prescribes that the worker must be offered a wage, insurances and other terms of employment that must not be inferior to those provided for in the relevant collective agreements or provided for by customs in the occupation or industry.[69]

The Migration Agency decides on work and residence permits. The Agency has designed a form called Offer of Employment that must be filled in and accompany the application for a work permit.[70] In the Offer of Employment, the employer must declare whether it is bound by a collective agreement and, in that case, which trade union is the party to the collective agreement. The Offer of Employment must also specify the working time, the applicable insurances, the kind of employment (indefinite or temporary) and the period of employment. The combined effect of the specified wages and the working time is also important to fulfil the last legal requirement for being granted a work permit, namely that migrant workers must be able to support themselves. This means that their total income must be higher than the level for upholding social assistance (13,000 Swedish Krona per month, around 1,200 Euro).[71] The relevant trade union must

---

65 Government Bill 2007/08:147 36 and 40 and Government Bill 2013/14:227 8.

66 Chapter 19 Section 5 Foreign Act (2005:716).

67 Chapter 19 section 3 Foreign Act (2005:716).

68 Government Bill 2007/08:147 27.

69 Chapter 6 section 2 Foreign Act (2005:716).

70 The form can be found on the website of the Migration Agency <http://www.migrationsverket.se/download/18.5e83388f141c129ba6312eab/1473238973457/anst_erbj_232011_sv.pdf> accessed 11 January 2017.

71 Chapter 6 section 2 Foreign Act (2005:716) and SOU 2016:91 (n 7) 45.

be given an opportunity to verify whether the offered terms are in accordance with the collective agreements or custom.[72]

All work permits are temporary. They are granted for the duration of the employment offered, but for a maximum of two years. Work permits may be extended an unlimited number of times, but the total period may only exceed four years in exceptional cases.[73] Each extension needs a new offer of employment from an employer.[74] After having worked legally in Sweden for four years within a seven-year period, the migrant worker may be granted a permanent residence permit.[75]

The work permit is tied to a specific employer and to a specific type of work (occupation) for the first two years. After two years, it is only tied to a specific type of work.[76] If the migrant worker wants to change employer or type of work, he or she must apply for a new work permit. That can be done from within Sweden, as long as the previous residence permit is still valid.[77]

The work permit and/or residence permit may be revoked if the employment has ceased and shall be revoked if the working conditions applied do not fulfil the requirements in the law, meaning for example that the wage is lower than the wage provided for in the relevant collective agreement or the employment has not begun four months after arrival.[78] To ensure that the migrant worker is not too dependent on the employer, they can stay in Sweden for three or four months to search for a new job if they lose the job that the work permit is connected to.[79]

6. How immigration law weakens the labour migrant's bargaining position

6.1 The Conclusion of the Employment Contract

From the above, one can conclude that when the migrant worker enters Sweden, he or she has been offered employment. This offer must include a level of wage and insurance conditions that correspond to a relevant collective agreement or

---

72 Chapter 5 section 7a Foreign Ordinance (2006:97).

73 Chapter 6 section 21 Foreign Act (2005:716).

74 See the Migration Authority website <www.migrationsverket.se/English/Private-individuals/Working-in-Sweden/Employed/If-you-are-in-Sweden/Extending-a-permit.html> accessed 15 January 2017.

75 Chapter 5 section 5 Foreign Act (2005:716).

76 Chapter 6 section 2a Foreign Act (2005:716).

77 Migration Agency Website (n 74).

78 Chapter 7 Sections 3 and 7e Foreign Act (2005:716).

79 ibid.

the custom in the industry. With regard to employment conditions, the Migration Agency only examines the wage level, the insurances applicable, and the working hours.[80] No other employment conditions are taken into account when it decides about the work permit.

The offer of employment is not an employment contract. That must be entered upon separately.[81] In many cases, this means that the labour migrant and the employer must agree on the wages and other employment conditions when the labour migrant is already in Sweden. At that point, all the sacrifices such a movement included for the labour migrant are already made. At this stage, the labour migrant is put into a very vulnerable situation. If the parties cannot agree on the conditions of the employment contract, the labour migrant will never enter employment. Besides the loss of income, the labour migrant's temporary residence permit shall be revoked if he or she does not find new employment within three months.[82] Until new employment is found – if it can be found– the labour migrant as a rule is not entitled to social assistance.

If, at that point, the employer only accepts conditions below the level prescribed for by the Foreign Act, the labour migrant would be put in a tricky situation. The residence permit will be revoked also under such circumstances, if the Migration Agency finds out. In 2016, the Migration Agency granted 12, 526 work permits to labour migrants.[83] In the same year, it carried out a couple of hundred inspections.[84] It is obvious that it is very difficult for the Migration Agency to detect abuse of the regulation. The most important check is made when a labour migrant applies for a renewal of the work permit. A renewal can only be granted if the legal requirements regarding the level of wage and insurance protection were fulfilled during the previous permit period.[85] In this situation, the labour migrant must choose between entering into a contract with employment conditions below the level required in the Foreign Act, including the related risks of loss of residence

---

80 However, the Migration Agency has introduced targeted controls of employers in the sectors most prone to abuse: berry picking, cleaning, hotels and restaurants, construction, retail, farming and forestry etc. See for example C Calleman, 'The Most Open System among OECD Countries: Swedish Regulation of Labour Migration' (2015) 5(1) Nordic Journal of Migration Research 28, 24.

81 Herzfeld Olsson, 'Empowering Temporary Migrant Workers' (n 7) 213.

82 Chapter 7 section 3 p, Foreign Act (2005:716).

83 Migration Agency statistics <www.migrationsverket.se/Om-Migrationsverket/Statistik/Arbetstagare---de-storsta-yrkesgrupperna.html> accessed 11 January 2017.

84 Riksrevisionen, 'Ett fungerande system för arbetskraftsinvandring?' RIR 2016:32, 109.

85 ibid 100 and 102.

permit, OR lose the total income and look for another job for a period of three months – and if none is found lose the residence permit anyway.

The employer, on the other hand, risks nothing. An inquiry has recently put forward a new legal proposal in order to make it less attractive for employers to enter into such employment contracts.[86] The proposal intends to increase the contractual equality between the employer and the labour migrant. Later in this chapter, to what extent the proposed solution is likely to have that effect will be discussed.

6.2 Employment Protection

It has been explained above how rigorous the Swedish law on dismissal is. It has also been explained that it is a criminal offence for employers to employ foreigners without the necessary permits, and that labour migrants only get temporary residence and work permits. In many cases, however, the migrant worker is offered an employment contract of indefinite duration in the employment offer.[87] As employing workers on indefinite contracts is the main rule in Swedish law, one may assume that many such contracts are entered upon.[88] It may seem illogical in a system where labour migrants can only be granted temporary residence and work permits. However, offering a worker an indefinite employment contract can be a comparative advantage for the employer, and contain an implicit promise of a longer relationship than the duration of the applicable permit.

But in order to make such a promise a reality, when the temporary residence and work permit expires, the employer must give the labour migrant a new offer of employment. That offer of employment is a necessary part of the application for a renewal of the residence and work permits. Without it, the permit will not be prolonged by the Migration Agency. The permit will expire and it will be a criminal offence for the employer to employ the labour migrant, and for the labour migrant to stay in Sweden. This obligation to renew the offer of employment is part of the immigration law regime, and the employer is not obliged to give any reason for denying the labour migrant a renewed offer of employment.

---

86 SOU 2016:91 (n7).

87 O Frödin and A Kjellberg, 'Arbetskraftsinvandring från tredje land i restaurang- och städbranscherna'. In C Calleman och P Herzfeld Olsson (eds) *Arbetskraft från hela världen: Hur blev det med 2008 års reform*? (DELMI 2015) 181: C Calleman, 'Arbetskraftsinvandring för arbete i privata hushåll'. In C. Calleman et al. *Rena hem på smutsiga villkor – hushållstjänster, migration och globalisering* (Makadam Förlag, 2013).

88 Section 4, Employment Protection Act (1982:80).

The question then arises how such behaviour should be looked at from the perspective of the law on dismissal. It is obviously criminal to employ the labour migrant if the permit expires. Does that mean that the requirements for a just cause do not apply? The Labour Court has clarified that if a work permit has expired and there are no remaining issues to take into consideration for the Migration Agency, as would be the case if the employer does not intend to offer the labour migrant new employment, the employer can immediately detach him or her from the employment without taking the provisions in the Employment Protection Act into consideration.[89]

It is obvious that employers have been given a legal vehicle to circumvent the right not to be dismissed without a just cause through the provisions in the Foreign Act. Such a vehicle can affect the parties' bargaining power during the whole employment relationship. The risk of not being entitled to a new offer of employment if a behaviour is not considered satisfactory can reduce the bargaining power of the labour migrant.[90] This is particularly the case if the labour migrant is active in a sector where there is no shortage of workers, which is the case for a huge number of Swedish labour migrants.[91]

Interestingly enough, the Labour Court included a remark in the judgement mentioned above, where it touched upon this relationship between the two legal regimes. The Court highlights the fact that there is a conflict between the Employment Protection Act and the criminal provisions in the Foreign Act. The Labour Court explains that it has put particular weight on the fact that an employer must not be obliged to follow provisions that will lead to criminal responsibility for him or her. At the same time, the Court continues, the outcome of this judgement leads to a remarkable weakening of a foreigner's social protection. Therefore, the Labour Court is highlighting the hardly satisfying outcome that the conflict of law situation leads too.[92]

So far nothing has been done to alter this situation. On the contrary, this judgement has been in place since 1979 and throughout this time the employers' role in the labour migration regime has been strengthened in a remarkable way, whilst the conflict between the two legal systems has been intensified. It is therefore even more accurate today to say that the fact that the employer does not have to take

89 Labour Court Judgment AD 1979 no 90.

90 See Anderson, *Migration* (n 4) 310.

91 Frödin and Kjellberg, 'Restaurang- och städbranscherna' (n 87) 151; L Pelling, 'Fristad Sverige? Om skyddssökande arbetskraftsinvandrares villkor' in Calleman and Herzfeld Olsson, *Arbetskraft från hela världen* (n 87) 245.

92 AD 1979 no 90.

the Employment Protection Act into consideration affects the contractual equality between the employer and the labour migrant.

7. Concluding remarks

The two examples identified above on how immigration law can derange the contractual equality between workers and employers established by labour law can be explained by at least two factors. Traditionally, upholding sovereignty through border control has been the responsibility of the state. The state is also the actor responsible for safeguarding the needs of the labour market. Labour law, on the other hand, is applied and monitored by the employers, employees and trade unions. Through the present labour migration system, the state has delegated parts of its control of its borders, as well as a responsibility for safeguarding the needs of the labour market, to the employers.[93] This power transfer is remarkable.[94] It is also not so surprising that such change in the power relationship affects the previous contractual equality between the parties. Many scholars have underlined that migration and immigration law has a role in 'jeopardizing labour law's worker-protective dimension, whilst privileging employers' interests'.[95]

Bridget Anderson has highlighted that 'the figure of the abusive employer throws a shadow over the role of the state in constructing vulnerability'.[96] Her comment is related to 'illegal immigrants', but is as relevant when talking about other categories of labour migrants. If the state is also interested in guarding the contractual equality between labour migrants and employers, additional measures must be taken. This takes us to the second factor influencing the effect of the interaction between immigration law and labour law. The problems identified related to the entering of the employment contract are mainly relevant in workplaces not covered by collective agreements and/or the monitoring of trade unions. In addition, the problems related to employment protection are most likely to occur in workplaces with no collective agreements and no local trade union branch. Otherwise, the trade union could safeguard that migrant workers were not exploited. In the Swedish system, where practically every step taken

93 See also the United Kingdom example in Ruhs, *Ideals versus Reality* (n 19) 66.
94 This problem has been discussed by many academic scholars, for example D Frank, 'Förändringar i svensk arbetsmarknadspolitik 1954–2014' forthcoming (2017) Arbetsliv & Arbetsmarknad and Andersson, 'Migration' (n 4) 309.
95 Freedland and Costello, *Migrants at Work*, based on the chapters by Menz, Ruhs and Davies, 14; Andersson, 'Migration' (n 4) 2010.
96 Anderson, 'Migration' (n 4) 211.

by the state related to the regulation of the labour market traditionally intended to promote collective agreements and the autonomy of the parties, the workers outside that context are left very vulnerable.

The labour migrants coming to Sweden tend to work in sectors where the coverage of collective agreements and trade union density is lower than average. They are also seldom members of trade unions.[97] This is the case for seasonal workers and workers in the hospitality sector and the information technology sector.[98] These three categories together represent almost two thirds of all the labour migrants who entered Sweden in 2016.[99]

Vulnerability is mainly associated with low skilled work. There are however indications that even highly skilled labour migrants in Sweden work for lower wages than comparable domestic workers.[100] Irrespective of the extent to which that is the case, it is likely to assume that labour migrants working at workplaces with no collective agreements and no trade union presence are very dependent on the employer. No authority is responsible for safeguarding such workers' rights and, of course, this applies also to labour migrants.

It has often been highlighted that the fact that a labour migrant is tied to a specific employer limits the workers freedom 'in ways which are unknown or virtually unknown to modern domestic labour law systems'.[101] As previously explained, this is also the case in Swedish law for the first two years of the labour migrant's stay.[102] This fact adds to the two problematic situations discussed. In a labour law system like the Swedish one, where collective agreements and trade unions play such a crucial role for establishing a contractual equality between workers and employers, the legislator must take into account that if it delegates additional powers to

---

97 Engblom (n 7) 355.

98 See for the berry sector (n 37) and IT-sector <www.arbetsvarlden.se/sa-manga-har-kollektivavtal-i-olika-sektorer/> accessed 11 January 2017 <www.arbetsvarlden.se/snabbvaxare-om-kollektivavtal-ingen-har-fragat-efter-det/> accessed 11 January 2017.

99 Migration Agency Statistics from its web <www.migrationsverket.se/Om-Migrationsverket/Statistik/Arbetstagare---de-storsta-yrkesgrupperna.html> accessed 18 January 2017.

100 H Emilson and K Magnusson, 'Högkvalificerad arbetskraftsinvandring till Sverige' in Calleman and Herzfeld Olsson, *Arbetskraft från hela världen* (n 87) 90.

101 Freedland and Costello, *Migrants at Work* (n 5) 11.

102 Section 6:2a Foreign Act (2005:716).

the employers, it will be even more difficult to uphold rights for workers active in sectors where trade union activity is low and many employers are unorganised.[103]

As mentioned before, a new Commission of inquiry has proposed measures to strengthen the position of the labour migrants in the Swedish labour market. The major measure proposed by the inquiry is to criminalize employers who apply working conditions that do not fulfil the requirements in the Foreign Act. It is doubtful if this is a step in the right direction. Still, labour migrants will not be compensated if they lose their employment and therefore their right to stay in Sweden because they try to enforce their rights. This issue has not been dealt with in this chapter. However, we can conclude that even if this proposal is adopted, it would only promote that the labour migrant is guaranteed a certain level of wages and certain insurances. An employment contract covers so many other aspects, and when these are negotiated, the proposed measures would play no role at all. Something has to be done in order to maintain the autonomy of labour law, and safeguard that the contractual equality between workers and employers can be a reality also for labour migrants. This is particularly urgent in a system like the Swedish one, where attracting labour migrants is considered a very important aspect of competitiveness and economic growth.

---

103 See also J Fudge, 'Lågkvalificerad arbetskraftsinvandring – En jämförelse mellan Kanada och Sverige' in Calleman and Herzfeld Olsson, *Arbetskraft från hela världen* (n 87) 484.

Authors and Editors

Kerstin Ahlberg is the Director of the Institute for Social Private Law, Department of Law, Stockholm University.

Alan Bogg is a Professor of Labour Law at the University of Bristol, United Kingdom.

Niklas Bruun is a Professor of Labour Law at Stockholm University and Hanken School of Economics, Helsinki, Finland.

Eberhard Eichenhofer is a Professor of Social Law and Civil Law at Friedrich Schiller Universität in Jena, Germany.

Judy Fudge is a Professor at Kent Law School, University of Kent, United Kingdom.

Patrick Gunnigle is a Professor of Business Studies at the University of Limerick, Ireland.

Petra Herzfeld Olsson is an associate professor at Uppsala University, Sweden.

Isabelle Van Hiel is a Research Associate at the Department of Constitutional and Administrative Law of the Vrije Universiteit Brussel, Belgium.

Mijke Houwerzijl is a Professor of Labour Law at Tilburg University. She also holds a chair in Comparative and European Labour Law at the University of Groningen, the Netherlands.

Jonathan Lavelle is a Senior Lecturer in Industrial Relations at the University of Limerick, Ireland.

Juliet McMahon is a Lecturer in Industrial Relations & Human Resource Management at the University of Limerick, Ireland.

Caroline Murphy is a Lecturer in Employment Relations at the University of Limerick, Ireland.

Kevät Nousiainen is a Professor of Comparative Law and Legal Theory, at the University of Turku, Finland.

Mike O'Brien is a Lecturer in Management Development at the University of Limerick, Ireland.

Michelle O'Sullivan is a Senior Lecturer in Industrial Relations at the University of Limerick, Ireland.

Jeremias Prassl is an Associate Professor in the Faculty of Law and Fellow of Magdalen College, University of Oxford, United Kingdom.

Martin Risak is an Associate Professor at the Department of Labour Law and Law of Social Security at the University of Vienna, Austria.

Lorraine Ryan is a Lecturer in Industrial Relations & Human Resource Management at the University of Limerick, Ireland.

Kari Tapiola is Special Adviser to the Director-General of the International Labour Organization.

Darcy du Toit is Emeritus Professor at the University of the Western Cape, South Africa.

Tom Turner is an Associate Professor in Industrial Relations at the University of Limerick, Ireland.

Joanna Unterschütz is an Associate Professor at the University of Business and Administration in Gdynia, Poland.

www.ingramcontent.com/pod-product-compliance
Ingram Content Group UK Ltd.
Pitfield, Milton Keynes, MK11 3LW, UK
UKHW020835290926
15470UKWH00004B/1359

9 783631 718506